A
GUIDEBOOK
TO
ENVIRONMENTAL LAW

AUSTRALIA
The Law Book Company
Brisbane · Sydney · Melbourne · Perth

CANADA
Carswell
Ottawa · Toronto · Calgary · Montreal · Vancouver

AGENTS
Steimatzky's Agency Ltd., Tel Aviv;
N.M. Tripathi (Private) Ltd., Bombay;
Eastern Law House (Private) Ltd., Calcutta;
M.P.P. House, Bangalore;
Universal Book Traders, Delhi;
Aditya Books, Delhi;
MacMillan Shuppan KK, Tokyo;
Pakistan Law House, Karachi, Lahore

A
GUIDEBOOK
TO
ENVIRONMENTAL LAW

By

Rosalind Malcolm LL.B. (Hons), Barrister
Lecturer in Law, University of Surrey

LONDON · SWEET & MAXWELL · 1994

Published by
Sweet & Maxwell Limited of
South Quay Plaza,
183 Marsh Wall,
London E14 9FT

Computer set by York House Typographic Ltd., London W13 8NT
Printed in England by Clays Ltd., St. Ives plc

A CIP catalogue record
for this book is available
for the British Library

ISBN 0 421 513500

No natural forests were destroyed to make this product:
only farmed timber was used and re-planted

The index was prepared by Hélène Plant

Preface

Environmental law is arguably one of the most dynamic and fascinating areas of law. Its sources are manifold. They range from the traditional role of common law judges and the British administrative regulatory system, to European legislation and policies and international agreements. The development of environmental law is influenced by politics at all levels – local, national, European and international, and by the phenomenal advances in scientific understanding and technology. Its topicality cannot be denied since it is a subject which in some way affects every person every day.

This book seeks to draw together these aspects of environmental law and to provide a cohesive perspective of the subject. Environmental law is a subject which now appears on undergraduate and postgraduate degree courses in law and other degree and professional courses relating to land or environmental health and management. It is also a subject with which many practitioners – new and experienced – have found it necessary to acquire some familiarity. This book endeavours to provide a grounding in the subject of environmental law for these readers by explaining the various sources of law relating to the different environmental media and by explaining the scientific and political context in which the law is developing. The first three Chapters deal with the essential framework in which environmental law operates in the United Kingdom; the fourth Chapter demonstrates, by means of a practical model, the range of environmental laws, while Chapters five, six, seven, eight and nine concentrate on the laws relevant (in the classical model) to earth, air, water, waste, radioactive and hazardous substances, and Chapter ten hazards a discussion of emerging trends in this fast-moving field of law.

The dynamic nature of the subject has meant that it has been necessary to incorporate changes at each stage of the publishing process and I am grateful to Sweet & Maxwell for their support in this. In particular, it has proved possible to incorporate the important changes in waste law effected by the long-awaited implementation of

Part II of the Environmental Protection Act 1990 and the Waste
Management Licensing Regulations 1994. However, as this
occurred at page proof stage, it was necessary to incorporate some
additional detail in an Addendum which appears at the front of the
book.

I am also grateful to my colleagues at the University of Surrey –
Leslie Blake, Amanda Cleary and Michael Winkler – who read and
made constructive comments on various chapters of the book, and
to Richard Nice, who never failed to help at those times when it
seemed that my manuscript had been irretrievably lost somewhere
inside my word processor.

My thanks finally to my brother Rodney, whose constant encouragement kept me on target, and to my husband Tom, who argued
each case with his wife.

I have endeavoured to state the law as at May 1, 1994.

Rosalind N. Malcolm
May 13, 1994

Addendum

On May 1, 1994, the Waste Management Licensing Regulations 1994[1] ('the Regulations'), came into force. One of their primary objectives is the implementation of the Framework Directive on Waste[2]. They are accompanied by a lengthy and detailed circular, *'Environmental Protection Act 1990: Part II; Waste Management Licensing: The Framework Directive on Waste.'*[3] The immediate import of the Regulations is that they implement practically all of the remaining sections of Part II of the Environmental Protection Act 1990. In particular, this means the implementation of sections 33(1)(a) and (b) dealing with waste licensing offences. In addition the definition of waste has been revised in the light of the Framework Directive.

The Circular is arranged into 10 Annexes dealing with:

1. The E.C. Framework Directive on Waste: this provides guidance on the objectives of the Directive.

2. The definition of waste (see below).

3. The disposal of waste at sea under Part II of the Food and Environment Protection Act 1985 and its interaction with land based disposal under Part II of the Environmental Protection Act 1990.

4. The waste management licensing system dealing, in particular, with the introduction of the new offences under section

---

[1] S.I. 1994 No. 1056.
[2] Council Directive 75/442/EEC as amended by Council Directives 91/156/EEC and 91/692/EEC.
[3] Circular 11/94, (D.O.E.); Circular 26/94, (Welsh Office); Circular 10/94, (Scottish Office Environment Department).

33 of the Environmental Protection Act 1990[4] and the provisions relating to the granting, variation, transfer, revocation and surrender of licences.

5. Exemptions from licensing[5]: this part is extensive because of the increased scope of licensing under section 33 of the Environmental Protection Act 1990 and the consequent need to extend the range of exemptions. In addition, there is an increase in the activities exempted from the Regulations because of the Government's presumption in favour of deregulation.

6. The registration of exemptions.[6]

7. The protection of groundwater[7]: this transposes into British law certain requirements of the E.C. Directive on the Protection of Groundwater against Pollution caused by Certain Dangerous Substances.[8] It provides for certain procedures to be followed where a disposal of waste might lead to a discharge into groundwater of one of the substances listed in this Directive.[9]

8. The registration of waste brokers.[10]

9. Environmental information: public registers[11] and annual reports.[12]

10. Waste management licensing and commercial confidentiality appeals and other provisions related to waste management licensing.

THE DEFINITION OF WASTE

The Framework Directive was amended partly to achieve a common definition of waste. The definition does not now permit waste to be defined in accordance with national laws. Article 1

---

[4] See Chap 8.
[5] Regulations 16 and 17 and Schedule 3 of the Regulations.
[6] Regulation 18.
[7] Regulation 15.
[8] 80/68/EEC.
[9] See Chap. 7.
[10] Regulation 20.
[11] See Chap. 3.
[12] Regulations 10 and 11.

provides that 'waste means any substance or object set out in Annex 1 which the holder discards or intends or is required to discard.'

In United Kingdom law, waste was defined in section 75(2) of the Environmental Protection Act 1990. Pending primary legislation, the Regulations modify this definition by implementing the definition as contained in the Framework Directive. The categories of waste referred to in Annex I of the Directive are contained in Part II of Schedule 4 of the Regulations.

The Circular provides detailed guidance as to the interpretation of the meaning of waste. Waste is considered to be something which poses a significantly different threat to human health or the environment partly because of the manner in which it may be disposed of and partly because the holder no longer has the same sense of obligation in relation to it. Waste, therefore, is something which falls out of the normal commercial cycle or chain of utility. This is the general test.

The fact that an object falls into one of the categories in Part II of Schedule 4 of the Regulations is not sufficient on its own. The question to be asked is: has the chain been broken? A milk bottle which is returned to the depot for reuse is part of an unbroken chain. A bottle put in a bottle bank has been discarded and requires some further act of recovery before it can be put to further use. It is, therefore, waste until it is recovered – the chain of use has been broken.

On the other hand, where an object is consigned to a landfill site or an incinerator, or one of the other disposal operations listed in Part III of the Regulations, then that is conclusive as to the determination of the question that the object is waste. In addition, if an object is abandoned or dumped in a manner which falls outside the categories of disposal operations in Part III, it is also waste.

Part IV of Schedule 4 to the Regulations lists a series of operations which are designed for the recovery of waste. For example, the recycling of metals, the reclamation of solvents and the use of waste as a fuel or for generating energy are all included as recovery operations. These operations are central to the debate as to the definition of waste which hinges on the issues of recycling and recovery. The circular suggests that if the substance can be used, and is likely to be used, in its present form without being subjected to such an operation, then it is probably not waste. On the other hand, if it can only be used after being subjected to a recovery operation as listed in Part IV, then that indicates it has been discarded and is waste. Therefore, it is not sufficient to ask simply whether the object has been consigned to a recovery operation in Part IV; the issue is more complex than that.

The Circular deals with the case when an object changes hands for value; for example, when a merchant pays cash for scrap metal it is considered to be waste. The Circular suggests four broad categories which may be considered in deciding the question as to whether an object is waste:

1. Worn but functioning substances or objects which are still usable (albeit after repair) for the purpose for which they were made are not to be considered waste. So, the transfer of an old car as a usable object by sale or gift, as opposed to its transfer to a scrap metal merchant, is not a disposal of waste.

2. Substances or objects which can be put to immediate use otherwise than by a specialised waste recovery operation or undertaking are, likewise, not waste. Included here are by-products such as the intestines of animals sent from abattoirs to the pet food industry. In one sense, the intestines are waste products, but they are not to be treated as such because they can be used immediately in the creation of another product without undergoing some specialised treatment.

3. Degenerated substances or objects which can be put to use only by establishments or undertakings specialising in waste recovery are waste. The important factor here is that the object needs to undergo some special treatment before it can be reused. The old freezer taken away by the scrap metal merchant requires special treatment before the steel in it can be recovered and returned to the commercial cycle. Such an operation requires the control of the waste licensing regime to ensure that the necessary safeguards for the protection of human health and the environment are taken. Once the steel has been recovered, then it will cease to be treated as waste once it is returned to the commercial cycle.

4. Substances which the holder does not want and which he has to pay to have taken away, are, again, waste where the holder intends that the object is to be discarded.

The intention of the holder may be a critical factor. If the holder intends the transferee to use the object in its present form or as an item of raw material, then this indicates that the object is not waste. The disposal of old clothes to the charity shop falls into this category. However, the action of the transferee also needs to be considered. If the transferee is merely making use of an item which would otherwise be waste, then it is waste. For example, if the farmer uses a waste product as fertiliser in circumstances where the holder needs to dispose of it and the farmer would not otherwise use such a product, then this is a disposal operation and the object is waste. The Circular draws a distinction where the producer of the object uses it in his own business or for his own purposes. For example, the farmer who spreads slurry from his own cows onto the fields as fertiliser is not operating a waste disposal business. But, this would not hold true if the slurry produced was in excess of the farmer's normal requirements; then, he is disposing of waste. This distinction suggested by the Circular is far from clear-cut and may create significant difficulties in its application to any particular case. Deducing the intention of any individual is notoriously difficult and any definition based upon such a subjective criterion is likely to create confusion.

The Circular also suggests that an item will cease to be waste once it has been recovered or recycled and is thereby restored to the commercial cycle or chain of utility.

The Circular only refers to the European cases of *Vessoso and Zanetti*[13] where the European Court of Justice decided that the concept of waste was not to be understood as excluding substances and objects which are capable of economic reutilisation. No English court cases are referred to on the grounds that they are not determinant of the definition of waste as prescribed by the Framework Directive. The question of definition remains, however, a complex matter and it is clearly envisaged that litigation will arise on this issue. It is unlikely that an English judge will ignore earlier decisions of the English courts even though, according to the rules of statutory interpretation, the Regulations must be interpreted to give effect to the purpose and aims of the Directive. The Circular only refers to this principle of statutory interpretation being applicable in a case heard before the European Court of Justice.[14] It is, of course, applicable to any domestic court insofar as that court is required to interpret legislation which originates from Europe.[15]

---

[13] Joined cases C-206/88 and C-207/88; [1990] 2 L.M.E.L.R. 133.
[14] Para. 2.12.
[15] Case C-106/89, *Marleasing SA v. La Commercial Internacional de Alimentacion*: [1990] 1 E.C.R. 4135, [1992] 1 C.M.L.R. 305.

Contents

Table of Cases

Table of Cases Before The European Courts

Table of Statutes

Table of Statutory Instruments

E.C. Treaties and Conventions

E.C. Regulations

E.C. Directives

E.C. Decisions

International Treaties and Conventions

National legislation

Chapter One

The Concept of the Environment

To many people the term "environment" conjures up ideas of global warming, the greenhouse effect, CFCs (chlorofluorocarbons) in aerosols, the vulnerability of certain species of animals or even the planet earth itself. The environment means different things to different people.

In its most general sense it means the surroundings, that which is encircling. This can relate to that which surrounds people and affects their health and the quality of their lives. Human beings can be perceived as the central unit in the environment, or as Plato said: "man is the measure of all things."[1] The environment then becomes that combination of material and social things which conditions the well-being of people. In the workplace, this could mean the measures which are available for the health and safety of the workers, the presence of asbestos on the construction site, or the fumes from the dry-cleaning solvents at the launderette. In the home, it could mean the absence of excessive noise from the neighbours, the freedom from smoke from a nearby demolition site or the impact of a proposed new motorway. In the countryside, it could be represented by the loss of amenity for nearby urban dwellers caused by the opening of an open cast coal mine or a stone quarry.

The environment is now normally perceived to have a wider meaning than that which affects the quality of life for people and their physical and mental well-being. Whether humans retain a central or primary role in the definition, depends on the depth of greenness of the individual. For the greenest of environmentalists, humans are of lesser importance than the abundant and diverse flora and fauna of the planet. Humans are defined as a recent addition to the livestock and are considered to have been a wholly disruptive influence on a world which was paradise before their arrival. For

---

[1] Ascribed by Plato in *Theaetetus* to Protagoras (430 B.C.).

these environmentalists, animal rights take priority over human rights. Environmentalism becomes a religion or a form of spiritualism; it certainly amounts to a creed.

A less extreme view sees humans as occupying a primary position but acknowledges the status of flora, fauna, the landscape and countryside and the environmental media as deserving protection in their own right. So, the extinction of whales should be prevented by regulation and international agreement and pressure not because they are of value to people, but because they have an independent right to exist. In fact, there may be a conflict between the material interest of people and the animal in question. The people of the traditional whaling villages of Norway have demanded the right to resume their whaling activities in the face of an international agreement and European Regulation prohibiting whaling. Although they are not nowadays economically dependent on whaling they demand it as a custom which stems from their cultural background and history. It is similar to the argument presented by native peoples such as the Inuit of Labrador who are granted the right to hunt unlimited numbers of caribou and seals because it is part of their cultural history. The conflict occurs between the preservation of an endangered species, such as the baleen and sperm whales, and the preservation of an indigenous people and their customary behaviour. However, even in this context, it can be seen that the interests of people are ultimately the overriding concern. None but the Zealots would argue that the wolf and bear, eliminated from Great Britain since the seventeenth century, should be reintroduced into the New Forest. Few would argue that a man-eating tiger in India should not be hunted and killed.

The concept of the environment can also be defined so as to extend beyond living objects. The 1985 European Directive on the assessment of environmental impacts[2] includes in the list of items to be considered, "cultural heritage and material assets." Thus, ancient artefacts and archaeological remains become part of the definition. The discovery of a Roman theatre on a construction site could therefore be classified as part of the environment. Norman churches and Victorian aqueducts could all fall within the definition. Such inanimate objects could then be weighed in the balance in analysing the cost and benefit of a proposed development as part of an environmental assessment.

---

[2] Directive on the Assessment of the Effects of Certain Public and Private Projects on the Environment; Directive 85/337: [1985] O.J. L175/40.

VALUES AND THE ENVIRONMENT

The link between economics and the environment reflects the change in thinking about environmental problems which has occurred in industrialised countries in the last few years. The emphasis has shifted from the "command and control," or regulatory, approach to an allegiance to market based instruments, such as taxes or charges, which give polluters an economic incentive to adapt their practices. Harnessing the market is a more efficient way of protecting the environment, it is suggested, particularly when coupled with the judicious use of regulations.

The role of economic analysis in environmental policy advocates a rigorous analysis of the facts on an economic basis which may not automatically coincide with the commercial interests involved.[3] It works by attributing a value to factors which have traditionally been left uncosted because they had no value to the trade. It is a form of cost benefit analysis. It is not an entirely novel attempt to use this form of economic assessment in the environmental field.

An early example occurs in the Report into the Third London Airport where the Commission were enjoined to apply cost-benefit analysis for the first time. The Commission concluded that they should make use of cost benefit analysis "as the best available aid to rational decision-making but the results must be subject to close scrutiny and discussion before any final recommendation."

The use of traditional cost-benefit analysis revealed some of the inadequacies of such an approach; in fact, the Commission were at the time more than conscious of the difficulties. They emphasised that in the end the decision-makers must make their own judgment, particularly in the face of conflicting expert opinions. They recognised the difficulties of placing money values on such factors as: "the historical and architectural qualities of Norman and Victorian churches, open countryside, the unique qualities of the ecology on the shores of Foulness Island and peaceful Sunday afternoons in the garden." However, in spite of the criticism that they were exclusively applying materialistic standards, they justified this approach on the grounds that it meant they could eschew purely subjective and arbitrary judgments. They argued that it would at least provide an opportunity to "measure and value factors which are external to ordinary market transactions."

---

[3] D. Pearce (ed.). "Blueprints for a Green Economy" (Earthscan Publications); D. Pearce (ed.), "Blueprint 2, Greening the World Economy" (Earthscan Publications).

Environmental values are not the only criteria to be weighed in the balance when decisions about development projects are made. In the planning system, various factors are weighed in the balance before a decision to approve a project is made. While environmental concerns may be taken into account, they may be outweighed by economic questions. The need for a factory which will create jobs and boost the local economy may take precedence. The need for housing may be more urgent than the need to preserve an open area. The need for a new road to aid the movement of freight lorries and limit accidents may take priority over an area of outstanding natural beauty. It will depend on a combination of factors, including, the circumstances of the project, the locality in which it is to be sited, the views of the politicians (local or national), and the degree of local support for the project. The environment will be only one of the features to be considered in the planning process.

POLITICS AND THE ENVIRONMENT

The topicality of environmental issues cannot be denied. No newspaper editor allows a day to pass without some reference to an environmental story. It might be a report of an international conference on the ozone layer, or a report of a protest group taking direct action to interrupt a project they consider damaging to the environment, or a report of a noise nuisance caused by the loud playing of a record-player in a block of flats. It could simply be the list of planning applications in the local newspaper or even be the subject matter of a series of editorials.

The topicality of environmental issues derives from their appearance on the political agenda. The environment is often considered to have emerged as a political force in the 1960s, and books such as Rachel Carson's "Silent Spring" bear testimony to this. However, environmental issues have emerged down the centuries. They appear most notably, and most recently, in the writings of Adolf Hitler, a vegetarian, who advocated protection of the environment and the countryside.

However, as a force in modern party politics, they emerged most vigorously in the European Parliamentary elections of June 1989 when the Green Party in the United Kingdom polled 14.5 per cent. in the elections to the European Parliament and their membership rose to 20,000. The various green parties within the European Community then gained considerable ground and credence in promoting their views. The subsequent decline of the Green Party might be ascribed to the fact that the mainstream political parties ensured that their manifestos were adjusted to reflect the growing importance on the electoral platform of environmental concerns. In addition, 1989 was a year when the economy appeared to be burgeoning, whereas, five years later the political agenda has become dominated by economic and social issues in the wake of a severe recession.

Outside the arena of party politics, the pressure groups have developed important power bases with increased membership. Such organisations as Greenpeace on the international scale, and Friends of the Earth and the Campaign for the Protection of Rural England have demonstrably become important lobbying organisations at national and European level. Animal charities such as the Royal Society for the Protection of Birds also feature as important organisations ready to campaign through the legal and administrative structures for the promotion of their charitable objectives. In addition to these major organisations are numerous groups set up for ad hoc purposes which campaign at various points in the hierarchy.

Within the United Kingdom, environmental questions have become part of the political agenda. In a notable speech to the Royal Society in 1988, Lady Thatcher, then Prime Minister, referred to this generation's responsibility for a "full repairing lease" on the planet. The White Paper[4] followed in September 1990.

However, with a deepening recession, it has become apparent that environmental protection is largely a luxury to be afforded in times of prosperity and that a redetermination of environmental priorities is taking place. Concern over the mounting cost of implementing the green initiatives is forcing a rethink of which policies should take priority. In the United States of America, the cost of the American Superfund, the compulsory insurance scheme for environmental clean-up, is now perceived as prohibitive. In the United Kingdom proposals for introducing a compulsory scheme of registration for contaminated land were dropped in the face of opposition from industry on the grounds of the cost of blighted land.

The review of priorities raises the question of the definition of the environment. The issue of whether it is centred on people or whether people are the stewards of the planet becomes central. Is the priority to be the health and safety of people or issues such as recycling or the development of renewable energy? Such issues as these have been at the forefront of the crusade by environmental campaigners. In New York, for example, it is an offence for householders not to sort their rubbish into separate sacks for recycling, and Germany, too, has

---

[4] *This Common Inheritance: Britain's Environmental Strategy*, Cm. 1200 (1990).

wholeheartedly adopted the policy of recycling. But the German waste recycling scheme, the Duales System Deutschland (DSD), was on the edge of bankruptcy before being propped up at the last minute by funds from industry.

The politics of the environment have important economic consequences. The German recycling scheme, for example, has had a devastating effect on the recycling industry in other European countries. The quantity of carefully sorted waste has exceeded Germany's capacity to recycle it and it has been exported to neighbouring countries at subsidised prices with deleterious effects on their recycling firms. In fact several United Kingdom firms have gone out of business as a result of German waste becoming available on the United Kingdom market at low prices.

SCIENCE AND THE ENVIRONMENT

The politics of the environment may not always equate with science. What may be top of the political agenda, may not be there because it has a clear scientific base. It may be there because of popular scientific misconceptions or without an agreed scientific base. For example, the threat posed by global warming, a topic much in the mind of ordinary consumers, is not agreed upon by scientists. Some argue that the threat of a rise in the planet's temperature from an increase in the concentration of carbon dioxide and methane might be counteracted by the natural action of the clouds and the oceans. The "hole in the ozone layer" has frightened many ordinary mortals, yet scientists fail to agree on the threat it poses. But, because of the degree of awareness of the ozone layer, agreements have been reached at international level, to limit the use of chlorofluorocarbons to minimise the risk. These agreements have a significant impact on industry yet, the scientific evidence supporting these assumptions remains debatable.

For environmental lawyers, who may or may not be environmentalists, the importance is to have an understanding of the scientific issues, to remain open-minded and to retain the lawyer's objectivity. Science is important in that it may be necessary to establish a known scientific consequence of a particular activity. Knowledge of the precise effect of global warming may not be critical to the outcome of a particular case. Nevertheless, a general understanding of the issues is important for an environmental lawyer, just as an understanding of medical terms and medical ethics is important for a successful outcome of an action in medical negligence. A cross-examination of an expert witness will be aided by a reasonably scientific approach. A key point to remember when dealing with evidence and witnesses, is that science seldom presents an absolute truth. It is more often based on probabilities. It is the task of the lawyer to test and challenge these probabilities.

All lawyers are familiar with the concept of the standard of proof and the way which this is interpreted in the courtroom. Every law student can state that the standard of proof in the criminal court is proof beyond reasonable doubt, and, in a civil court, on the balance of probabilities. So, in a case concerning environmental pollution the prosecution must establish proof beyond reasonable doubt or, in the civil context, the plaintiff must prove their case on the balance of probabilities. The evidence which is to be tested will largely be based on scientific issues given in evidence by expert witnesses. In a case concerning a criminal offence such as murder, scientific and forensic evidence may be called, but much of the evidence will be factual. So proof beyond reasonable doubt must be adduced of such questions as to the whereabouts of the suspect and the strength of an alibi, for example. Where environmental damage is alleged, then the issues may be predominantly concerned with whether the particular damage alleged was capable of being caused by the activity of the defendant. The main issue may well be the validity of the scientific evidence.

For example, in the case of *Reay* v. *British Nuclear Fuels*,[5] the overwhelming bulk of the evidence concerned the evidence of expert witnesses as to whether exposure to radiation could have caused the workers at Sellafield nuclear power station to have defective sperm which caused their children to have a propensity to leukaemia. Numerous experts were called and reports received which the judge considered and to which he applied the legal standard of proof finding that the plaintiffs had failed to prove their case on the balance of probabilities.

This calls in question the basis on which scientists are able to aver that a particular state of affairs is scientifically proven. What standard do scientists use to establish that a certain fact is proved or otherwise? In 1968, Sir Peter Medawar, an eminent scientist, wrote:

"Ask a scientist what he conceives the scientific likelihood to be, and he will adopt an expression which is at once solemn and shifty-eyed: solemn because he feels he ought to declare an

---

[5] *Reay* v. *British Nuclear Fuels plc; Hope* v. *British Nuclear Fuels plc* 1990 R. No 860; 1989 H. No. 3689 (unreported).

opinion: shifty-eyed because he is wondering how to conceal the fact that he has no opinion to declare."[6]

This remark, superficially flippant, reveals a major debate in the scientific establishment and the community at large as to the value of science and its ability to present objective truths. The difficulty is in part because over periods of time a set of scientific theories, standards and methods may be accepted by the scientific establishment and therefore perceived as "truths." Then, a major breakthrough is made which, like a revolution, turns everything on its head and challenges many assumptions previously accepted. It might seem at these points, that science is not about truth and reality but about transient vogues.[7] There is also currently in fashion, an anti-science movement; a movement which rejects science and scientists as the perpetrators of all that has gone wrong with the environment. This movement leans towards a spiritual relationship with nature and the earth, sometimes described as a Gaian approach to life.

The approach by many environmentalists is that science, because it is constantly evolving, makes it impossible to prove that any particular substance is harmless. It is argued that because no apparent harm has been caused that does not mean that the substance is harmless. Ill effects may emerge at some time in the future. This approach would mean that the burden of proof is shifted from the environmentalist who must currently show harm, to the producer who will have to show that it is harmless.[8] This involves the use of the precautionary principle.[9] This blatantly overlooks the fact that science has established many certainties and provided many explanations for global phenomena.

From the lawyer's perspective this presents certain problems. For instance, there may be an unspoken assumption held by many people that nuclear power is bad. This assumption is based not on scientific evidence but on an unformulated fear. Factual evidence showing that more people are killed in road accidents in a year than have ever been killed by nuclear accidents may have no impact on this attitude. Such an attitude kindles an approach which is anti-science. This approach may appear to undervalue the validity of scientific evidence as presented in a courtroom. In fact, if taken to its

---

[6] P. B. Medawar, *Induction and Intuition in Scientific Thought* (Methuen, London, 1969), p. 11.
[7] T. Theocaris & M. Psimopoulos, "Where Science Has Gone Wrong" (1987) 329 *Nature*, October 15.
[8] S. Mayar & B. Wynne, "How Science Failed the Environment" (1993) *New Scientist*, June.
[9] See p. 27.

extreme it makes scientific evidence impossible since the environmentalist can always claim that although harm has not yet been proved, that does not mean that it is harmless.

It needs to be understood that scientific evidence may be based on statistical evidence and the use of proven methodologies. The testing of such evidence, therefore, requires the testing of the methods on which it is based and the statistical validity of the results. If a method is discredited by another scientist then it throws doubt on the results produced by the expert who has been called to establish a certain fact. If another scientist has been unable to repeat the experiment with the same results this has the same effect. For instance, in 1990, two scientists claimed that they had been able to generate heat by a technique known as cold fusion. This revolutionary claim was subsequently tested by numerous scientists, the majority of whom were unable to repeat the results. They used the same method but obtained different results. Thus, the evidence of the original two was discredited. In the same way, if their evidence was to be presented in court, the evidence of the other scientists would be brought to weigh against theirs and their credibility would be destroyed. On the balance of probabilities their case would fall.

Science establishes partial or provisional truths. It is a tenet of science that all scientific statements are known to be wrong insofar as they can be expanded and qualified. The criminal court, however, requires truth beyond reasonable doubt, not a scientific debate about the validity or otherwise of some scientific statement or method.

Any case which a lawyer may handle may require the assimilation of information which is unfamiliar. Indeed, it is one of the skills of a lawyer to absorb new information quickly and accurately. Some competence in the environmental terminology is, therefore, critical when dealing with clients in conference or when exhibiting forensic skills in the courtroom.

For a detailed grasp of the science behind these concepts, reference should be made to scientific text books and journals. The following definitions should prove useful, however, for an elementary guide to the language of the environmentalist.

Global warming

This is sometimes known as the greenhouse effect. This is because certain gases form an insulating blanket round the earth. They allow in the energy provided by the sun. This warms the earth. Then, in turn, the insulating gases prevent the warmth from escaping. This effect is what makes this planet habitable; without it most of the earth would be frozen. The problem is that if these gases become too concentrated, they work too well, keeping in too much heat, (or at least more than we are used to). These gases include carbon dioxide which is produced by burning fossil fuels and by deforestation, (trees absorb carbon dioxide). Methane is another greenhouse gas and is produced by agriculture, (by cows in particular), old mine workings and landfill waste. The gases which do not occur naturally are the chlorofluorocarbons (CFCs).

The effect of global warming is debatable. Some argue that it will result in the thawing of the polar ice caps and the thermal expansion of the oceans and cause devastating flooding; that up to a third of rainfall will be lost in some areas such as, for example, the grainbelts of the United States and the wheatfields of the Caucasian steppes. Low lying areas such as Bangladesh, already periodically subject to catastrophic flooding, will be permanently under water.[9A]

The hole in the ozone layer

This in itself is a misdescription. What has been observed has been a depletion in the ozone layer. The ozone layer is a screen of ozone gas about 25 kilometres above the earth. This gas prevents some of the ultra-violet radiation from the sun passing through. Excessive exposure to ultra-violet rays causes skin cancer in some human beings and restricts the growth of plants.

Certain gases, notably CFCs, destroy ozone gas. Scientific observations have shown that certain areas, particularly those above the North and South Poles have a depleted layer of ozone gas in the stratosphere. It has only been possible to record the concentration of the ozone layer this century. It is arguable that changes in the ozone layer have occurred naturally over the centuries and are affected by natural phenomena such as volcanoes more significantly than man-made activities. However, industry has been forced to change its practices as a consequence of political pressure.

Acid rain

Rain is normally slightly acidic. The problem referred to in relation to acid rain is where rain has become more acidic than normal. This does not cause a problem if it falls on the Chiltern Hills, a range of chalk hills where the alkaline soil neutralises the acid. However, if it falls on soil which is acid, then the problem is compounded and the inland waterways become too acid. Acid rain also has the effect of removing ammonium and calcium ions from

---

[9A]   See the Government strategy document "*Climate Change – The UK Programme*".

the soils, this gets in the waterways, acidifies the lakes and affects plant life on the land such as forests. Buildings may also be damaged by the effect of an overly acid atmosphere. Acid rain occurs when acid gases enter the atmosphere and then come back to earth in the form of rain, mist or snow. Sulphur and nitrogen oxides are the main acid gases and are produced by large combustion power stations which burn coal and by motor vehicles which burn oil.

Microbiological contamination

The microbiological quality of water concerns the presence in water of certain bacteria. Sewage contaminated water, for example, can carry different bacteria which constitute a health risk. One bacterium in particular has been used as a measure of water quality. Escherichia coli, or E.coli, indicates the presence of faecal pollution and therefore the possible presence of other pathogens.[10] Salmonella is an example of such a pathogen. Some naturally occurring bacteria may also cause infection.

Life cycle analysis

Life cycle analysis or assessment (L.C.A.), is a new concept which explores the life cycle of a product from cradle to grave, (or, in the case of recycled products, from conception to resurrection). Frequently, it challenges assumptions about the viability of recycling products as an environmentally sound goal. For example, if newsprint is recycled, the energy involved in the process far exceeds the benefit derived from the recycled material. It would be less damaging to grow and chop down another tree. The trend towards recycling household waste is another case in point, particularly if the example of the German system is taken. In Germany the domestic waste industry cannot cope with the mountain of household waste enthusiastically sorted and saved by German householders. As a consequence, it is being transported mostly by lorries which emit exhaust gases and which create noise and have other damaging effects. Then the waste must be washed and graded. The cost in environmental terms can be greater than the benefit.

[10] D. Wheeler, "On the Beach" 39 *Laboratory Practice* (No. 4) 19–23.

Biodiversity of species

This is normally considered in the context of the threat to individual species of wild life; the threat that they may become extinct. This may occur because their natural habitat has disappeared – a forest chopped down for its timber, for example. Plant and animal communities are never static, they are always dynamic. Their abundance and distribution may change from time to time. Changes in water table levels, for example, can cause dramatic changes to the local flora and fauna.[11] The last 300 years have seen a dramatic increase in exterminated life forms. An attempt to classify species according to the risk of extermination has been made by the International Union for the Conservation of Nature in the form of the Red Data Books. A species may be endangered, that is in danger of extinction unless the current factors affecting its existence are changed; vulnerable, that is, on the brink of endangered; or rare, that is, having a small world population. Such classification may be critical in determining protective legislation at national or international level. The evidence in the decline of certain types of whales, for example, led to an international convention protecting them. There is also the International Convention on International Trade in Endangered Species of Wild Fauna and Flora (CITES), which has been implemented by Regulation in the European Community.[12] This convention introduced a system of licensing for trade in certain species and prohibited trade in the most endangered species.[12A]

Sustainable development

This concept refers to the objective of continuing to develop the economies of the world while protecting the environment for the benefit of all present nations of the world, and all future generations. The next generation should not have to pay the bill for the activities of its ancestors. It was developed in "Our Common Future," the report of the World Commission on Environment and Development, (the "Brundtland Report"), and has most recently appeared in the Fifth Action Programme of the European Commission. The Rio Earth Summit of 1992 endorsed it as a principle to guide future development and the United Kingdom Government has issued a consultation paper which "seeks to provide a focus for continuing

---

[11] I.F. Spellerberg, "Ecological Evaluation for Conservation" (1981) *Studies in Biology* (No. 133).
[12] For further reading see S. Lyster, *International Wildlife Law* (1985).
[12A] See the Government document: "*Biodiversity – The U.K. Action Plan*" (Cm. 2428).

public debate about the preparation of a United Kingdom strategy [for sustainable development]."[12B] It is one of the best examples both of the idealism of the environmental movement, and of the failure to accord environmental initiatives a scientific base.

The concept of sustainable development seems impossibly vague and idealistic. Yet, the Town and Country Planning Association, an independent charity, has produced a document, "Planning for a Sustainable Environment,"[13] which attempts to elaborate a strategy for the achievement of this goal. This report accepts that formidable changes in attitudes, institutions and ideologies are required. The Town and Country Planning Association defines sustainable development as including four aspects: the conservation of the stock of natural assets; the need to avoid damage to the regenerative capacity of ecosystems; the need to achieve greater social equality; and the need to avoid leaving future generations to pay the bill for today's damage to the environment. There is an acceptance in the report that the strategy is not simply about environmental protection but is also about politics. It requires a change in social political circumstances which, given the political priorities of most of the present governments in the world, are largely unthinkable.

There are various features of sustainable development. It advocates the development of renewable energy resources so that they can be replaced as fast as they are used. Renewable energy resources should replace non-renewable sources such as coal, gas and oil. New products should be manufactured which involve the use of clean technology, minimising the production of waste and using the by-products or based on the use of recycled products.

At the international level, draft articles on sustainable development are included in the legal principles adopted by the World Commission on Environment and Development and in a draft charter by the Council of Europe on Environment and Development.

Risk analysis

This is linked to the concept of hazard assessment. It is a method of determining the level of risk involved in a certain operation. There are numerous examples from the health and safety sector. The risk involved in undertaking a major project, such as the building of the Channel Tunnel, can be viewed in terms of the likely number of

---

[12B] See the strategy document issued by the Government: "*Sustainable Development – The U.K. Strategy*" (Cm. 2426).

[13] Earthscan (1993).

deaths which will occur during construction. One death could be discounted in terms of the decision to go ahead and build. Five hundred anticipated deaths would cause the project to be viewed in a different light. Under such circumstances, it may not be worth building it.

Similarly, the cost in the number of lives that would be saved if a new road were to be built will be a factor in considering the cost of construction. At planning inquiries these figures are routinely taken into account. At the planning inquiry for the construction of that stretch of the M3 across Twyford Down, the figure of 42 personal injury accidents per year was cited. The calculation is not simply in terms of the number of lives in question. Lives are given a putative value. The Ministry of Transport assigns a monetary value to each human life.

Environmental risks may also be calculated. A risk analysis of a nuclear power station would consider the chances of an accident occurring and the possible consequences of such an accident.

THE SCOPE OF ENVIRONMENTAL LAW

The term "environment" might convey an image of sandals, beards and flowers, of blue painted people demonstrating on construction sites rather than a group of sober suited lawyers. Indeed, 20 years ago a book on environmental law would have seemed a dangerous novelty. Yet now the subject has achieved respectability. It features regularly on degree courses, both at undergraduate and at post-graduate level, and a growing number of practising lawyers now style themselves environmental lawyers. The development of the subject within the legal profession follows hard upon the heels of the rise in public consciousness of the state of the environment. But, although the subject has acquired a status of its own, its range remains open to debate. Established subjects can be clearly defined, but environmental law has yet to acquire a conventional syllabus.

The problem stems to some extent from the way in which the legal profession has approached the subject. In the United Kingdom, an environmental lawyer has typically evolved from a property lawyer who has specialised in administrative, local government and plan-ning law. Many courses, therefore, concentrate heavily on land use planning law as a key component. Sometimes, the environmental law course has simply replaced the planning law course. Whereas in continental Europe, the environmental lawyer has frequently pre-viously specialised as a consumer lawyer, and, therefore, views environmental law from the perspective of the individual member of the public. Food law might, therefore, be perceived by a continental lawyer as a proper topic to be included within the field of environmental law. A student considering the selection of a course on environmental law would do well to study carefully the individual syllabus to discover its content.

For the practitioner, the need to acquire some expertise within the field might spring from the commercial activities of the firm. A commercial client, accustomed to seeking advice on conveyances, take-overs and mergers, might need legal advice on the liability for contaminated land or on the implications of a European Directive on environmental auditing. An industrial client might require advice on integrated pollution control. A local authority might require legal expertise on the implications of new waste laws. A personal client, however, may raise a problem that bears on the health implications of a local industrial activity. An allegation that an adverse health effect has been suffered because of the presence of toxic fumes in the atmosphere may raise the possibility of litigation. Such litigation is likely to be vigorously defended since the implications of a successful claim could be devastating financially for the defendant company. Or, the solicitor might be consulted by a local pressure group campaigning against a new development such as a new road or airport. A residents' association might be formed which is seeking to use the legal system as part of its weaponry, perhaps to seek judicial review of the actions of a government Minister in the High Court, or to seek legal representation in a planning inquiry, or which is even contemplating pursuing the campaign at European level.

Frequently, the practitioner may work as part of a team alongside environmental consultants, experts in technical fields such as noise levels and water quality, and scientists and engineers. Formal legal action, such as seeking injunctions, may only be one weapon in the armoury of these clients. The legal process may be used alongside political lobbying which may be at local, national or, as is increasingly the case, at European level. The role of the European Parliament is notable in environmental cases. Members of the European Parliament have shown themselves to be very willing to raise questions on national environmental issues. For the lawyer, not only legal skills are required but also the facility to co-ordinate a campaign or to work alongside other professionals as part of a team under the leadership of a campaign manager.

So, the range of topics under the general heading of environmental law is extensive. It could include planning law, the law relating to the quality of air and water, the disposal and transport of waste, control of the nuclear industry, statutory nuisances. It represents a new classification which absorbs many areas previously considered to fall under different headings, public health, for instance, or, planning law, or certain aspects of housing law. It includes new areas, such as energy law and the law relating to the countryside and to animals. It can even extend beyond planetary boundaries outwards to outer space. Dumping in near space is becoming a serious problem although not, as yet, for the ordinary man in the street.

THE PUBLIC AND THE ENVIRONMENT

Redress for environmental grievances

The involvement of the practising lawyer in issues of environmental law, is likely to arise where an individual's interests are directly affected by some environmental activity, or where a group are campaigning against some activity perceived as "damaging to the environment." Environmental law can either arise as an aspect of private law protecting persons or their property, or as an aspect of public law. In the former context, the legal recourse might be achieved by a tortious action, in the latter, through an administrative action or criminal prosecution. River pollution has historically been challenged by angling associations using the tort of nuisance to protect their fishing rights. Now, the administrative agency, the National Rivers Authority, might bring a criminal prosecution in addition to such a private action. The loss of light brought about by a new skyscraper might be challenged by an action for loss of an easement of light. Alternatively, or in addition, a judicial review might be sought of the decision of the local planning authority not to undertake an environmental assessment of the proposed skyscraper. A smoking bonfire might give rise to an action in nuisance or a local authority environmental health officer might bring a prosecution for statutory nuisance.

The growth of administrative agencies and the power given to them by an increase in regulation means that environmentally damaging activities may be controlled to an increasing extent by the State. Increased penalties, (in many cases the magistrates' courts are now able to fine up to £20,000), means that breaches are taken seriously by offenders. In many instances this means that cases are more vigorously defended involving the use of expert witnesses and relying more on the skills of environmental lawyers. A case may be brought as a result of a complaint by an individual member of the public or as a result of a routine inspection by an officer of the agency.

Actions on behalf of private clients would rarely take the form of criminal prosecutions. More usually, they would be based on classic forms of common law actions or on administrative actions. Actions for damages or an injunction in the county or High Court or appeals on a point of law to the High Court or an application to the Queen's Bench Division of the High Court are the most likely avenues for legal redress.

Class actions have not traditionally been part of the English legal system. Normally, people must sue as individuals or join together on a writ as named individuals. However, one recent example has indicated a change in this. Residents of the London Docklands instituted proceedings against the London Docklands Development Corporation, Olympia and York, the builders of Canary Wharf and the Docklands Light Railway.[14]

It is also clear since the decision of the House of Lords in *R v. Secretary of State for Employment, ex parte Equal Opportunities Commission*[15] that if persons with a proper interest can show that the government is in breach of European law, they are entitled to use judicial review proceedings to seek a declaration from the court. There is already a greater willingness by the pressure groups to use the courts to achieve their environmental objectives. For example, Greenpeace brought an action against British Nuclear Fuels on the ground that the Government had acted unreasonably in approving the commissioning of the THORP nuclear reprocessing plant, in the High Court, (March 4, 1994).

Such actions are more common in the United States of America, where well-funded pressure groups, such as the Sierra Club, can afford to run the risk of losing such an action. In the Greenpeace action against British Nuclear Fuels, costs were not awarded against the plaintiffs as they did win the point that the Government was obliged to justify the decision to start up the THORP plant. Such an outcome in future cases cannot, however, be assumed, and, while major pressure groups such as Greenpeace and Friends of the Earth are presently attracting substantial donations,[16] costs awards against them would quickly eat into their funds.

---

[14] A. Mumma, "Protection of the Water Environment Through Private Court Action" (1992) *Water Law* 51–54, March.

[15] *R. v. Secretary of State for Employment, ex parte Equal Opportunities Commission, The Times,* March 4, 1994.

[16] In 1993, Greenpeace U.K. received £6.6 million in donations before fundraising costs; Friends of the Earth – £4.5 million on the same basis.

HISTORY OF ENVIRONMENTAL LAW

The Development of environmental law

Modern environmental law, therefore, can be seen to have a wide range drawing on public and private law, criminal and civil law, common law and administrative regulatory law. Its sources are local bye-laws, national and European legislation, and international conventions and agreements.

Whilst its classification is modern, its origins are not entirely novel. Although environmental law may have emerged as a new discipline for formal study, environmental laws are not new.[17] There are examples of medieval statutes on environmental issues, and King James I, who found that smoke got in his eyes, passed a law banning the burning of sea coal in London. In the nineteenth century, however, with the Industrial revolution, the need to regulate industry to control its effects became apparent. The pressure on urban areas became particularly acute with the population drift from the countryside into the cities and the population increase. Thus, the landmark legislation on public health, housing and town and country planning was initiated.[18]

HISTORY OF ENVIRONMENTAL CONTROL

The current growth in public awareness of environmental issues sometimes obscures the fact that, just as environmental law is not new, neither is the manipulation of the environment. As the social organisation of mankind developed, so did his desire and ability to control the environment.

As a gatherer and hunter, an activity which would seem to have a minimal impact on the environment, mankind sought to control the environment in order to provide a better living. The native Americans burned the plains of America in order to provide better grazing for the buffalo. When mankind ceased to rely exclusively on gathering and hunting as a way of living, it became necessary to clear land

---

[17] Garner, "Environmental Law – A Real Subject?" (1992) New L.J. 1718, December 11.
[18] D. Hughes, *Environmental Law* (1992), Chap. 1; S. Ball & S. Bell, *Environmental Law* (1991), Chap. 1.

to grow crops. While this is occurring now in Latin America with the clearances of rain forests, it has been happening in Europe over the last 3,000 years. A modern example is the agricultural practice of removing hedgerows to create larger fields.

The greatest protection to the environment in northern Europe has been the climate, the soil structure and the use of primitive tools. Primitive tools and techniques have limited the ability of their users to have a massive impact on the environment. Even so, in prehistoric times much of Europe was covered by forest. The forest was lost, not through climatic change, but by systematic clearance by people. Subsequently, many places were turned into moorland or even desert.

Environmental control has grown exponentially with social organisation. The Romans, for example, developed a far reaching social organisation. With it, came a concern for the environment. This concern was not altruistic, nor was it based on an understanding of the consequences of environmental control in the long term. Instead it was based on a realisation that the environment could be controlled to the economic and social advantage of the State. So, the marshes of Italy were drained and the port at Brindisium was built. Once the social structure of Rome broke down, the organisation capable of controlling these environmental changes collapsed, the marshes returned and eventually the Vandals launched their successful invasion.

Examples of such links between social and economic structures and environmental control are manifold. Alexander the Great developed the irrigation wells in ancient Persia; during the reign of King Cnut draining of the Fenlands continued, leaving the best agricultural soil in Britain; the English lairds cleared the highlands of Scotland removing the crofters and replacing them with sheep – a more profitable venture – thereby changing the character of the country which had already been changed from a forested land by the crofters themselves. Modern examples abound. Hydro-electric power projects all over the world and the building of dams, where valleys are flooded and natural rivers dammed, reflect social organisation at the highest level. The environmental control achieves an economic end in the production of electricity or in the supply of water for irrigation. Such production has the potential of improving the living conditions of ordinary people as well as enhancing the prosperity of groups of people within society.

The difficulty occurs where a gap is perceived between the gain achieved by the environmental control and the devastation rendered by it. Yet, to express the control in such terms as "devastation" can, in itself, be highly misleading. Where a long history of environmental control has already completely changed the face of the countryside, one more change may simply be a new chapter in the planning history of the landscape.

For example, such changes as the opening of a new open cast coalmining site can readily be demonstrated to have a devastating effect. Even so, British Coal Opencast are always ready to explain the long term benefits of aftercare conditions and to demonstrate that, ultimately, the environment will enjoy an improvement. Such an assurance can be comprehended in the context of sites which are, for example, contaminated and blighted from previous industrial uses. They are less readily accepted where they involve land which is treated by local people as a natural asset, albeit, it is not truly "natural" in the sense of being untouched by humans. Other examples, such as dam projects in Russia and China, and the project to change the course of the River Danube, are projects of a tremendous magnitude with huge environmental consequences. The benefit from these projects, which require a highly sophisticated level of social organisation, is of high economic value in that they will provide irrigation and supplies of drinking water. The conflict can be plainly seen.

Thus, the breadth of environmental control can be seen to have a long history. The modern era of environmental awareness seems to date, at least on a mass scale, from the 1960s. It coincides with the space exploration which led to men walking on the moon and pictures becoming available of the earth as it was seen from outer space. It has a romantic imagery in the minds of some:

> "In my mind there are hardly any pictures which have made a more fundamental impact on modern thinking. The exquisite beauty and vulnerability of this small planet is there for anyone to see. We are no longer only the inheritors of the earth, we are also Earth's children, fellow travellers on a ship in space. And a growing number of people are prepared to act on this new view of the world. This is in a sense a Copernican counter-revolution. Earth has again become the centre of the universe."

(Professor Anders Victorin)[19]

The same thought is expressed in the report of the World Commission on Environment and Development, "Our Common Future," (the "Brundtland Report"):

---

[19] Environmental Law Symposium, 1990, University of Surrey.

"Historians may eventually find that this vision had a greater impact on thought than did the Copernican revolution of the 16th century, which upset the human self-image by revealing that the Earth is not the centre of the universe. From space, we see a small and fragile ball dominated not by human activity and edifice but by a pattern of clouds, oceans, greenery, and soils."

International activity in the environmental context began from this period. One of the key examples of this activity, and of co-operation at an international level, is the United Nations Conference of the Human Environment at Stockholm in 1972. This conference called for a determination to shape human actions according to their environmental effects. It also looked to the problems for developing countries in achieving an improved standard of living and, at the same time, not causing environmental harm.

DEVELOPMENT OF ENVIRONMENTAL LAW IN:

1. The Nordic programmes

The Nordic countries saw the development of a number of environmental programmes from this era. In 1974, three articles were included in the Helsinki agreement of 1962. These articles stated that the environmental interests of the other Nordic countries should have the same standing as national interests, harmonisation of legislation should be sought on environmental questions, and there should be a co-ordinated policy on setting aside areas for nature protection and recreation as well as on the protection of wild animals and plants. This was followed in 1976, when a convention was agreed which implemented the proposal that the environmental concerns of each of the Nordic states should be taken into account when permits for polluting activities were being considered. So, if a paper and pulp mill was being proposed in Norway, the Norwegian authorities would be obliged to consider the potential polluting effects that this would have in Sweden as well as in Norway. This involves the principles of environmental assessment at a trans-boundary level.

In fact, there are many instances of Nordic advances in the environmental field in advance of such developments in the rest of Europe or at European Community level. In 1988, the Nordic Council of Ministers proposed two programmes: a Nordic environ-mental Programme and a Plan of Action on Marine Pollution. The latter was primarily in response to the pollution incidents in the

North Sea in 1988. It deals with the reduction of harmful substances in the marine environment, such as nitrogen and phosphates and heavy metals. The Swedes at one time were even planning to close their nuclear reactors by 2010, a decision that appears to have been held in abeyance.

In many respects the Nordic countries are in advance of the European Community. As part of the extended European Union, Sweden and Norway will be disadvantaged in respect of their trading arrangements as part of a single market. There is no encouragement for one Member State to have stricter environmental controls than the rest. Such an approach would prejudice their national business and industrial interests. It is that criticism which is most effectively levelled at the Community. Environmental control progresses at the rate of the most conservative member.

Yet, although Sweden and Norway appear to be in advance of the rest of the Community, there are deficiencies within their own systems. Some are deficiencies which find their reflection in British environmental law. For example, one criticism made of Swedish law is that there is no coherent approach to legislation and enforcement. There are overlapping controls for projects. A more sophisticated criticism is that one single project may create pollution problems not simply at source but throughout the life of its product. For example, if a mine applies for a permit to extract coal, there are no harmonised controls over the lifetime of the coal that is mined; there is no cradle to grave control.[20] A Commission has, however, been set up in Sweden to review their system of environmental law. What will be of much interest will be the impact on European environmental law as Sweden and Norway join the Community.

2. United States of America

The United States is notable for its development of environmental law and its use of judicial proceedings to determine liability. In fact, Canada, Australia and New Zealand also have advanced frameworks of environmental law although they are not recognised as having the same influence on the development of European environmental law as the United States.

---

[20] Dr. G. Michanek, "Swedish Environmental Law: As Good as its International Reputation?" (University of Uppsala, Sweden), Environmental Law Symposium, 1992, University of Surrey.

In 1969 the United States passed the National Environmental Policy Act (NEPA) to improve the environmental assessment procedures of federal agencies. Its object was to improve the policy-making and data-gathering of environmental issues by the agencies. The major innovation of NEPA was, however, the requirement of environmental impact statements. NEPA requires that an environmental impact statement be filed for "major federal actions significantly affecting the quality of the human environment." NEPA was one of the major influences on the development of the European Directive on environmental impact assessment.

Under NEPA the Council on Environmental Quality (C.E.Q.) was set up and based in the President's Office. C.E.Q. has a number of responsibilities including the review of federal programmes and the development of national environmental policies.

The United States also has an Environmental Protection Agency which is the model for the proposed European Agency.

A further influence on the development of European policy on the environment has been the United States policy on measures to clean up hazardous waste. In 1980, the US Congress introduced the Comprehensive Environmental Response, Compensation and Liability Act, (CERCLA) which is commonly known as Superfund because it established a US $1.5bn fund to pay for clean-ups where the parties responsible for the sites were not in a position to pay for the work. The idea was to identify hazardous sites and to require them to be cleaned up either by the parties responsible or by the government. It soon became apparent that these funds were woefully inadequate for the task and further contributions amounting to US $13.6bn have been made. Superfund also receives contributions from various tax sources and from cost recovery actions.

Under the Superfund legislation, the parties responsible are strictly liable and are also subject to joint and several liability. So, a company which disposed of hazardous waste at a landfill site which is now leaching dangerous chemicals into the watercourses could be liable for the whole cost of clean up. Such a company may seek contributions from other users of the site, but the usual problems of insolvency or liquidation on the part of the other users may bar such an action. The legislation has the potential for an inequitable distribution of liability. This liability will in most cases fall on the insurance industry.

The draft European Directive on civil liability for damage caused by waste has many of the characteristics of the United States Superfund legislation and this has resulted in much opposition to its proposals by the waste management industry.

3. European Union environmental law

The European Union originally came into existence as the European Economic Community. Then "economic" was dropped from the title and now, since, the ratification of the Maastricht Treaty, a Union has been created. This change in nomenclature is not unrelated to the growing importance of environmental issues within Europe. In 1957, when the Treaty of Rome was concluded, the issue of the environment was not paramount. The post-war demand was for European stability and economic growth. The ravages of war on the economies of the Member States made urgent the need for expansion and for the improvement of the conditions for the citizens of these countries. That economic development could only take place within a framework which guaranteed a period of peace. The objectives of the Treaty, in effect, furthered the resolution of the Congress of Europe at the Hague in May 1948 for "a united Europe throughout whose area the free movement of persons, ideas and goods is restored." In the Treaty establishing the European Coal and Steel Community, concluded in Paris on April 18, 1951, the emphasis was on the need for "world peace." The Euratom Treaty, which established the European Atomic Energy Community and was concluded on the same day as the European Economic Community, March 25, 1957, also emphasised the raising of the standard of living for ordinary people:

"It shall be the task of the Community to contribute to the raising of the standard of living in the Member States and to the development of relations with the other countries by creating the conditions necessary for the speedy establishment and growth of nuclear industries."

(Article 1, Euratom Treaty.)

Environmental issues, insofar as they were considered at all, would have been specifically relegated to the imperative requirement of reorganising industry and re-establishing shattered economies.

The establishment of the European Economic Community created, however, a structure which was eventually to make the rise of environmental issues possible. The Treaty of Rome did not simply establish a series of common objectives; it also established a structure with institutions and a bureaucracy to enforce and execute those objectives. The Union comprises a supra-national organisation which is capable of having direct effect within the Member States. It has been held to create a new legal order, a description reminiscent of Hitlerian objectives and the establishment of the Third Reich. The similarity is striking; the Union of Europe achieved by the Treaty of Rome and later amending Treaties has achieved much of the organisational structure for which Hitler unsuccessfully strove.

The Union is unique amongst international organisations in that it has power to regulate the actions of its members. Further to the amendments introduced by the Maastricht Treaty, there will be increased powers of enforcement in respect of defaulting partners. The Declaration on the implementation of Community law stresses the importance for the coherence of the Union that Community Directives should be transposed, within the deadlines, into national law. The Commission is empowered to publish periodically a full report, which will amount to a league table of the extent of compliance by Member States with Union law.

Existing powers of enforcement under Article 169 of the Treaty of Rome mean that the Commission can issue proceedings against a Member State where there has been a failure to transpose a Directive properly or at all into national law. These proceedings take the form of a reasoned opinion which usually follows a period of informal negotiations. If no settlement is achieved then the Commission can bring the matter before the European Court of Justice.

The European Court of Justice is also unique, (with the possible exception of the European Court of Human Rights which exists by an international agreement). The European Court is alone in the international context in that it has the power to adjudicate the legality of the actions of members of the Union. Weaknesses are apparent, however, in that while the Court may adjudicate that a State has infringed Union law, powers of enforcement are limited. They amount to little more than the power to repeat the Article 169 proceedings by declaring that the State has failed to comply with an order of the Court. The effect of the establishment of a new legal order on environmental issues has been to give the European Union authority to determine policy and to legislate so as to bind in a detailed and specific manner the actions of the Member States. In particular, this affects the economic development of the members in the fields of energy, transport, the chemical, waste and construction industries. The water Directives require environmental standards relating not only to the quality of the water we drink, but also to the aesthetic appearance of the water in which we bathe for recreational purposes. As such, they impose considerable burdens on the water and sewerage industries to increase standards. In the wake of the privatisation of the water industry in the United Kingdom, the Government has shown itself reluctant to impose these burdens on the new water companies. As a consequence, infringement proceedings have been successfully brought against the United Kingdom for failing to implement the drinking water Directive. This relates, in particular, to the levels of nitrates present in the water in certain parts of the country.

The impact of European legislation falls, not on the individual in the first instance, but on industry. It is not, therefore, surprising, that industry has shown itself concerned at the quantity of environmental legislation and has lobbied with varying degrees of success against certain environmental proposals. There are two specific examples worthy of note. The Environmental Protection Act 1990, s.143, contained a proposal to create a register of contaminated land sites. In a statement on March 24, 1993, Michael Howard, Environment Secretary, announced the formal abandonment of the proposals. He stated that "the proposed registers would have reduced confidence in the value of sites placed on the register, thereby exacerbating blight without giving any clear indication on how such sites could be brought back into good condition and confidence restored." The proposals had been vigorously opposed by the construction industry. The Royal Institution for Chartered Surveyors had backed an alternative scheme involving the provision of land quality statements at the pre-development stage.

The second example relates to the European proposal for environmental audits. The original proposal was for all companies to undertake an environmental audit of their activities. This audit, as its financial counterpart, would have been mandatory. This proposal has again been watered down and it would seem that the eventual policy will be to adopt a voluntary code.

There is one area where environmental legislative intervention is noticeably lacking at European level. This is nuclear energy. The Euratom Treaty calls for the development of nuclear energy with the expressed objective of raising the standard of living of the Member States. Although there are requirements for the health and safety of workers in the nuclear industry and for general emission limits, there is not the wealth of legislation that can be found in other areas of the energy industry. There are various treaties at international level and most of the sources of supra-national intervention can be found at that level. Given the importance of nuclear power as a source of energy, (for example, in France it provides over 70 per cent. of the nation's energy requirements), this omission is remarkable. Nuclear power does, however, have the potential for military use. In the United Kingdom, the nuclear industry is largely occupied with recycling nuclear waste and the production of plutonium which has military uses. It would seem that, for this reason, European intervention at the environmental level is perceived as too sensitive and too close to a nation's individual defence systems.

One of the key features of the impact of European law on the United Kingdom has been the development of guiding and fundamental principles. Some of the principles are self-explanatory, others are more esoteric. A familiarity with the concepts they represent is critical to an understanding of environmental law. There are four basic principles set out in the E.C. Treaty:

"Community policy . . . shall be based on the precautionary principle and on the principle that preventive action should be taken, that environmental damage should as a priority be rectified at source, and that the polluter should pay."

(Article 130r(2)).

The precautionary principle. The evolution of this principle is striking. Whereas the other principles can be traced to the Action Programmes, this principle emerges suddenly in the Treaty on European Union. At first sight, it might appear to be identical to the preventive principle, but, in fact, it is markedly different. It implies that, even where there is no scientific evidence available to support a particular theory, precautions should be taken. It is striking evidence that the challenge to the scientific community and the challenge to the concept of scientific truth and objectivity has made its mark at the highest level of government.[21] If an assertion is made about the potential polluting effect of a certain substance, based on a popularly held view, then steps will be taken through legislative intervention to prevent environmental damage occurring even where it is not clearly established that the alleged culprit is to blame. The justification for this approach is that if subsequently the culprit is found to be to blame, it might be too late to save the earth. It is better to err on the side of caution than to take risks with the environment. For instance, there is much debate about the impact of global warming and its causes. It will probably take the scientific community decades to reach a conclusion about the validity of these theories. Yet, steps have been taken at an international level to control the production of the gases which are alleged to be the trouble-makers. The impact of these steps on the industrialised countries and the developing countries is tremendous, nevertheless limits have been imposed. The presumption, where the risks are not actually known, is against the discharge of potentially harmful or accumulative contaminants –

---

[21] See p. 6.

the environment must not be left to show harm before action is taken.[22]

The preventive principle. This principle emerges at the earliest stage in the development of European environmental policy and is based on the maxim that prevention is better than cure. As a principle it is eminently sound but only achievable when starting with a clean slate. If industry is already emitting smoke into the atmosphere and effluent into the rivers, then a damage limitation exercise is the appropriate and most feasible way forward. In fact, the preventive principle has only been clearly achieved in a limited number of Directives. The Environmental Impact Assessment Directive[23] is a prime example in that it requires an assessment of the environmental effects of major construction projects to be assessed before they are approved and given the go-ahead to be built. The sixth amendment to the Chemicals Directive[24] is another example. It requires new chemicals to be tested not only for their health effects but also for their effect on the environment in general, before being launched on the market.

By comparison, many other environmental Directives limit the amount of pollution. For example, the water Directives prescribe limits for certain substances present in water. It is possible to argue that they are also preventive in that they prevent excessive levels of lead, nitrates, etc., in the water. But, essentially, they achieve a compromise by permitting a certain amount of pollution which is generally agreed to be harmless.

The proximity principle. The principle that environmental damage should be rectified at source could be likened to the exhortation found on municipal billboards that you should take your rubbish home with you. The effect of pollution can be like a snowball, multiplying as it rolls onwards. The transportation of waste is an illustration. If a factory in Germany produces waste which is then transported to a landfill site in the United Kingdom the transportation itself creates pollution and the risk of accidental

---

[22] See "Greens' Bogus Science" *Financial Times*, August 1993.

[23] Council Directive on the Assessment of the Effects of Certain Public Private Projects on the Environment; Directive 85/337: [1985] O.J. L175/40.

[24] Directive amending for the sixth time Directive 67/548: J.O. 196/1 on the approximation of the laws, Regulations and administrative provisions relating to the classification, packaging and labelling of dangerous substances; Directive 79/831: [1979] O.J. L255/10.

spillage and contamination is increased. Consideration of the proximity principle within this context took place in the case of the *Wallonia*,[25] a decree of the Walloon Regional Executive which banned the import of waste into Wallonia was held effective insofar as it related to waste other than special waste. The court accepted the view that waste should be disposed of as near to the point that it was produced as possible.

The polluter pays. The meaning of this principle is clear. However, its interpretation in practice has been the subject of differing political views. The polluter may pay in a variety of ways. In the first instance, various polluting activities require a license or permit. For example, major industrial units in the United Kingdom require permits from Her Majesty's Inspectorate of Pollution before they can start operating. The National Rivers Authority also operates a licensing system for the discharge of effluents into the waterways. Fees are charged for these permits and are payable on an annual basis. If operations are conducted in breach of the licensing regime then they are punishable in the criminal courts and subject to a fine. So, there exists an administrative control which the "polluter" must pay for, and there exists the range of criminal penalties. Within the existing system of English common law, the liability for damages as a compensatory measure exists as a parallel to the administrative and penal controls.

A controversial application of this principle has been the proposal to introduce a system of taxation on polluters – the more you pollute, the more tax you pay. These are sometimes referred to as carbon taxes or eco-taxes. One proposal was specifically related to the production of carbon dioxide. It would have applied to all industries and individuals that were responsible for producing carbon dioxide. This would have affected a range of different interests from coal-fired power stations to the owners of old cars. Europe has not yet shown itself ready to agree to this innovative extension of the principle that the polluter should pay for the damage caused.

In the United States, the principle has been enacted through the Superfund scheme introduced in the Comprehensive Environmental Response Compensation and Liability Act of 1980 (CERCLA). This Act is retrospective and obliges owners to clean up sites polluted by hazardous waste. In fact, the liability, (projected to cost between $150 and $300 billion), will fall largely on the insurance industry.

---

[25] Case C-2/90, *Commission* v. *Belgium*: [1992] 1 E.C.R. 4431, [1993] 1 C.M.L.R. 365.

Proposals for a European Superfund have been made, (see above, p. 23).

So, the principle can be viewed in two ways. Firstly, it can be seen as an instrument which requires the polluter to bear the financial consequences of his activities. Secondly, it can be seen as a method of causing the polluter to finance the system necessary to monitor, inspect and prevent pollution.[26]

The Council of the European Communities expressed the principle in this way:

> "The Council stresses that in the interests of more efficient environmental protection in the context of effectively integrating environment and economic policy and meeting the fundamental objective of sustainable development, in particular while complying with the 'polluter pays' principle, it is necessary to back up current, direct environmental regulations, based on the command and control approach, with economic and fiscal instruments aimed at influencing the reasoning and behaviour of producers and consumers, to discourage wasteful and polluting processes and products and to promote technologies and productive processes which are consistent with resource conservation."

The principle of subsidiarity. The debate on the Maastricht Treaty brought to the forefront the issue of subsidiarity. Subsidiarity is the principle which states that if something can be carried out more effectively at a level in the hierarchy lower than Community level, then that is where it should be effected. It is the principle of the lowest common denominator.

The principle was not introduced by the Maastricht Treaty. It appears in the First Action Programme and became part of the E.C. Treaty as one of the amendments introduced by the Single European Act. The discussion arose in the context of the environment, however, when issues of federalism were raised during the progress of the Maastricht Bill through Parliament. It was argued by the United Kingdom Government that environmental issues are apt for the application of the principle of subsidiarity. In many instances, pollution can be a local matter and this may be particularly relevant for an island. For continental Europe, where rivers flow across state boundaries and the winds blow inconveniently from one country to the next, the argument is poorly made. When the Sandoz factory

---

[26] Dr. Marisa Meli, "The Polluter Pays; Some Conceptual Problems" (1992) 3 *Water Law* (No. 3) 79–81, May.

spilt chemicals into the Rhine, it had the potential to pollute riparian owners in five other Member States. Coal fired power stations may have the potential to cause acid rain which damages the Norwegian forests. When the fast flowing rivers of the United Kingdom dump waste into the North Sea it may reappear on the coastal borders of the Netherlands. Roads may also appear to be a local issue to be dealt with on a national basis. But a transport policy in favour of roads instead of railways can cause harmful gases which might have a global effect. There is also an economic question. If a single market is to become a reality, then the constraints on economic development should also be harmonised across the Member States.

The Fifth Action Programme seems to have been written with subsidiarity in mind. Unlike the earlier programmes which contained specific and detailed proposals, the Fifth Programme is general and seeks to "initiate changes in current trends and practices which are detrimental to the environment." Although it details priority themes it is expressed to be drafted "pursuant to the principle of subsidiarity." It is almost apologetic in stating that the programme "contains matters of particular seriousness which have a community-wide dimension, either because of the internal market, cross-boundary, shared resource or cohesion implications and because they have a crucial bearing on environmental quality and conditions in all regions of the community."

4. The United Kingdom

The United Kingdom has a body of environmental law which has developed through the system of common law which will be examined in detail in Chapter 2.

The major impact on the development of United Kingdom law has undoubtedly resulted from membership of the European Union. The obligation to implement Directives so as to harmonise standards across the E.C. has created a considerable tension between the United Kingdom and the European Commission. Nevertheless, despite popular opinion to the contrary, the United Kingdom is amongst the first of the Member States to take steps to implement European legislation in accordance with the timetables imposed by the Directives. The effect of adherence to the doctrine of subsidiarity may, however, be the major direction for the future development of environmental legislation, both in the United Kingdom and in Europe.

5. The international context

Environmental law at international level is created largely through the medium of treaties, agreements and conventions.[27] The most significant organisation other than the European Community, (which has been covered above), is the United Nations. The UN, through its Environment Programme, has made a major contribution to the development of environmental law on the international field. The first most significant conference of the UN was the Conference on the Human Environment (UNCHE) at Stockholm in 1972. The Conference established an Action Plan for environmental policy; an Environmental Fund; the UN Environmental Programme which comprised an administrative machinery and a Declaration consisting of 26 principles on the environment.

The World Health Organisation, the Food and Agriculture Organisation and the International Atomic Energy Agency are all examples of specialised UN agencies.

6. The developing nations

For the developing nations environmental protection has proved a double-edged sword. On the one hand many of their valuable resources are sited in areas regarded as areas of great environmental wealth by the rest of the world. Yet, the rest of the world has already removed its own forests, drained its own wetlands, ploughed its own meadows and has otherwise artificially controlled its immediate environment for thousands of years. If the Third World is to progress to a standard of living enjoyed by the rest then it is difficult to avoid the conclusion that a similar plundering of assets must take place. On the other hand, the developing countries have shown themselves to have a high level of concern about their own environment and to have a readiness to protect it. There is a need for the industrialised countries to be more ready to transfer technologies and to give the developing world ready access to the resources of research and development which will enable the industrialised countries to be at the forefront of the development of cleaner technologies and processes.

---

[27] For a detailed exposition see Birnie & Boyle, *International Law and the Environment* (1993).

Chapter Two

Sources of Environmental Law

INTRODUCTION

The bases for liability

Environmental pollution may give rise to the possibility of actions in public and private law, in civil and criminal law. An individual may be advised to seek the support of one of the enforcement agencies in seeking a remedy for the pollution. The enforcement agencies have statutory authority to act and can normally rely on statutes which create criminal offences. They may also have powers to issue and revoke licences to operate or to attach new conditions which will control the polluter's activities.

Within the United Kingdom, criminal liability within the field of environmental law is linked to the administrative regime. Most breaches of statutes dealing with pollution control are subject to criminal prosecution and are punishable by fines and/or imprisonment. There is, however, a considerable gap between pollution offences and "mainstream" crime. Pollution offences are prosecuted by the administrative agencies responsible for that aspect of pollution control. So, the National Rivers Authority brings enforcement proceedings for breaches of the Water Acts which cause pollution of the waterways. The waste authorities enforce breaches of the waste laws and local authority environmental health officers bring actions in respect of noise nuisance, local air pollution and breaches of the food hygiene rules. The criminalisation of pollution is linked to the administrative system. The police and the Crown Prosecution Service are not involved.

Administrative officers of these agencies are, therefore, responsible for the whole procedure. They have duties to inspect and monitor for incidents of pollution. They have the initial decision whether to negotiate a compromise solution or to instigate criminal proceedings or to serve one of the administrative notices available. For example, a local authority environmental health officer may decide to serve an abatement notice for a noise nuisance in the first instance. Failure by the culprit to observe this would then lead to criminal proceedings. The decision to issue proceedings may lie in the hands of the legal department of the local authority in the case of environmental health officers, or with the lawyers in other administrative agencies. The initial preparation of the evidence is, however, likely to be in the hands of the enforcement officer.

The enforcement officers of the various agencies are not lawyers and they, therefore, require the expertise of a lawyer to advise on the preparation of evidence for court and the procedural and evidential rules. In the past, there was a tradition for enforcement officers (such as environmental health officers, factory inspectors and trading standards inspectors) to conduct legal proceedings themselves. As a result those officers gaining this experience became very expert. This custom has largely disappeared mostly as a result of policy decisions that lawyers should be involved in the conduct of legal proceedings. This means that there may be a gap between the highly expert technical skills of the enforcement officer and the forensic skills of the lawyer that may lead to disasters in the courtroom. For a lawyer brought in to conduct a prosecution in a pollution case, early liaison with the enforcement officer is crucial. The enforcement officer is usually responsible for taking the witness statements and these should be carefully examined for admissibility according to the rules of evidence. The hearsay rule, for example, is complex, even for those trained in evidential matters, and can be a minefield for the uninitiated. The evidence may include photographs and video-tapes and these must be checked to ensure they contain no prejudicial matter which would cause them to be excluded at the trial.

The elements of criminal guilt

The elements constituting guilt in the pollution offence are different from the traditional concepts of "guilty conduct" and "guilty mind" invariably found in "offences of true criminality," such as criminal damage. The pollution offence is normally an offence of strict liability so that a "guilty mind" does not have to be proved, and so that the circumstances of the crime may be a state of affairs rather than a positive act or culpable neglect. The punishment is likely to be a fine. The level of fines has been sharply increased of late, permitting magistrates on a summary trial to fine up to £20,000, (a tenfold increase from £2,000). Imprisonment is rare, although there are some reported prison sentences for waste offences.[1] These changes in enforcement patterns reflect a growing concern with environmental crimes. In many civil law jurisdictions, some pollution offences have the same status as "mainstream" crime.[2] Offences which cause serious harm to the environment or endanger public health and safety are subject to criminal enforcement proceedings, not by the pollution enforcement agencies, but by the police and the criminal justice system. It would seem that the United Kingdom is unlikely in the near future to adopt such an approach. The favoured solution has been to increase the powers of the enforcement agencies and to increase the penalty for the offence.

Acting for the individual

If an individual wishes to seek compensation for the damage, however, then it is more appropriate to bring civil proceedings for an award of damages.

This could be done in addition to the action of an enforcement agency as proof of a criminal conviction can be used as evidence in the ensuing civil action, (Civil Evidence Act 1968, s.11).

An individual only has limited weapons to control the future operation of the polluter. An injunction may be available and, in some instances, there is scope for a private individual to use the administrative procedures available to the agencies. But the ability of an individual to monitor and enforce such a method of control is inevitably limited compared to the organs of the State. Therefore, in many instance, the appropriate advice to a personal client would be to lobby the appropriate enforcement body directly or through a representative politician such as a Member of Parliament or a councillor.

When giving general advice on liability to a client, then the usual sources of law must be consulted. The common law provides a range of actions which may be relevant. Parliament has also legislated on numerous issues. In the field of environmental law, Europe has been uncommonly active and has issued numerous Directives. There are

[1] See [1994] Env.L.R. 41.
[2] For a discussion see Owen Lomas (ed.). *Frontiers of Environmental Law*, Chap. 6; Gunter Heine, *Environmental Protection and Criminal Law* (1991).

also a number of international conventions which are pertinent to environmental law.

Environmental policy

It is also imperative to be familiar with the development of policy on the environment, particularly in Europe. European environmental policy is developed through the medium of the Action Programmes and presages changes in United Kingdom legislation. For example, the debate on the means of disposal of waste is relevant to the draft European Directives on packaging and recycling. There are two means of disposing of waste currently in dispute; one is incineration, the other is recycling. Incineration could, in the past, be a dirty method of disposal. Modern incineration methods, however, burn cleanly, eliminating many of the unacceptable substances such as ash, grit and poisonous gases. They may also be capable of using the energy thereby produced. A new plant in France, for instance, burns 630,000 tonnes of garbage a year and uses the energy produced to heat 70,000 flats in Paris. The incinerated waste is then put in landfill sites. The outcome of the debate will have repercussions for the packaging and waste management and recycling industries. Clients will be concerned either simply to be aware of the debate in order to make informed decisions about their future development, or to participate in it in order to influence the outcome.

The process of consultation at European level can be bleak. There is no formal consultative process and new proposals are normally conducted under a cloak of secrecy. However, lobbying occurs through interest organisations and pressure groups and can be developed through these means.

In the United Kingdom, policy is developed in the normal way through the means of consultation papers and Green and White Papers issued by the Department of Environment or some other relevant Ministry. The procedure for consultation is apparently more open than in Europe, although it is frequently criticised on the ground that minimum time is permitted for a response or that responses are ignored.

Familiarity with environmental policy is more important in environmental matters than other fields of policy, partly because the construction of European legislation can be more fluid and general in form than United Kingdom laws. Indeed, an understanding of the jurisprudence of European law has become vital for the United

Kingdom lawyer not just in the context of environmental law. United Kingdom laws must be interpreted in the light of European Directives, (*Marleasing*[3]) and the doctrine of direct effect means that an individual can rely directly on a European law even if it has not been implemented in the United Kingdom, (*Van Duyn* v. *Home Office*[4]). Further, if it can be shown that a Directive has conferred clearly identifiable individual rights and an individual had suffered loss as a result of the Member State's failure to implement the Directive, an action for damages could be brought against that State, (*Francovich* v. *Italian Republic*[5]). In the light of these developments in European jurisprudence, it is necessary to keep abreast with policy-making initiatives at European level.

THE COMMON LAW

In the United Kingdom the control of environmental damage and pollution has historically been through the action of the common law. Liability in tort is the classic form. This liability could be via the torts of negligence and nuisance or the doctrine of strict liability established in *Rylands* v. *Fletcher*. The primary vehicle for actions in environmental cases has been the tort of nuisance.

Tort of nuisance

Private nuisance is available as a cause of action where there has been an actionable interference with the use and enjoyment of another person's land. It is a private, civil action unlike public nuisance which is a criminal offence. Statutory nuisances are also criminal offences and are committed when a breach of statute, primarily the Environmental Protection Act 1990, occurs.

The nuisance complained of must normally represent a continuing or repetitious state of affairs. The emission of noxious fumes from a factory or the discharge of effluent into a river over a prolonged period of time would be actionable under the heading of private nuisance. The harm complained of must either amount to an interference with the beneficial use of the property, or cause actual, physical damage to the property.

---

[3] Case C-106/89, *Marleasing SA* v. *La Comercial Internacional de Alimentación:* [1990] 1 E.C.R. 4135, [1992] 1 C.M.L.R. 305.

[4] Case 41/74, *Van Duyn* v. *Home Office:* [1974] E.C.R. 1337, [1975] 1 C.M.L.R. 1.

[5] Cases 6/90 & 9/90, *Francovich* v. *Italian Republic:* [1992] I.R.L.R. 84, [1991] 1 E.C.R. 5357, [1993] 2 C.M.L.R. 66.

A difficulty for cases seeking compensation for environmental harm is contained in the famous formula of Thesiger J. in the case of *Sturges* v. *Bridgman*,[6] "What would be a nuisance in Belgrave Square would not necessarily be so in Bermondsey." This policy imperative means that a degree of environmental pollution might be acceptable in one locality but not in another. It is relevant where personal harm is alleged. Then, the particular circumstances of the case are taken into account and this includes locality. In cases where damage to property is alleged then the principle does not apply. In *St. Helens Smelting Co.* v. *Tipping*[7] copper smelting premises emitted noxious vapours which damaged the plaintiff's trees and shrubs. Because the pollution resulted in damage to property the plaintiff won the action.

The nineteenth century policy which underlay this decision is clear. Actions in nuisance are primarily concerned with protecting the rights of landowners. This is not necessarily inimical to the interests of the environment insofar as those interests include the health and welfare of human beings. If the environmental damage affects the value of the land then it is actionable in nuisance. The individual landowner will pursue the polluter for compensatory damages. The courts do not compensate for damage to the environment *per se*; there must be a link to the material interests of the owner of that piece of the environment. At first sight, this might seem to be a case where economic values are attributed to aspects of the environment. But the detriment for which compensation is awarded is the damage caused to the property. In the *St. Helens Smelting Co.* v. *Tipping* case damages of £361 18s 2d were awarded for the damage to the trees and shrubs, a substantial sum in 1865. However, it is worth reflecting on the nature of the landowner's interest. The plaintiff was described as being the proprietor of an estate of great value. The damages reflect the diminution in value of the estate, not the cost of replacing the trees or shrubs.

Another case concerning environmental issues is *Halsey* v. *Esso Petroleum Co. Ltd.*[8] The defendants owned and operated a depot which was used for the distribution of oil. They were held liable in private nuisance for the damage caused by the action of acidic smuts to the plaintiff's laundry, the nauseating smell and noise caused by the operation of the plant and the movement of tankers. The character of the locality was relevant in determining liability for the

---

[6] (1879) 11 Ch. D 852, 865.
[7] (1865) 11 H.L.C. 642.
[8] [1961] 2 All. E.R. 145.

smell and noise since it was a matter of personal discomfort and inconvenience which did not affect property values. This is reflected in the amount of damages awarded, £200. The economic value attributed by the judges to the damage caused to the health and wellbeing of humans was trivial.

In the *Cambridge Water Company v. Eastern Counties Leatherwork plc*[9] case, the rights of landowners in relation to water flowing under their land was considered. The House of Lords accepted that an action in private nuisance to protect such property rights would succeed provided that the damage was reasonably foreseeable. They considered the earlier decision of *Ballard v. Tomlinson*[10] which concerned the natural right to receive ground water in an uncontaminated state. An interference with that right, which is a property right, constituted an actionable nuisance.

Natural Rights. There are two natural rights which attach to the freehold ownership of land which are relevant within the context of environmental law. One relates to air, one to water. These are the right to receive water in an uncontaminated state, (see *Cambridge Water Co. v. Eastern Counties Leather plc*, above), and the right to receive an unpolluted flow of air through a defined channel. The right to clean water applies to water percolating underneath land or flowing in defined channels, (*Ballard v. Tomlinson*), and the right of a riparian owner to have the water flowing in a state which is not noticeably altered in terms of its character, quality or quantity, (*Young & Co. v. Bankier Distillery Co).*[11]

The water itself is not the subject of a proprietary right. The natural right is to take the water. It follows that anyone taking the water must not contaminate it in such a way so as to interfere with another's natural right. So there is a right of action in nuisance against anyone who is contaminating water which is being used by a property owner as a natural right incident to that property ownership.

There are several nineteenth century cases besides *Ballard v. Tomlinson* which deal with this issue. They consider the question whether the contamination results from the exercise of a "natural" right. For example in *Smith v. Kenrick*,[12] the defendant worked his mine in such a manner that the water which naturally percolated in his mine was able to flow down into the plaintiff's mine which was at

---

[9] [1994] 1 All E.R. 53.
[10] (1885) 29 Ch. 115.
[11] [1893] A.C. 698.
[12] (1849) 7 C.B. 515.

a lower level. This was held not to be actionable since he was working his mine in a proper manner and was not negligent or malicious. In *Baird* v. *Williamson*,[13] however, the facts were similar, except that the water flowed into the lower mine by the action of the defendant who was pumping it from another source. The defendant was actively controlling the flow of the underground water and was therefore liable for interfering with the plaintiff's natural right. The distinction seems to be that if the defendant's action constitutes a non-natural use, that is, if the defendant puts poison into the water or interferes with its natural flow by diverting it, then this is actionable. If, however, the action of the defendant is part of the exercise of a natural right, such as abstracting the water, then it is not actionable.

In *Cambridge Water Co.* v. *Eastern Counties Leather plc* it was arguable that the spillage of a solvent used for degreasing leather called perchloroethene, ("P.C.E."), which then filtered into the underground water, was a breach of the natural right of the water company to abstract water in the state in which nature had supplied. This breach was actionable under the tort of nuisance subject to the prerequisite that the damage caused was reasonably foreseeable. Mann L.J., in the Court of Appeal, argued that *Ballard* v. *Tomlinson* established a natural right in relation to land for which liability was strict regardless of whether it was reasonably foreseeable. This action was, in the opinion of the Court of Appeal, independent of the ordinary law of nuisance. However, in the House of Lords, Lord Goff discounted this approach, holding that the tortious liability in *Ballard* v. *Tomlinson* arose either on the basis of the rule in *Rylands* v. *Fletcher*, or under the law of nuisance. He also held that the rule in *Rylands* v. *Fletcher* was part of the law of nuisance, not a separate tort.

In *Ballard* v. *Tomlinson* the contamination was caused when the defendant put sewage and refuse from his printing works into his well. This contaminated the water in the chalk aquifer and the plaintiff was no longer able to use it for his brewing processes. In *Cambridge Water Co.* v. *Eastern Counties Leather plc* the spillage was accidental, no negligence was established. However, the House of Lords emphasised that, while liability was strict under the tort of nuisance, the damage must have been reasonably foreseeable. In the case, it was found that the environmental contamination was not foreseeable by a reasonable supervisor.

---

[13] (1863) 15 C.B. (N.S.) 376.

It is worthy of note that the plaintiff and defendant were not adjacent landowners as they were in the earlier case of *Ballard* v. *Tomlinson*. In the *Cambridge Water Co.* case the pollutant dissolved into the percolating flows of groundwater and was carried down the catchment at an estimated rate of 7 metres a day towards the plaintiff's borehole which was *1.3 miles away*. The ability of the hydro-geological inquiry conducted by the British Geological Survey to identify the source is remarkable. Even so, much is left to conjecture because the working scientific knowledge of the action of the contaminant, P.C.E., is still limited. Much of the current scientific knowledge now available has been gained as a result of the scientific inquiry into the *Cambridge Water Co.* case. The room for dispute over technical matters in cases of this sort is large and a careful preparation of the expert technical evidence will be of the utmost importance. It was found on the balance of probabilities that Eastern Counties Leather plc were at least materially responsible for the concentrations of P.C.E. found in the borehole belonging to the Cambridge Water company. There are various technical questions which are remarkable in this case. Most significant was the ability of the British Geological Survey to trace the source of the contamination. The spillage of the P.C.E. was relatively small, (3,200 litres), in relation to the total amount of P.C.E. used on the premises, (50,000 to 100,000 litres per year used from sometime in the 1960's until 1991). P.C.E. is a chemical which evaporates rapidly in air but does not dissolve readily in water. In fact, it might have been expected that most of the spillages would have evaporated before soaking into the ground. P.C.E. is familiar in the domestic context in the form of cleaning agents used to remove grease. The British Geological Survey were able to trace the source of this small quantity of the chemical because of their findings in relation to the structure of the underlying land. They found that the P.C.E. travelled down through the chalk lying under the tannery until it was stopped 50 metres down by a layer of sedimentary rock, a chalk marl, which was relatively impermeable. Pools of P.C.E. formed at that point and gradually dissolved in the groundwater. Once dissolved it passed along a deep and narrow pathway which found its way to the borehole. This ability to pinpoint the source of the contamination is an indication that one of the most notable problems of establishing liability, that is, proving causation, may be diminishing given the judicious use of scientific and technical evidence.

Thus both of the so-called natural rights, as property rights, are protected by the tort of private nuisance. They do not constitute a further level of protection for the environment nor do they further the principle that the polluter should pay. The polluter might be required to pay for the environmental damage but only if that damage constitutes an interference with a landowner's property right and if it was reasonably foreseeable.

The tort of negligence

The tort of negligence relies on establishing the existence of a duty of care owed by one person to another, that there has been a breach of that duty and that damage has resulted. This is the classic *Donoghue* v. *Stevenson* model. It is a liability based on fault and the damage must have been reasonably foreseeable.

It is necessary in the first place to establish that a duty of care exists. So, the manufacturer owes the ultimate consumer of the product a duty not to cause harm from any negligent failure in relation to the product. In relation to environmental damage it would be necessary to establish that the defendant owes such a duty to the plaintiff. Even if the harm is proved, in the absence of a duty of care, no liability in negligence arises. In *Gunn* v. *Wallsend Slipway and Engineering Co. Ltd*[14] no duty of care was established between an employer and the employee's wife who had died from a lung disease brought about by the presence of asbestos dust brought home from the shipyard on her husband's clothes. The decision to extend the categories of duty of care is a policy issue and one which the courts may be reluctant to make.

The requirement of reasonable foreseeability implies that there must be some relationship between the harm occurring and the harm that was foreseen. If there is a major spillage, such as occurred when the Shell oil company discharged fuel oil into the River Mersey, then a reasonable site manager or foreman could have reasonably foreseen some specific environmental damage. It does not require expert scientific evidence to deduce that fish would die and the water would be unsuitable for drinking, irrigation purposes or fishing.[15]

However, environmental damage may not always be caused by such dramatic spillages or be so clear-cut in its effects. If a chemical is spilt over a large number of years in relatively small quantities, the reasonable foreman is unlikely to envisage any particular harm occurring. But, the environmental consequence could be very significant. In the *Cambridge Water Co.* case the leakage was caused when the solvents were tipped from the 40 gallon drums into the

---

[14] (1989) *The Times*, January 23.
[15] *Pride of Derby Angling Assoc.* v. *British Celanese Ltd.* (1953) 1 Ch. 149; (1953) 1 All E.R. 179.

machinery. It was reckoned that the daily losses of a few gallons of solvent occurred in this way. While the supervisor must have known of the spillages which were wasteful and careless, he could not have been expected to know of their particular behaviour in causing pollution to the aquifers which would be apparent some fifteen to thirty years later. In the *British Nuclear Fuels* case,[16] a similar argument was raised in relation to the alleged effect on the genetic make-up of the sperm of a worker within the nuclear power plant at Sellafield. It is reasonably foreseeable that exposure to radioactivity could have both immediate and longer carcinogenic effects on the worker himself. It was arguable that it was not foreseeable that actual harm would be caused to the sperm, even if this had been the cause of the leukaemia, (which was not proven to be the case).

The chain of causation must be established between the breach of the duty of care and the harm. Frequently this will involve the use of expert scientific advice. This evidence will normally be couched in probabilities not certainties and the weight of it may depend on the ability of the witness in the witness box. Expert witnesses have special privileges beyond that of the ordinary witness. They may, (and should), remain in the courtroom throughout the trial. Their presence is important as they will be able to hear the evidence of the other side, particularly of the other side's experts. They can then brief their lawyer on the weight of the evidence and provide ammunition for cross-examination or re-examination. They are also able to attend the lawyers' conferences before the trial. It is critical that these opportunities are taken to test the strength of the evidence where it depends on scientific proof. If the expert has any doubts or there are any weaknesses in the evidence it is vital they are explored at the pre-trial stage.

There are clearly difficulties in establishing an action for environmental damage based on the tort of negligence. Fault liability is justifiable as an action within private law on the grounds that a person should not in general be liable for action except where they could have prevented the damage by behaving with care and without negligence. If a doctor prescribes a drug to which the patient is allergic and the patient as a consequence dies, then it is necessary to establish whether the doctor was negligent in prescribing that drug. The consequence is that one injured person may receive damages, another may not. The philosophical questions relate to the disparity

---

[16] *Reay* v. *British Nuclear Fuels plc* and *Hope* v. *British Nuclear Fuels plc* 1990 R. No. 860; 1989 H. No. 3689 (unreported).

between individuals suffering the same damage but in different circumstances.

For the environment, the question has similarities. For one case of environmental damage, the polluter may not be liable, for another compensation may be payable. The consequences may be the same, the river may be polluted and the fish killed, but the outcome of the actions may be quite different. This belies the general principle that the polluter should pay.

The doctrine of strict liability

In some countries, this problem has been confronted by the development of the doctrine in *Rylands* v. *Fletcher*. This case does seem to have been designed for environmental litigation. In Blackburn J.'s judgment in the case, he refers to the "person whose grass or corn is eaten down by the escaping cattle of his neighbour, or whose mine is flooded by the water from his neighbour's reservoir, or whose cellar is invaded by the filth of his neighbour's privy, or whose habitation is made unhealthy by the fumes and noisome vapours of his neighbour's alkali works." This provides some excellent examples of environmentally damaging activities. The rule provides for the escape of something which is potentially dangerous from land where, as a consequence, damage results. It applies where the object was brought and collected and kept on the land in circumstances where it was not a natural use of that land. The potential danger must have been reasonably foreseeable as the liability is strict, not absolute. In the United Kingdom, unlike other jurisdictions such as Australia, the development of the doctrine of strict liability has not progressed at the same rate as the tort of negligence. The doctrine has seldom been pleaded and it has been criticised by the Law Commission.[17] Judicial decisions have also severely limited its scope. The definition of what constitutes the natural use of land has been surprisingly extensive.

Natural use of land

The question to be decided is whether the use is natural or non-natural. The test inadvertently raises some of the same questions which relate to the definition of the word "environment." However,

---

[17] Report of the Law Commission on Civil Liability for Dangerous Things and Activities, Law. Com. No. 32

it would seem that this factual question is one which will be determined by the judge in the light of human activity.

In *Rylands* v. *Fletcher* itself the item was water. Water is a "natural" commodity, but it was accumulated on the land by the defendants. It did not arrive there by the action of rainfall. It is not the object itself, but the action in bringing the object onto the land, and the consequences of an escape, which are critical in determining liability.

Would the escape of hazardous waste from a landfill site or dioxin from a chemical plant be actionable under the doctrine? The first question is whether they constitute a non-natural use of land and the second is whether they are likely to do mischief if they escape.

The second question is more easily resolved. The escaped object does not have to be inherently dangerous; water is not, in itself, a dangerous object but has the potential to cause damage if it escapes, as in *Rylands* v. *Fletcher*. Hazardous waste and dioxin are in themselves dangerous things so this requirement is easily satisfied.

But are they a non-natural use of the land? In *Cambridge Water Company Limited* v. *Eastern Counties Leather plc* this point was considered in the High Court and the House of Lords. The case concerned a leak of a solvent, perchloroethene ("P.C.E"), from the defendants' leatherworks into the groundwater supply. The leak occurred during the ordinary operations of the tannery on the site during the period prior to 1976 when the solvents were delivered in drums. In the High Court, Kennedy J. held that the storage of solvents on the manufacturing premises was a natural use of the land. The judge took into account the benefits to society of the presence of small works up and down the country with drums stored in their yards. In a manufacturing society the presence of such drums, some of which must inevitably pose a potential hazard, are part of the life of every citizen. The judge stated that, while it was foreseeable that some damage would occur from an escape of the contents of these drums, their storage on the site did not constitute a non-natural use of land for the purposes of the doctrine. Likewise, in *W.H. Smith Ltd.* v. *Daw*,[18] the Court of Appeal held that sewage which had escaped from a lavatory pipe fell within the exemption of the natural use. In the *Cambridge Water Co.* case, in the Court of Appeal, Mann L.J. stated obiter, that in the court's view, the spilling of P.C.E. did not amount to an escape. He stated that the rule makes a person liable for an escape but in this case the liability arose because of the action of the defendants in spilling the P.C.E. The

---

[18] (1987) 2 *Environmental Law* (No. 1) 5.

judge suggested that it might have been different if the chemical had got into the groundwater system by leaking through cracks in a storage tank. The rule in *Rylands* v. *Fletcher* was not applicable apparently in either the High Court or the Court of Appeal although on different grounds.

The decision in the High Court was in line with past precedents which have restricted the scope of *Rylands* v. *Fletcher*. This part of the decision was, however, overruled in the House of Lords. Lord Goff held that the concept of the "industrial village" and the notion that the advantages of employment for the local community would cause a use to be regarded as a natural or ordinary use of the land were untenable. Although he did not embark on an extensive redefinition of the concept of natural use, he was satisfied that the storage of chemicals in substantial quantities, and their use in the manner employed at Eastern Counties Leather plc, did not constitute a natural use. Indeed, he stated that "the storage of substantial quantities of chemicals on industrial premises should be regarded as an almost classic case of non-natural use; and I find it very difficult to think that it should be thought objectionable to impose strict liability for damage caused in the event of their escape." Therefore, had the damage caused by their escape been reasonably foreseeable, Eastern Counties Leather plc would have been strictly liable for the consequences of their escape.

Thus, although the House of Lords' decision in the *Cambridge Water Co.* case has made it clear that the rule in *Rylands* v. *Fletcher* is only an application of the tort of nuisance and is subject to the prerequisite of reasonable foreseeability, it has limited the exception for natural use. It has been considered that the decision is a retrograde step for the protection of the environment. Insofar as it limits the concept of strict liability to those who might reasonably have been expected to have foreseen the consequences of their acts, it has had that effect. However, such is the advance in technical knowledge and public awareness of the dangers of pollution to the environment that the issue of what is reasonably foreseeable may not be insurmountable in future cases. For example, the knowledge gained as to the action of organochlorines in underground water as a result of this case must mean that the standard expected of the reasonable supervisor and the working practices adopted must have increased. The impact of European environmental Directives and rules relating to health and safety and the concern amongst the general public about health hazards must have affected the objective standards of knowledge and foreseeability. This will be the position where polluting events arise in the future. There are, however, a number of cases where pollution has occurred in the past and land has been contaminated before the activity became unlawful. These cases are known as cases of historic pollution. In the *Cambridge Water Co.* case, the House of Lords considered it inappropriate to impose liability retrospectively where it was not so imposed by statute.

The House of Lords were also not prepared to extend the rule to cases of extra-hazardous activities. The argument put was that persons conducting such operations should be liable for the extra-ordinary risk to others involved in such operations. Lord Goff, however, took the view that such a development of the law was a matter for Parliament and not for the judges. It was a situation where Parliament should lay down precise criteria for the incidence and scope of such liability particularly as Parliament was currently concerned to establish an extensive statutory regime for environmental liability.

STATUTORY NUISANCE

The common law rules on nuisance are supplemented by statute. The object of this was to pass control of public health into the hands of the administration and to criminalise, within the system of regulatory controls, public health offences. The primary statute dealing with nuisance is now the Environmental Protection Act 1990, ("E.P.A"), although nuisances relating to watercourses, ditches and ponds are still covered by the Public Health Act 1936, ss.259–265.

The E.P.A. covers a range of issues: litter to abandoned shopping trolleys, waste on land to pollution at sea, clean air to stubble burning, genetically modified organisms to dogs, nature conservation to statutory nuisance. It was the Act which the Conservative Government hoped would establish their environmental credentials and was presaged by the White Paper, "This Common Inheritance,"[19] It is an Act of nine Parts, 164 sections and 16 Schedules. It contains an attempt by Parliament to introduce a system of integrated pollution control providing for the improved control of pollution arising from industrial and other processes. This part is dealt with in Chapter 6.

The E.P.A. restates and updates the law relating to statutory nuisance. It also contains improvements in the summary procedures for dealing with such nuisances. There is a common factor linking

---

[19] "This Common Inheritance: Britain's Environmental Strategy," Cm. 1200 (1990).

those nuisances listed in the E.P.A. They must be prejudicial to health or a nuisance. These are alternatives. Nuisance is not defined within the Act and the common law must be called in aid to supplement the statute on this point.[20] Prejudice to health is defined in the Act, section 1(7), and means injurious or likely to cause injury to health. Statutory nuisances are designed to deal with aspects of public health; that is the historical origin. They date from the great Public Health Act of 1936 and have their roots in earlier Victorian legislation. Although the commission of a statutory nuisance may involve other aspects of environmental harm, enforcement action will only occur if some injury has occurred or is threatened to people. Local authority environmental health officers are responsible for enforcement.

The provisions relating to statutory nuisance are now contained in Part III of the E.P.A. which came into force on January 1, 1991. This repealed the relevant sections of the Public Health Act 1936, sections 91–100, and also the Public Health (Recurring Nuisances) Act 1969.

Section 79 consists of a list of matters which can constitute a statutory nuisance. The list is an expanded version of the previous statute. It is not an exhaustive list.

The provisions relating to housing remain unaltered: "any premises in such a state as to be prejudicial to health or a nuisance";(s.79(a)). This covers extreme dampness and structural defects in properties. In some modern flats the problem of condensation has become particularly acute. In *Greater London Council* v. *Tower Hamlets L.B.C.*[21] it was held that extensive dampness and mould growth were sufficiently bad in the circumstances of the case to constitute a statutory nuisance.

Noise can also be a factor making premises injurious to health. In *London Borough of Southwark* v. *Ince*[22] the noise from the nearby Old Kent Road was sufficient to constitute a nuisance in the light of the Council's failure to insulate the flats adequately so as to minimise the noise.

Premises is defined so as to be wide enough to include land even where that land is in a natural state. In *Leakey* v. *National Trust*[23] it was held that a hill which slipped after severe weather onto the

---

[20] *National Coal Board* v. *Thorne* [1976] 1 W.L.R. 543.
[21] (1983) 15 H.L.R. 57.
[22] (1989) 21 H.L.R. 504, C.A.
[23] [1980] 2 W.L.R. 65.

plaintiff's land was part of the premises. The defendants were liable in nuisance for failing to prevent the landslip.

Provisions relating to clean air are included for the first time alongside other statutory nuisances, although the Clean Air Act 1993, which consolidated and updated the Clean Air Acts 1956 and 1968, and which came into force on August 27, 1993, makes further provision in respect of air pollution.

Section 79(1)(b) provides that "smoke emitted from premises so as to be prejudicial to health or a nuisance" shall constitute a statutory nuisance. This does not cover smoke from chimneys of private dwellings in smoke control areas, dark smoke from boilers or industrial plants, smoke emitted from railway locomotive steam engines, or any other dark smoke from industrial or trade premises. The protection afforded to steam engines was achieved by a steam engine enthusiast in the House of Lords.

So, the E.P.A. 1990 extends statutory nuisance to cover smoke in domestic premises, such as the weekend bonfire.

The original legislation relating to smoke was prompted not by industrial polluters, but by domestic coal burning. The infamous London smog of 1952 prompted the Clean Air Act 1956 which introduced the present system of smoke control.

Dark smoke and black smoke from industrial premises are now covered by the Clean Air Act 1993. Dark and black smoke are determined by comparison with a shade card known as the Ringelmann chart, but experienced environmental health officers appear to rely on their own judgment which is acceptable as evidence in a court.

In respect of private premises only, the emission of fumes or gas is covered (s.79(1)(c)). Fumes includes solid airborne matter smaller than dust, and gas includes vapour and moisture emitted from vapour.

Under the former provisions, dust and other effluvia were covered. Smell and steam are, therefore, new (s.79(1)(d)). It applies to industrial, trade or business premises. It may have particular application to restaurants and launderettes. Again, the steam rail enthusiast succeeded in excluding steam engines from this provision.

The provisions relating to accumulation or deposits (s.79(1)(e)) and animals (s. 79(1)(f)) are repeated from the former Public Health Act.

Under section 79(1)(g) noise emitted from premises so as to be prejudicial to health or a nuisance is covered. This was previously covered by the Control of Pollution Act 1974, ss. 58 and 59. Noise complaints received by local authority environmental health departments have increased significantly. The courts are prepared to take a pragmatic view – in *Coventry City Council* v. *Harris*,[24] the Crown Court accepted that a top brass band player should be allowed to practice his cornet in a semi-detached house, but limited it to one hour a day.

The increasing concern about noise nuisances is reflected in the implementation of the Noise and Statutory Nuisance Act 1993, which came into force in January 1994. This Act inserted "noise . . . emitted from or caused by a vehicle, machinery or equipment in a street" into the list of statutory nuisances in section 79 of the E.P.A. It also inserted a new section 80A which deals with abatement notices in respect of noise in the street. The 1993 Act also provides for noise caused by burglar alarms and loudspeakers in streets.

It is a defence to prove that the best practicable means were used to prevent, or counteract, the effects of the nuisance, (s.80(7)). The defence is limited. In the case of premises, dust, steam, smell or other effluvia, accumulations or deposits, animals or noise, the defence is only available where the nuisance arises on industrial, trade or business premises. In the case of smoke the defence is only available where the smoke comes from a chimney. The defence is not available at all where the nuisance consists of fumes or gases, or any other nuisances declared by any other enactments.

Best practicable means cover the design, installation, maintenance and manner and periods of operation of plant and machinery, and the design, construction and maintenance of buildings and structures.

Reasonableness is a factor in determining what is practicable. Local conditions and circumstances can be taken into account, together with the current state of technical knowledge and the financial implications.

The local authority has a duty to inspect its area from time to time to detect any statutory nuisances. If a complaint is made by a local resident, the local authority must take such steps as are reasonably practicable to investigate the complaint.

This double duty will operate to oblige those local authorities who had previously declined to inspect council premises to reverse their policy. Noise nuisance, in particular, is likely therefore, to be a matter which will feature greatly in the activities of the local authority.

Where the local authority are satisfied that a statutory nuisance exists or is likely to occur or recur, then they must serve an abatement notice. This must require the abatement of the nuisance,

---

[24] (1992) 4 Land Management and Env. L. R. 168.

or its prohibition or restriction, and will require the execution of such works, and the taking of such other steps, as are necessary (s.80(1)).

It is to be served on the person responsible, or if the nuisance arises from a structural defect, on the owner of the premises. If the person responsible cannot be found, then it must be served on the owner or occupier (s.80(2)).

The E.P.A. 1990 introduces a new right of appeal (s.80(3)). The person served has a right of appeal within 21 days from service, to the magistrates' court. The grounds of appeal are circumscribed by the Statutory Nuisances (Appeals) Regulations 1990.[25] This prevents appeals being automatically lodged without any justifiable grounds in order to defer the effect of the abatement notice.

While an appeal is pending, the abatement notice may be suspended. In order to prevent this, the local authority may insert a declaration in the abatement notice that it will remain effective on grounds set out in the regulations.

If the person served contravenes or fails to comply with the notice, without reasonable excuse, then a criminal offence has been committed (s.80(4)). The local authority are not obliged to prosecute for failure to comply with a notice.

However, whether or not they prosecute, the local authority may abate the nuisance and do whatever works are necessary (s.81(3)). They may recover any expenses they reasonably incur in doing this (s.81(4)), although they are often reluctant to do so because of the disputes which afterwards arise about the cost of the work or the efficacy of it, or the need for it.

Section 81A, inserted by the Noise and Statutory Nuisance Act 1993, provides that, where the local authority incurs expenses in abating or preventing the recurrence of a nuisance, these may be charged on the property to which they relate.

It remains possible for a private individual who is aggrieved by a statutory nuisance to bring private proceedings in the magistrates' court. The court has power to make an order requiring the defendant to abate the nuisance and carry out necessary works (s.82).

This will, therefore, continue to be useful where a local authority declines to act for whatever reason. This may occur where the nuisance arises in respect of local authority accommodation.

Where premises are unfit for human habitation, the court may issue an order prohibiting their use for human habitation.

---

[25] S.I. 1990 No. 2276.

The person aggrieved must serve notice on the person responsible stating the intention to bring proceedings and setting out the matters complained of. This is a new provision. The notice must be at least 21 days, unless it is in respect of noise, when it can be three days. The person to be served must be the person responsible, unless that person cannot be found, when the owner or occupier is liable, or the nuisance arises from a structural defect, when the owner is liable.

Costs, now, are no longer in the discretion of the court where the nuisance is proved, but are automatically granted to the complainant.

Breach of the order constitutes a criminal offence.

EUROPE AS A SOURCE OF LAW

There are two aspects to the contribution Europe makes to the development of environmental law: that is, the development of policy and the issuing of secondary law, primarily Directives.

The development of european environmental policy

European environmental policy is developed through the medium of the Action Programmes. These are documents which establish a proposed action plan for environmental developments over a period of time, usually about five years. They form the basis for policy development in the environmental arena. The Action Programmes are resolutions of the Council of the European Communities and of the representatives of the governments of the Member States.

The first Action Programme resulted from a meeting of the Heads of State or Government in Paris on October 19 and 20, 1972. The importance of a Community environmental policy was emphasised at this meeting and the Community institutions were invited to establish a programme of action before July 31, 1973. A further meeting of environment Ministers took place in Bonn on October 31,1972 to elaborate the procedure to be adopted in producing the Action Programmes. Their decisions were communicated to the institutions of the Community and in due course resulted in the first Action Programme on November 22, 1973.[26] The first Programme

---

[26] [1973] O.J. C112/1.

was for the period 1973–1976. There have since been four Programmes: second: 1977–81[27]; third: 1982–86[28]; fourth: 1987–92.[29] The fifth programme takes European environmental policy up to the end of the century.[30]

The first Action Programme sets out 11 general principles. The first principle states that "the best environmental policy consists in preventing the creation of pollution and nuisances at source, rather than subsequently trying to counteract their effects." The second states that "effects on the environment should be taken into account at the earliest possible stage in all technical planning and decision-making processes." Thus, the basis for preventative action was established.

The detailed programme in Part II is divided into two parts. Title I deals with measures to reduce pollution and nuisances and covers, for example, the setting of standards for certain pollutants: lead, mercury, cadmium, organic chlorine compounds, toxic chemical substances and micro-organisms present in drinking water. Title II deals with action to improve the environment. Environmental assessment is specifically foreshadowed in the first Action Programme which has both positive and negative aspects. That is, it deals reactively with pollution problems already in existence, and deals proactively with ideas to improve and protect the environment.

The third Action Programme emphasises the preventive side of environmental policy and seeks to strengthen it in the framework of the overall strategy. There are 11 declarations. The first is for action to be taken to integrate the environmental dimension into other policies; the second is for action to be taken to set up an environmental impact assessment procedure.

Although the first programme deals with the preventative principle, it is in the third programme that it reaches maturity. The development of the system of inspection and notification of new chemical substances, (the "sixth amendment," Directive amending for the sixth time Directive 67/548/EEC on the approximation of the laws, Regulations and administrative provisions relating to the classification, packaging and labelling of dangerous substances, 79/831/EEC[31]) was treated as a milestone in the development of the

---

27 [1977] O.J. C139/1.
28 [1983] O.J. C46/1.
29 [1987] O.J. C328/1.
30 COM (92) 23.
31 [1979] O.J.L 259/10.

preventative principle. The development of an overall strategy coun-
tenances three principles: the principle of subsidiarity, that each
action must be applied at the most appropriate level, the principle
that prevention is better than cure, and the principle that restoration
should take place wherever possible. So, the Community approach
reflects the approach outlined in the first programme. That is, a
balance between reactive and proactive policies.

The Fifth Action Programme: "Towards Sustainability." This is
the current programme which covers the period up to the turn of the
century. Its primary theme is of sustainable development, the concept which has now gripped current thinking on environmental
issues. It acknowledges that there will be an increased trend in
economic and social activities that will have a further impact on the
environment. The possible extension of the Union to include countries in central and Eastern Europe is foreseen as increasing the
pressure on the environment. There is a recognition that the policy
of sustainable development will not be achieved during the life span
of the programme and that further measures will be necessary in the
future. The maintenance of public health and economic and social
welfare at a high level is advocated as the objective of a policy of
sustainable development.

The Fifth Programme advocates three approaches to deal with
these pressures on the environment. These are the development of
life cycle management of products and processes, (particularly in
relation to waste), the use of cleaner technology and the substitution
of less hazardous processes where this can be achieved in a cost
effective way. These objectives are costly for industry. Yet, on the
other hand, they have the potential for creating economic activity
and generating wealth. The development of new cleaner and safer
methods of production will create new opportunities for research
and development and for engineering. The encouragement to seek
and use cleaner technology will in itself create industrial activity.
The proposals in the fifth programme will provide an impetus which
will have greater consequences than simply improving the environmental performance of industry. It will provide a boost for economies in recession and in the course of improving environmental
performance, general improvements in processing and productivity
will undoubtedly ensue. Industry will wholeheartedly support improvements which are cost effective in relation to existing processes
and which comply with environmental regulations and improve the
public relations profile.

In order to achieve these policy objectives, the Fifth Action Programme sets out a number of financial measures, such as the use of market-based and other economic instruments.

The Treaty of Rome

In the original Treaty of Rome there was no reference to the environment. Such a reference was not to be expected. The purpose of the Treaty was to establish an economic community:

"The Community shall have as its task, by establishing a Common Market and progressively approximating the economic policies of Member States, to promote throughout the Community a harmonious development of economic activities, a continuous and balanced expansion, an increase in stability, an accelerated raising of the standard of living and closer relations between the States belonging to it."[32]

In the United Kingdom, environmental issues did have a part to play. The 1947 Town & Country Planning Act created the framework for a planned redevelopment of urban areas. Yet, even here the purpose behind the legislation was to improve basic living conditions for people. The concept of the environment as including the whole of the animal kingdom and all vegetation was not considered as an issue in its own right. Its only relevance was to the extent that it had an impact on people.

It can be argued that a concern for the environment remains a luxury that can only be afforded in times of prosperity. When people are under pressure, whether through the adversity of war or the failure of post-wartime economies, then the interests of people become paramount. When a choice has to be made, it is invariably made in favour of the material welfare of mankind or in the interests of the State.

The legal basis for european environmental legislation

As has been shown the original Treaty of Rome contained no reference to the environment. The Action Programmes were the first instruments of policy-making within this field. However, this lack caused no embarrassment and the Community succeeded in producing a considerable amount of environmental legislation.

---

[32] Article 2 of the EEC Treaty.

The legal basis for this legislation was Articles 100 and 235. Article 100 deals with the approximation of laws:

> "The Council shall, acting unanimously on a proposal from the Commission, issue directives for the approximation of such provisions laid down by law, regulation or administrative action in Member States as directly affect the establishment or functioning of the common market."

This provides the authority for the issuing of Directives. This authority was only exercisable, under the terms of the original Treaty, on a unanimous basis.

Article 235 provides general power to further the objectives of the Treaty in the absence of a specific power:

> "If action by the Community should prove necessary to attain, in the course of the operation of the common market, one of the objectives of the Community and this Treaty has not provided the necessary powers, the Council shall, acting unanimously on a proposal from the Commission and after consulting the European Parliament, take the appropriate measures."

The "Single European Act"

The omission of environmental policy from the Treaty of Rome, was resolved, however, by amending the Treaty of Rome to include a chapter on the environment. The "Single European Act," as it was known, was adopted by Parliament in the European Communities (Amendment) Act 1986 and came into force on July 1, 1987. The intended effect of this amendment to the Treaty of Rome was to sweep away the remaining barriers by December 31, 1992.

The rules on the free movement of goods and other rules on trading, such as competition rules, sought to achieve a single, common market. Anyone travelling through the Member States, however, would have been conscious that this objective was not reflected in reality. Long queues of lorries and cars, and border and custom controls, belied the ideal of free inter-state movement.

Prior to the adoption of the "Single European Act," the Commission published a White Paper in June 1985, ("Completing the internal market, White Paper from the Commission to the European Council,"[33]) which established a legislative programme, designed to

---

[33] COM (85) 310 final.

remove the various barriers, whether fiscal, physical or technical, to free trade. The time-scale allowed for the achievement of these proposals, (numbering more than 300), was between 1985 and 1992.

The Single European Act was passed as a result of this White Paper, and operates as an amendment to the Treaty. The main aim of the Single European Act was to achieve a completely free market by the end of 1992. There were various specific means to achieve this.

First, it sought to enhance the decision-making powers of the Community by removing the right of veto (Article 100A). As has been seen, the original Article 100 provided, that the Council had power to issue Directives provided that it acted unanimously. The new Article 100A provided that Council decisions could be achieved by a qualified majority in all cases which sought to establish the internal market. However, excluded from this provision were all "fiscal provisions." This exclusion, included to protect national sovereignty over internal national tax rates, meant that such decisions still had to be reached unanimously. The possibility that tax rates will be harmonised still remains remote. Excluded also were provisions relating to the free movement of persons and to the rights of employed persons.

Specifically mentioned in Article 100a(3), however, were proposals concerning health, safety, environmental protection and consumer protection. These were clearly referred to as areas envisaged in paragraph (1) as subject to the qualified majority procedure. It is stated that these areas would take as a base, a "high level of protection," thereby indicating the importance that would be attached to them. Paragraph 4 of Article 100a permitted a Member State to adopt national measures in the face of a Council harmonisation measure, where it related to the protection of the environment and on the grounds of major needs further to Article 36. Article 36 permitted prohibitions or restrictions on imports, exports or goods in transit justified on the grounds of protection of health and life of humans, animals or plants, *inter alia*, provided that it was not being used as a method of discrimination.

This provision was considered in the Wallonia[34] case where it was held that waste was a good which could, therefore, be covered by these provisions. It was also held that the Wallonian prohibition on the import of waste was justifiable on grounds of environmental

[34] Case C-2/90, E.C. *Commission* v. *Belgium*: [1992] 1 E.C.R. 4431, [1993] 1 C.M.L.R. 365.

protection. Article 100a(3), therefore, envisaged that it may be appropriate in certain limited cases for a Member State to adopt national measures to control a particular threat to the environment. The Community cannot legislate for every eventuality faced by every member. It leaves open the possibility, therefore, for individual measures to be taken at local level. This admits the principle of subsidiarity although there is control at Commission level. The Commission must be notified of such a measure and has power to confirm it provided it is not masking some discriminatory act. The sanction that the Commission may wield is to bring any offender before the Court of Justice.

Other matters incorporated into the Treaties by the Single European Act, other than the chapter on the protection of the environment, were, co-operation in the sphere of foreign policy, the establishment of a legal framework for activities in the sphere of science and technology, the Regional Development Fund, a reference to Economic and Monetary Union, and the role of the European Parliament.

The European Parliament has, in many respects, played a limited and marginal role in the Community. Article 100a allowed a greater role for the Parliament in terms of co-operation with the Commission.

The Maastricht Treaty

The Treaty on European Union was signed in Maastricht in the afternoon of February 7, 1992 by the 12 Member States. This Treaty, "marks a new stage in the process of creating an ever-closer union among the peoples of Europe, in which decisions are taken as closely as possible to the citizen," (Article A of the preamble). The union "shall be founded on the European Communities, supplemented by the policies and forms of cooperation established by (the) Treaty. Its task shall be to organise, in a manner demonstrating consistency and solidarity, relations between the Member States and their peoples." An underlying principle is to create a social cohesion between the peoples of the Member States going beyond an economic union.

The environment, and, in particular, the principle of sustainable development, feature prominently in the Treaty on European Union. Article 2 states that the task of the Community is to promote:

"a harmonious and balanced development of economic activities, sustainable and non-inflationary growth respecting the environment."

The principle of sustainable development, initiated by the Brundt-land Report (above, p. 12), is elaborated significantly in the Fifth Action Programme (above, p. 54). It reflects the future for environmental policy development in Europe.

The Treaty on European Union was subjected to a referendum in some of the Member States. Following its rejection by the Danes in 1992, and the reluctance of the United Kingdom to accept aspects of it relating to the part known as the "social charter," its future was rendered uncertain. It was eventually formally ratified by the United Kingdom on August 2, 1993. The last country to ratify, Germany, did so in October 1993 further to a decision by their constitutional court which ruled that the principle of democracy did not prevent Germany joining a supranationally organised community of states.

Certain of its principles do seem to be taking shape already. For example, the principle of subsidiarity has already been welcomed by the United Kingdom in such fields as environmental regulation and control. The principle of subsidiarity states that the Community should only take action where the objectives of the proposed action cannot be sufficiently achieved by the Member States.

The principle of qualified majority voting is further extended by this Treaty. In the field of environmental law, in particular, the principle of majority voting is extended significantly. Water Directives, for example, where the United Kingdom has already been subject to enforcement proceedings under Article 169, could in future be passed by a qualified majority.

In many ways Europe has become the focus for the development and enforcement of environmental law. The Maastricht Treaty currently holds centre stage in the political arena and environmental questions are not divorced from the discussion. The principles of subsidiarity and proportionality, the clash between economic development and environmental protection, the founding of rights for individual citizens to pursue actions for damages based on European legislation are all part of the general political debate surrounding the adoption of the Maastricht Treaty. Title XVI, the chapter on the environment originally inserted by the Single European Act, is expanded under the Treaty on European Union.

Title XVI, the Chapter on the Environment

Article 130R(1) sets out the objectives for the Community:

" (i) to preserve, protect and improve the quality of the environment;
 (ii) to contribute towards protecting human health;

(iii) to ensure a prudent and rational utilisation of natural resources."

The Maastricht Treaty adds a fourth:

"promoting measures at international level to deal with regional or worldwide environmental problems."

Article 130r(2) sets out the key principles on which environmental policy shall be based. These are the preventive principle, the principle that pollution should be rectified at source and the principle that the polluter should pay. The Maastricht Treaty adds the precautionary principle and establishes that Community policy shall aim at a high level of protection.

The principle of subsidiarity

Fundamental to the Maastricht debate is the principle of subsidiarity; the principle of the lowest common denominator. Action should be taken at the most appropriate level. Action should not, therefore, be taken at Community level if it is more appropriate to take the action at national or, even, regional level (see above, p. 30).

INTERNATIONAL LAW

The United Kingdom is part of a world community as well as part of the European Union and is subject to international law, either as an individual nation, or as a member of the Union. Within the corpus of international law there is a developing body of environmental measures. These measures encounter similar difficulties to other aspects of international law.

The world community consists of widely disparate nations. Some, for example the countries within the European Union and the countries of North America and Australia and New Zealand, have highly developed capitalistic economies. While these economies are ostensibly based on the theory of the free market, they are, in fact highly regulated. A glance at the simple number of environmental regulations alone highlights this feature. Some countries, frequently described as developing countries, are characterised by expanding populations which are not supported by an industrialised base. Their agricultural and extractive economies are unable to maintain a standard of living for their growing populations which are therefore subject to declining health standards and are therefore vulnerable to such diseases as cholera, typhoid fever, dysentery, influenza and tuberculosis, (one-third of the world's population are infected with this last disease). Countries in Latin America fall into this category. They are frequently concerned to develop a system of environmental law primarily to improve the basic standards of human health but also to protect many of the rare ecological sites, such as rainforests, which exist within their borders. There are examples of these countries developing regulatory systems of greater import than in the United Kingdom. For example, in Peru, the Government is seeking to establish an inspectorate for drinking water which will have far more resources and more extensive powers than the equivalent agency in the United Kingdom. The concern of such countries, and those in the Indian subcontinent, to establish an environmental code, is, in many respects, perceived as a higher priority than in the industrialised countries. These countries with a developing industrialised base, therefore, form a strong lobby within the international community. There are difficulties in establishing a consensus on environmental measures across the world community. The larger the number of partners, the greater is the difficulty in achieving an agreement and the outcome of the debate is likely to be diffuse. Problems of enforcement are also abundant. Yet, there is an extensive body of environmental measures developing at international level which have an impact on the economies of the partners. Agreements at international level on acid rain and on the ozone layer, when implemented at national level, mean that industry may have to adapt its practices or individuals may have to pay greater taxes. For the environmental lawyer, therefore, it is necessary to be aware of international agreements which will rapidly dictate internal measures.

International environmental law is also concerned with those areas which are not subject to the control of individual nations. Territorial boundaries cease at certain prescribed points and areas beyond them are referred to as the global commons. Agreements relating to the oceans and outer space have environmental features. For instance, the problem of dumping waste, both in the oceans and in outer space, is a matter of international concern for the environment. Accidents on the high seas causing major pollution incidents are subject to control at international level.

The principles of international law as they affect the environment are no different from any other fields of international law. The sources can consist of "soft" law, such as declarations which are not binding but which establish principles for behaviour or norms, or "hard" law, such as the provisions of treaties which are binding.

"Soft law"

Soft law is not a traditional source of law and is sometimes viewed with disfavour by lawyers as not being "proper law." It is not binding, so how can it constitute law at all? But the concept of "soft law" is particularly relevant in the field of international environmental law. Agreements within the arena of environmental law are very likely to have an impact on the economic activities of nations. As such, it may be difficult to achieve a binding treaty restricting economic development. The concept of soft law permits an agreement to be reached which recommends a certain course of action and which permits some flexibility for individual nations to incorporate it into their system. Such an approach may be more successful in achieving an environmental objective than an attempt to prescribe a solution which individual countries, for political or other reasons, may be obliged to reject out of hand. Examples of soft law can be found in the United Nations Environment Programme and include decisions on the Principles of Conduct on Shared Natural Resources and the Provisions for Co-operation between states in Weather Modification.[35] It may also be the case that where the scientific basis for a decision is unclear or subject to debate, a binding legal obligation is inappropriate. On the other hand, there may be concern that a particular activity is potentially damaging and some precautions should be taken in the event that scientific knowledge will eventually show conclusively that environmental harm will occur. Soft law is the appropriate mechanism for such an interim solution. An example is the debate over dumping in the North Sea. The 1990 Third North Sea Ministerial Conference adopted a precautionary principle to deal with the potential risks to the quality of the North Sea and its fish though these were not clearly supported by scientific evidence.

"Hard law"

The Statute of the International Court of Justice, (Article 38(1)), sets out the various sources which the court may consult. These consist of customary law, treaties (sometimes called conventions, protocols or agreements), judicial decisions, academic texts and decisions of international governmental organisations and general principles of law.

---

[35] Decision 8/7/A of the Governing Council of UNEP of April 29, 1980.

General principles of law. This means those legal concepts which are recognised by all systems of national laws. Such general principles can be used by international courts or tribunals to aid their decision-making process. For example, the concept of an equitable doctrine might be adopted by a court in reaching its decision. The general principles may relate to procedural and evidential matters as well as substantive issues of law.

The application of these general principles permits a degree of flexibility to the judicial processes. Unlike the other sources which require a positive assent on the part of the other nations signing them, they allow the introduction of certain concepts and doctrines which may not be universally applicable. One example of a concept that was rejected by the International Court of Justice was the doctrine of estoppel.

While it seems clear that this source will include such rules as pertain to a fair and equitable system of justice, such as the rules of natural justice, it remains unclear whether it will include principles going beyond the scope of that. For example, within the context of environmental law, there are a number of emerging principles: the precautionary principle, the principle of sustainable environmental development, the principle that the polluter pays. It would seem that there are no decisions at international level so far which accept these principles as a source of law. Some development of the jurisprudence of the International Court of Justice may, in time, throw some light on this.

Customary law. Historically, this has been the major source of international law. It has developed from patterns of usage which have crystallised into law. The Greek city states of the classical world operated together on the basis of customary law. A customary law may eventually be accepted by a national or international court as the formal expression of law within that field. It usually derives from diplomatic relations between states, the practice of international bodies such as the International Labour Organisation, and, at municipal level: national laws, judicial decisions and administrative practices.

Customary law is not a significant source of environmental law. There are some general principles such as the obligation on one state not to injuriously affect another state by such of its activities that might have a transboundary impact. One decision, the *Trail Smelter* arbitration[36] exemplifies this. This famous case involved the deleterious activities of a Canadian smelter which had caused air pollution damage across the border in the United States of America. The tribunal accepted the principle that no state had the right to cause damage by fumes to the territory of another state.

There is considerable difficulty in the modern world, however, in establishing customary laws. There are many more states in existence than ever before, (over 170 and still proliferating). There are also numerous international bodies which could be the source of customary law. It is now the case that customary law has receded in importance as a source of international law, in part, as a result of the growth in treaty making which has been evident since the nineteenth century.

Treaties. These may take many forms. They may set out rules which are to be implemented by the states which are parties to the treaty. Some treaties establish a framework within which states are to take action. Some may establish a broad framework which is supplemented by narrower agreements on specific issues. The Stockholm Conference of 1972 and its Declaration on the Human Environment is an important example of treaty-making within the environmental context. The Declaration sets out a number of principles. These are broadly drafted leaving a degree of discretion to the Member States as to their implementation.

In the United Kingdom, treaties affecting domestic law require parliamentary approval. The timescale for making a treaty may, therefore, be lengthy, although the example of the Vienna Convention for Protection of the Ozone Layer, which took less than a year to come into force belies this.

There are now a number of treaties within the environmental field. Many of these treaties have been developed under the aegis of international bodies such as the United Nations Environment Programme. They cover a range of topics such as whaling,[37] the protection of the ozone layer,[38] the control of hazardous waste,[39] nuclear accidents[40] and transboundary air pollution.[41]

---

[36] (1939) 33 A.J.I.L. 182; (1941) 35 A.J.I.L. 684.
[37] International Convention for Regulation of Whaling, 1946.
[38] Vienna Convention for the Protection of the Ozone Layer, 1985.
[39] Convention on the Control of Transboundary Movements of Hazardous Wastes and their Disposal, 1989, Basel, (in force May 24, 1992).
[40] Vienna Convention on Early Notification of a Nuclear Accident, 1989, (in force October 27, 1986).
[41] Geneva Convention on Long Range Transboundary Air Pollution, 1983, (in force March 16, 1983).

Judicial decisions. The International Court of Justice, (the Permanent Initial Court of Justice until 1946), is the only international court with a general jurisdiction. In addition, there is the European Court of Justice, which has particular relevance within the European Union. There is no concept of judge-made law on the international plane as there is no system of judicial precedent. Courts at international level do, however, have a role to play in acknowledging customary law and interpreting treaties. The courts at European and national level also, by their decision making process, throw light on the interpretation of international law.

Academic texts. These may also be used as a secondary source of law. In the Statute of the International Court of Justice these are referred to as "the teachings of the most highly qualified publicists of the various nations." They are persuasive only. International bodies may also come under this heading to the extent that they make pronouncements on international law. The value of these sources is evidential, they do not constitute declaratory sources.

The United Nations, as a world assembly, is clearly an influential voice in the determination of environmental policy. While its pronouncements are not a formal source of law, they are undoubtedly of great weight. A Resolution of the General Assembly of the United Nations is not "hard law," however, insofar as it is acted on by Member States, it may eventually be adopted by usage as customary law.

Chapter Three

Who's Who in the Administration and Enforcement of Environmental Controls

SECTION 1: THE UNITED KINGDOM

INTRODUCTION

In the United Kingdom there is a Department of the Environment which is headed by a Secretary of State who holds a key position within the Cabinet. It might seem, therefore, that, by its title, all control of environmental pollution is centred there. In one sense that is true. The Secretary of State for the Environment is ultimately accountable to Parliament for environmental issues. But this control is remote in most cases. Actual enforcement of the environmental regulatory regime is diverse. It is scattered around a number of different bodies, some of which are directly accountable to central government, while others are accountable at local level.

The title Department of the Environment is also somewhat misleading, implying that the Secretary of State and that branch of the civil service are exclusively concerned with environmental matters. In fact, the department is also responsible for local government, an area which is subject, as on many occasions in the past, to reform which engenders much political controversy. Local government finance is no small part of the work of the Department of the Environment and that is an area which again has absorbed much of the working time of the Secretary of State.

Environment agency. There is now a firm commitment to set up an environment agency in the United Kingdom. Although this idea was originally rejected by the government in the White Paper "This Common Inheritance," a change of heart occurred. There is now a

Bill waiting to go before Parliament on this issue but there still appears to be a lack of readiness to promote it at government level. The proposal is to establish an agency which will combine controls over land, air and water. It will combine the functions of Her Majesty's Inspectorate of Pollution, the National Rivers Authority and the waste regulation authorities.

THE ROLE OF CENTRAL GOVERNMENT

The key department responsible for environmental matters is the Department of the Environment. In addition, however, the Departments of Energy, Trade and Industry, and Transport, amongst others, also have a contribution to make.

Department of the Environment

The Secretary of State for the Environment occupies the prime role within the context of environmental policy and management and has a number of functions. This government department has particular responsibility for planning and environmental protection, water, countryside matters and local government. The department is divided into different groups. Those relevant to the environment include the Planning, Rural Affairs and Water Group, and the Environment Protection Group.

The key function is the *development of policy*. This is undertaken through the usual medium of issuing consultative papers and Green and White Papers. For example, the White Paper, "This Common Inheritance: Britain's Environmental Strategy"[1] has been the most important example of a formulation of environmental policy. It has been followed by two progress reports[2] issued by the Government. These progress reports have attempted to assess the Government's performance against their environmental objectives. The second report for 1992 contains a list of 479 commitments set out in the White Paper with summaries of the action taken and an indication of the commitments for future action. These represent important documents in terms of policy development. For example, the Second Year Report contains a statement by the Secretary of State that there is to

---

[1] Cm. 1200 (1990). For a discussion of the White Paper, see Tromans, (1991) 3 J.E.L. 168.

[2] This Common Inheritance: The First Year Report, Cm. 1655 (1991); This Common Inheritance: The Second Year Report, Cm. 2068 (1992).

be a change of direction in favour of economic instruments for environmental control rather than regulation. There are a number of proposals contained in the report for the different types of instruments which might be used, such as recycling credits and tradeable credits for sulphur dioxide emissions (the chemical emitted by coal fired power stations – one of the factors held responsible for acid rain), and credits for fuel efficient cars.

These documents represent policy development on a grand scale. The Secretary of State also issues a host of *consultation papers* on all aspects of planning and environmental matters.

There are also a series of *Pollution Papers*, (currently numbering 27), which are issued by the Central Unit on Environmental Pollution, a unit within the Department of the Environment. These report on such issues as dioxin in the environment,[3] and nitrates in water.[4] The series also contains the papers which are the Government's response to the reports of the Royal Commission on Environmental Pollution, and the reports of working parties.

More formal guidance is contained in *circulars* which explain the manner in which the Government expects legislation to be applied. These circulars can be very detailed and provide quite explicit guidance on the manner of interpretation of legislation. For example, the circular on environmental assessment explains the manner in which the Town & Country Planning (Assessment of Environmental Effects) Regulations 1988 are to be interpreted. It provides a number of thresholds which define the point at which an assessment of the environmental effects might be expected. These thresholds are quite specific. One example is that an application for a pig farm is likely to require an assessment of its environmental effects if there are more than 400 pigs. If a local planning authority chose to ignore such a guideline, they would clearly be in peril of being overruled on an appeal to the Secretary of State. It would be for the local authority to prove that there was excellent reason for them to ignore the ministerial circular. The burden would, in effect, shift to the local authority as respondent on the appeal. The circular, therefore, is an important method by which government policy is imposed on the bodies which are operating the regulatory regime on a day-to-day basis.

In common with other areas of administrative law, environmental law is characterised by a large number of *statutory instruments*. Broad brush Acts of Parliament lay down general principles and

---

[3] Pollution Paper No. 27, "Dioxins in the Environment" (H.M.S.O. 1989).
[4] Pollution Paper No. 26, "Nitrate in Water" (H.M.S.O., 1986).

concepts and leave the detail to be filled in by the Secretary of State by means of regulations. These abound in the control of waste, water, hazardous substances, air, noise, – in other words, in all fields of environmental law.

The role of the Secretary of State and the use of statutory instruments and other administrative measures as part of the regulatory regime emphasises the fact that environmental law is a branch of administrative law. It also raise a fundamental question about the status of environmental law and its future development. The United Kingdom has an elaborate system of environmental controls administered through the Executive. Europe has issued a large number of Directives which have required implementation by a change in the law, (usually through the medium of a statutory instrument), rather than a change in administrative practice. This is the command and control method of the environmental regime. It imposes solutions on industry and individuals by decreeing prescribed emission limits or procedures. The indications now seem to be in favour of a change from this heavily regulated system of environmental control to a system based on market principles; a system where the environment is regulated by providing industry with financial incentives or penalties to ensure control. This policy change seeks to make the polluter pay either by imposing a tax on pollution, or by imposing fines and clean up costs, or by charging the potential polluter for the cost of monitoring and enforcing pollution control. This policy change may occur as part of a drive towards the deregulation of environmental pollution controls and a lessening of the role of government.

Other central government departments also are concerned with environmental issues. Although this feature of the administration of environmental control is sometimes voiced as a criticism, in fact, it can be argued that it is appropriate that environmental concerns should permeate other departments. It is an aspect of European policy that all decisions should contemplate their environmental effect. However, the role of other departments in environmental questions is not as extensive as this approach recommends. The role of other departments is historical and accidental rather than a matter of policy.

Department of Trade and Industry

This department has a major impact on environmental issues. The plans announced in the autumn of 1992 to close all but 19 of Britain's remaining 50 coal-pits and to privatise those that are left by 1995, have implications not just for the mining industry but also for

the environment. The Department of Trade and Industry and the
Department of Energy are responsible for the energy industry. Such
issues as the so-called "dash for gas" policy by virtue of which the
national grid is developing 31 power stations – all but one of which
will use gas – has environmental consequences.[5] Coal-fired power
stations, which are responsible for a large part of the emission of
sulphur dioxide which can cause excessive acidification of the
rainfall, are being dismantled. This may appear to be a bonus for the
environment but the environmental cost of extracting gas must be
weighed in the balance. The thirty-first power station uses nuclear
power; it is the Sizewell B power station in Suffolk. It can be argued
that nuclear power is clean and cheap and a further 14 power
stations are run on this source of energy, although it depends on the
method of cost accounting adopted particularly in relation to capital
charges. But environmental concerns are particularly high in relation to nuclear power as a source of energy. Widely publicised
accidents at Chernobyl, in the former Soviet Union, and Three Mile
Island in the United States of America, and less well known leaks at
Sellafield in the United Kingdom, (formerly known as Windscale),
have confounded the pro-nuclear lobby. The development of alternative sources of energy fall under the aegis of these two departments.
Yet environmental arguments surround the development of wind
power as an alternative source of energy. Planning permission has
been given for a number of wind farms around the country in spite of
objections on the ground of their adverse impact on the landscape
and the noise.

The Department of Transport

This is another government department where decisions will be
made that affect the environment. The development of the road
network in the United Kingdom and the proposed privatisation of
the railways are decisions that have largely been taken without a
comprehensive consideration of the environmental consequences.
The environment is considered on an ad hoc basis. The planning
inquiry which considers the new road or the extension of an existing
road will take environmental questions into account. This may be
through the formal means of an environmental assessment under the
regulations, or it may be raised by an objector or a pressure group.
But the consequences of a national policy which supports road

---

[5] For a discussion of some of the issues surrounding the government policy on pit
closures see R. Malcolm, "In the Black" (Central Television (pub.), 1993).

building in preference to public transport have not been reviewed from the environmental viewpoint. The environmental questions are not necessarily inimical to the economic issues. For example, the idea of a free public transport system has environmental benefits in reducing the number of vehicles on the roads which emit fumes and spoil the towns and countryside as pleasant places to live. It would save government expenditure on roads and reduce the dependence on imported petroleum products. It would harm the motor manufacturing industries but would enhance the development of the railway industry and would create a valuable infrastructure for the country.

The difficulty arises from the need to make economic decisions relating to issues such as energy or transport, while evaluating their environmental impact, when the decision-making process must occur in a political context with the many vested interests that demand acknowledgment.

The Department of Transport is also concerned with sea transport and, therefore, is concerned with marine oil spills.

The Department of Health

This is a further department with extensive responsibilities for public health. This department has specific responsibility for medical services.

The Department of National Heritage

This is a new department, which was created in 1992. Conservation and tourism fall now to this department, although it is also responsible for other matter such as sport and tourism.[6] Specific responsibilities are for the listing of buildings and their subsequent maintenance.

The Ministry of Agriculture, Fisheries and Food

This is responsible for policy development within its named areas. This extends to aspects of food safety and quality. To this end it is responsible for monitoring levels of radioactivity in water and soil and to check such levels in food. When the Chernobyl accident occurred, and when leaks from Sellafield occur, it is this Ministry

---

[6] Transfer of Function (National Heritage) Order 1992 (S.I. 1992 No. 1311), Circular 20/92.

which proscribes the movement and sale of livestock, such as sheep, which may be affected. Agriculture is a major source of pollutants of the environment in the form of pesticides and fertilizers, and the Ministry issues Codes of Practice in relation to these issues.

The government departments are assisted by other bodies which can deliberate issues relating to the environment in a context which is more remote from the immediate hurly-burly of politics. These include the Royal Commission on Environmental Pollution and various other parliamentary committees.

Royal Commission on Environmental Pollution

This Commission has been producing reports of exceptional quality and influence since the early 1970s. It is a standing committee; that is, it has a permanent status and therefore has a permanent staff. The Commissioners are appointed for periods of three or four years. It prepares its reports by taking evidence from experts. This can be done orally or in writing. The Commission can be directed by a Minister to look at an issue, or it can choose to look at specific issues such as oil pollution of the sea,[7] or the emissions from heavy duty vehicles.[8] Broader reports include the Sixth Report on Nuclear Power and the Environment,[9] the Seventh Report on Agriculture and Pollution,[10] and the Tenth Report on Tackling Pollution: Experience and Prospects.[11]

Government agencies

English Heritage is the name adopted[12] by the Government's main agency for carrying out the day-to-day work on historic buildings and monuments. It has about 400 properties under its care. English Heritage has an advisory role not just to the Government but to local councils and to the owners of historic properties or conservation areas. It is responsible for administering the grant

---

[7] Eighth Report of the Royal Commission on Environmental Pollution, Cmnd. 7644 (1979).

[8] Fifteenth Report of the Royal Commission on Environmental Pollution, Cmnd. 1631 (1991).

[9] Cmnd. 6618 (1976).

[10] Cmnd. 7644 (1979).

[11] Cmnd. 9149 (1984).

[12] Under the Planning (Listed Buildings and Conservation Areas) Act 1990, this agency is called the Historic Buildings and Monuments Commission.

system which is available for the restoration or repair of these properties.[13]

The National Rivers Authority is the regulatory body which was set up when the water industry was privatised in 1989. Prior to that date the water industry fell within the public sector and it was not considered necessary to separate the regulatory functions from the duty to provide for water and sewerage. However, when the water companies were set up as profit-making companies limited by shares, it was deemed appropriate to separate the public duty of enforcing water quality. Thus the NRA is a public body which is constituted under section 6 of the Water Resources Act 1991.

The NRA is responsible for the protection of watercourses and groundwater. It issues licences permitting industry to discharge effluent into waterways and has power to attach conditions. If there is a breach of these regulations, the National Rivers Authority is the enforcing agency with power to prosecute in the criminal courts. One newsworthy prosecution against Shell for pollution of the River Mersey resulted in a fine of £1 million. However, the average fine has increased from a figure of £883 for 1989/1990 to £1,962 for 1991/1992. The number of successful prosecutions is, however, barely one percent. The first annual report of the NRA shows that out of some 28,143 water pollution incidents, only 272 resulted in a successful prosecution. This figure may improve as the NRA acquires experience in prosecuting in the light of a developing attitude which expects enforcing agencies to take formal action rather than seek a solution by negotiation and compromise.

The NRA also grants licences permitting the abstraction of water from rivers and groundwater. Industry is a heavy user of water. This is the reason that industries are frequently sited on riverbanks, in part originally for the advantages of navigation, but also to take the water for use in their production processes. The water might be taken to cool the machinery and would then be discharged back into the river. Difficulties arise if the temperature of the water in the river, (the ambient temperature), rises as a result of this activity and this is one matter for which the NRA monitor.

The NRA is also responsible for monitoring the quality of bathing water further to the E.C. Directive on Bathing Water.

---

[13] The equivalent organisations in Scotland and Wales are the Countryside Council for Wales and the Scottish National Heritage.

The Drinking Water Inspectorate is concerned to ensure that the standards set for the quality of drinking water which cover health, taste and appearance are met by the privatised water companies. However, the inspectorate is not resourced to enable it to carry out a system of sampling and monitoring itself. It is only able to oversee the water companies which are expected to monitor their own water for compliance with the standards.

The inspectorate are the enforcing body and can prosecute the water companies for breaches of the regulations. They also provide advice to central government and local government.

Her Majesty's Inspectorate of Pollution is the national authority responsible for the system of integrated pollution control introduced by Part I of the Environmental Protection Act 1990. HMIP was set up in 1987 and absorbed the existing inspectorates for Industrial Air Pollution, Radiochemicals and Hazardous Waste. It also absorbed the newly created Water Pollution Inspectorate. It is part of the Department of the Environment and has regional divisions. As part of the ethos of the integration of pollution control the inspectors are responsible for enforcing pollution control within each of the media. There are not separate divisions within the inspectorate. So, if an inspector is monitoring a particular factory, then potential emissions into the air, the water and the land will be checked.

HMIP's specific responsibilities under the Environmental Protection Act 1990 are to authorise particular processes which involve the emission of particularly risky substances into the atmosphere or into the water. There is a potential overlap with the activities of the NRA but it is resolved in that HMIP controls the emission into water of a particular group of substances known as the "red list" (see Chapter 7).

HMIP is not only responsible for enforcing legislation relating to integrated pollution control under the Environmental Protection Act 1990, but also deals with the legislative requirements in respect of controlled waste and radioactive substances.

The Health and Safety Executive is a body which deals exclusively with the work environment. Factory inspectors, employed under the Health and Safety at Work Act 1974, inspect work premises to ensure the safety of the workers. They, like environmental health officers, are empowered to bring criminal prosecutions for breaches of the regulations. For example, during the building of the Channel Tunnel, it was the Health and Safety Executive which was responsible for prosecuting the employers in respect of the number of accidental deaths which had occurred during construction.

The Nuclear Installations Inspectorate is part of the Health and Safety Executive, and, as its name implies, has the task of inspecting nuclear sites. It is also responsible for issuing licences to nuclear powered generating stations which will be subject to safety conditions.

THE ROLE OF LOCAL GOVERNMENT

Local authorities[14]

These have a greater range of enforcement functions than any of the central government agencies which tend to a more narrow specialism. Local authorities have a long history of dealing with public health matters which has developed to include housing, land use planning, regulation of food hygiene, building control, conservation, refuse collection and waste management, trading standards and statutory nuisances. Local authority officers will deal, therefore, with noise complaints, smoking bonfires, fumes from the local factory, food poisoning, rats in houses, overcrowded dwellings, applications to build locally and planning policy. They are the enforcement officers for breaches of the food hygiene regulations, Part III and Part I of the Environmental Protection Act 1990 and planning and conservation control. All these items have an immediate effect on the human environment and the importance of this local control should not be underestimated.

Local authorities are organised into boroughs in the cities where there is only one layer of local government. Outside these metropolitan areas, local authorities are presently organised into two layers: one at county level which is then subdivided into districts. These districts can cover a local town or a rural area. Each of these councils has an elected body which governs it and this elected body is supported by a number of officers who are full-time paid employees. Elected councillors receive expenses but no salary for their position and usually retain their full-time employment.

Local councils are ancient in origin and some retain their traditional names. For example, the council covering a city or town, which falls within the category of district councils is frequently known by its original title of a borough. Their powers and responsibilities are those of district councils. Reforms currently taking place

---

[14] For a detailed exposition of the organisation and history of local government see; Davies, *Local Government Law*; Cross, *Local Government Law* (1991).

will replace the present dual system outside the metropolitan areas with a single layer of councils known as unitary authorities. The boundaries for these new authorities are being determined by the Boundary Commission. They will inherit many of the present responsibilities which are now divided between county and district authorities.

There is a further subdivision which will remain unaffected by these proposed changes. These are the parish councils in rural areas, (or the community councils in Wales), and town councils in urban areas. These councils have few powers but can represent an important local political force. They have legal personality so can take legal action in their own name. The parish or town councillors are locally elected. Some may also be elected onto the county council and then have the opportunity to bring parish matters forward onto the county agenda.

When the authority is constituted for its different functions it is described by the name of the function. So, when an authority is deciding a planning application, it is called the local planning authority; when it is acting as the waste manager for the locality, it is called the waste management authority. Other titles are the minerals authority, the local housing authority, and so on. These are not separate groups of people. They are the same councillors sitting in the same town hall but constituted as a different legal entity with a different purpose.

The councillors sit on committees which are responsible for different functions. It is important to remember that the councillors are politicians and for the most part stand for the same political parties as are represented in the House of Commons. However, although much allegiance will be shown to the national party, of whatever colour that may be, local issues will have a considerable influence on the decision-making of the local councillors.

The officers of the authority are organised into departments. There are two departments which have most responsibility for environmental matters. These are the environmental health department and the planning department. There is also a department which deals with building control. This department is responsible for ensuring compliance with building regulations. These regulations ensure that buildings are structurally sound and accord with the best building practices currently enforceable by the authority which will promote health and safety.

The planning department of the local authority receives applications for the development of land in its locality. The planning officers have power to take a number of decisions on their own behalf where such power has been delegated to them by the council.[15] Most councils, however, make these decisions through the planning committee which will receive a report and recommendations from the planning officer.

The planning committee and department will also be involved in any planning applications which are accompanied by an environmental statement under the Town & Country (Assessment of Environmental Effects) Regulations 1988. This assessment of the environmental effects is a procedure which starts with the statement produced by the developer. It is for the local planning authority then to take the statement and any other information from concerned bodies into account before reaching their decision on the planning application. This may involve the authority in some form of analytical assessment of the environmental effects.

Local planning authorities are also responsible for the development of local planning policy and have to undertake the preparation of development plans at county and district level.

The environmental health department of the local authority has, as its name implies, the greatest involvement with public health in particular, and environmental issues in general. It is responsible, alongside Her Majesty's Inspectorate of Pollution, for atmospheric pollution,[16] and for the control of smoke.[17] Environmental health officers, who have an extensive period of training, are the enforcement officers for statutory nuisances,[18] and for breaches of the food laws.[19] This ensures that they have a wide range of environmental responsibilities.

Local authority environmental health officers have powers of inspection and sampling in relation to food and are enabled to serve various notices such as improvement and prohibition notices. It may prove necessary to establish that the food is unsafe by a scientific analysis. When a sample is taken it may either be sent to the *public analyst* or the *food examiner*. These are scientists who undertake a microbiological analysis of the food, looking for such things as the presence of salmonella.

In respect of nuisances and air pollution, environmental health officers can serve abatement notices. As the offences under all these statutory provisions are criminal, the officers have the same duties

---

[15] Local Government Act 1972, s.101.
[16] Environmental Protection Act 1990, Pt. I
[17] Clean Air Act 1993.
[18] Environmental Protection Act 1990, Pt. III.
[19] Food Safety Act 1990 and the Food Hygiene Regulations.

and responsibilities as the police investigating any crime. They must, therefore, comply with the Police & Criminal Evidence Act (PACE) 1984 and its codes and must adhere to the rules of evidence if court proceedings are anticipated.

Trading standards inspectors have responsibilities for consumer protection. This may involve ensuring that products are safe and do not pose a threat to public health and safety.

The *public* have a right of access to council meetings and to the papers relating to those meetings. They may even, with the permission of the chair, speak at a council meeting although this is not commonly done. The council meeting is representative of the local community and at this level democratic control can be effective. Local people or local campaigning groups have an enhanced opportunity to participate in local decision-making, whether it is by lobbying their local councillor or by making formal objections to planning applications. This is only possible, however, where the council retain responsibility for making the final decision. Where it is made by the officer, then the process whereby the decision is made is not open and not, therefore, subject to the same democratic control. Hence, the criticism of the British system of secretive decision-making by the Executive.

SECTION 2: EUROPE

INTRODUCTION

Europe is not simply a source of Directives. The involvement of Europe in terms of the enforcement of its provisions is growing. This enforcement occurs at a political, executive and judicial level. An understanding of the European context of environmental law is critical as it offers a means of dispute resolution. European law will in the future form an integral part of a lawyer's training in the United Kingdom. This is an outline of the institutions with a more detailed look at the role of the Commissioner for the Environment and his directorate.

The four institutions of the European Community

These were set up by the Treaties. They are the Council, the Commission, the European Parliament and the European Court of Justice.

1. The European Parliament is the one institution over which the people of the Member States have direct control since they can elect its members. Originally, the European Parliament had no powers to legislate or to raise taxes. In fact, it was originally called the "Assembly," its name being changed by the Assembly itself; a move which created confusion, and a false illusion of democratic control.

Its role was to advise and supervise. The Single European Act introduced a co-operation procedure between the Council, Commission and Parliament, otherwise its powers remained unchanged. The Treaty on European Union gave Parliament the right to be consulted on various matters by the Council which then adopts a "common position." Parliament can then approve it, reject it, or propose amendments. Council then makes its final decision according to the procedure detailed in Articles 189b and 189c. These are known as the co-decision and co-operation procedures.

As part of its supervisory role, Parliament can question and censure. The power to question, which applies to both the Council and the Commission, is widely used, unlike the power to censure, which is limited to the Commission. The Commission must also report to Parliament on Community activities.

2. The Council is the political body of the Community. Its role was, originally, to achieve co-ordination of the economic policies of the Community. Since the Single European Act and the Treaty on European Union, this role has been extended to policies within social, environmental and other fields. The Council has power to make Regulations, issue Directives, and take Decisions in accordance with the procedures detailed in Articles 189, 189a, 189b and 189c.

Each government sends a representative to the Council. The Council is not a fixed body. When there is a general meeting of the Council, the representatives are normally the national Ministers responsible for foreign affairs. However, if the Council is dealing with a specialised matter, such as agriculture or the environment, then the national minister responsible for that area normally attends.

Voting is increasingly by a majority of the Member States where the voting is weighted. There are a total of 76 votes distributed amongst the members. The four largest members, Germany, France, Italy and the United Kingdom, have 10 each. The remaining votes are distributed amongst the other members. Fifty-four votes in favour are required before the adoption of an Act.

In addition to the meetings of the "general" Council and the specialised groupings, the European Council meets at least twice each year. This consists of the Heads of State or of Government. In general this meeting deals with broad policy issues.

3. The Commission Although the Council is the legislative body and the Commission can correctly be described as the executive body, it does have a major role to play in formulating legislative proposals which are then passed to the Council. As an executive body it administers financial matters and implements Community policy. The Commission is sometimes described as a guardian of the Treaties. As such it has enforcement powers to ensure that no infringements of Community law are taking place. In addition it acts as a negotiating body in the international arena, leaving the final agreement to the Council.

At present, there are 17 Commissioners. The United Kingdom, France, Italy, Germany and Spain have two. They must be independent, competent and a national of a Member State. They are however, nominated by their national governments, although their appointment is by common accord of the governments of all the Member States and is also subject to the approval of the European Parliament, (Article 158). Their independence must be beyond doubt since they must be able to act in the general interests of the Community, even if this requires them to act against the national interests of their own, or any, state.

The civil service of the community is organised into *Directorate-Generals*. Directorate-General XI, (DG XI), is responsible for the environment, nuclear safety and civil protection. It employs about 450 people. Within DG XI there has been set up a small enforcement unit which has both the task of dealing with complaints and generating complaints. The unit consists of approximately one lawyer per country. This goes some way to explaining the time delay experienced by the Commission in dealing with complaints. In 1991, there was a delay of one year.

When a complaint comes in, it is initially registered with the enforcement unit who report it to the policy unit which gives scientific and technical advice. The enforcement unit then advises the Commission whether there has been a breach of European law.

Article 169 of the Treaty of Rome is the principal remedy available to the Commission where a Member State has infringed European law. It provides that the Commission shall deliver a reasoned opinion on the matter after giving the state concerned the opportunity to submit its observations. If the Member State fails to comply then the matter may go before the European Court of Justice. Most cases are settled by negotiation during the preliminary stages.

Under Article 171, where a Member State has failed to comply with a judgment of the Court of Justice, then the matter can be brought back before the Court. The Court then has power to impose a lump sum or penalty on the Member State if it finds that the Member State is in breach.

There have been cases where the European Court has been prepared to order interim measures against Member States in proceedings brought by the Commission. These proceedings are brought under Article 186.[20] Such a step may be taken if there appears no prospect of a negotiated settlement. If court proceedings become inevitable they are likely to take not less than two years, given the backlog of work at the Court. In the meantime, environmental damage may be occurring. For example, in the case of the alleged failure on the part of the United Kingdom to implement the Directive on Environmental Assessment properly, work was continuing on a number of projects even while Article 169 proceedings were underway.

4. The European Court of Justice This consists of 13 judges, one from each Member State and a President of the Court, who are assisted by six Advocates General. All are appointed for six years. The Advocates General make submissions to the court in which they lay out the facts and law and make recommendations. The Court is not obliged to follow the recommendations. It operates on Continental practices and procedures, thus it does not follow the practice of judicial precedent as in common law systems.

The Court is the supreme authority on all matters of Community law. Cases may be brought directly to it or referred by national courts. Its jurisdiction includes determining whether a Member State has failed to fulfil an obligation under the Treaty, giving preliminary rulings at the request of a national court or tribunal and deciding in disputes between Community institutions.

The workload of the Court has become so great that the Single European Act provided for a Court of First Instance to be established. This new court commenced proceedings on November 1, 1989. There are 12 members of this court appointed by common accord of the governments of the Member States for six years. Its jurisdiction is limited to disputes between the institutions and their servants, cases involving Community competition law, and actions concerning matters relating to the European Coal and Steel

---

[20] See for example Case 42/82R, *Commission* v. *France*: [1982] E.C.R. 841.

Community. There is a right of appeal from the Court of First Instance to the Court of Justice.

Courts within the United Kingdom can refer questions relating to the interpretation of the E.C. Treaty or the validity and interpretation of acts of the institutions of the Community directly to the European Court of Justice under Article 177. So, if there is some question about the interpretation of a Directive on environmental issues which the national court is unable to determine, then that issue can be referred straight to the European Court. This procedure is available to any court or tribunal in the United Kingdom.

The European Environment Agency is being set up to co-ordinate an information network. It will collect national data on the environment and provide information to form the basis for new European legislation. It will be responsible for drawing up expert reports on environmental issues and will establish uniform criteria to ensure the harmonisation of environmental controls across the Member States of the European Community. The Regulation dealing with the establishment of this agency, came into force the day after it was decided that the agency was to be located in Copenhagen, Denmark.[21] This decision was taken in October 1993 at the same time that the Maastricht Treaty was ratified formally by the 12 Member States and a number of decisions concerning the location of other Community institutions was taken.

SECTION 3: INTERNATIONAL INSTITUTIONS

INTRODUCTION

Enforcement of environmental law at national level where a governmental structure is in place backed up by the various means of enforcement provided by a state, is relatively straightforward. Arguments can be made about the enforcement policies adopted by certain of the agencies but the mechanism is in place. The means are available to bring a polluter to book. At European level the problem of enforcement becomes more acute. There may be judicial and

---

[21] Regulation 1210/90: [1990] O.J. L120/1.

administrative structures in place, but what powers do these bodies have in practice to force a defaulting state to comply with the common will of the European Union? At international level the difficulties are magnified. An international treaty may have been achieved after a long and delicate period of negotiations. If one party defaults what powers have the other parties to enforce the agreement against the defaulting party? Measures of censure may be available but may fall short of ensuring compliance with the environmental policy which was the subject of the treaty. There is no world government to enforce international law[22] and the various institutions operating in the international field normally have specific and narrow concerns and are not subject to open control. While the world is interlocked both economically and ecologically, the institutions controlling these aspects are fragmented and diverse. This is hardly surprising as it reflects the institutional arrangements within individual countries. One national ministry is concerned to promote industry while a separate department is concerned to clean up the waste generated by that industry. While environmental concerns are not part of the development of economic policy at national level it is no wonder that they are treated separately at international level.[23] For example, the World Health Organisation corresponds with the ministries of health, while the Food and Agricultural Organisation corresponds with the ministries of agriculture. Fragmentation at national level is bound to be reflected on the international plane.

There are changes coming about, however. The Maastricht Treaty has sought to make environmental concerns part of policy-making across the European Community. Financial agencies like the World Bank originally introduced the concept of environmental assessment in the early 1970s and this became a requirement for relevant projects in 1984. But these initiatives were, at first, largely cosmetic.[24] The World Bank eventually came to recognise the effect that its economic decisions to make major loans to developing countries for engineering projects had had on the environment. Such projects as the Carajas Iron Ore Project in Brazil, established with funding from the World Bank, have had devastating effects on the environment

---

[22] P. Alliolt, *Eunomia* (1990).
[23] "Our Common Future" (World Commission on Development), p. 9.
[24] Brian Clark, Chief Executive, Centre for Environmental Management and Planning, World Bank, "*Environmental Assessment in the World Bank*," "Advances in Environmental Assessment" Conference, October 29–30, 1992.

which were not examined in advance of the project. Since 1989, the World Bank has had a formal procedure in place for the environmental assessment of projects which seeks to ensure that development options are environmentally sound and sustainable. The European Bank for Reconstruction and Development has also undergone a "greening" process, adopting in January 1992 an environmental policy. Whether these environmental policies can successfully be integrated with the economic policies of these major international financial institutions is another question.

There are a number of institutions at international level. Some, like the World Bank and the European Bank, are concerned with development lending, trade regulation and agricultural development. They develop environmental policies which are taken into account when making economic decisions. Others, such as the United Nations, have broad concerns relating to world order and international co-operation. Environmental issues may be part of their remit as an offshoot of their primary activities. Some organisations are commissions set up under specific treaties to supervise implementation of the treaty objectives.

THE UNITED NATIONS

The UN is a premier international organisation whose Charter was agreed in 1945 by the original 46 nations. Present membership now exceeds 100. In 1945 environmental issues were not paramount compared to the need to secure world peace, and the UN Charter contained no specific reference to the environment. However, in the same way that the European Community was able to legislate on environmental issues despite the absence of any provisions in the Treaty of Rome, so has the UN been able to take on environmental matters within the general context of its work on social matters.

The UN is a highly developed organisation with a number of constituent parts. It has a judicial body: the International Court of Justice and a number of bodies with specific responsibilities such as the World Health Organisation and the Food and Agricultural Organisation which have environmental responsibilities within their remit.

In 1972 the UN held the influential Conference on the Human Environment in Stockholm as it perceived the urgent need to limit and, if possible, eliminate the impairment of the human environment. The UN environment programme resulted from this conference and there were four parts to it. Firstly, there was a Declaration of 26 principles which were to act as a guide to the international community for the preservation and enhancement of the human environment. Secondly, there was an Action Plan which contained 106 recommendations which included the proposal to set up Earthwatch, (a Global Assessment Programme). The object of Earthwatch was to gather information, to warn and to promote research. The third achievement of the Conference was to set up an Environment Fund which would be funded on a voluntary basis by the states, and the fourth element was to set up the U.N. Environment Programme.

The United Nations Environment Programme

This has a separate organisational structure with a General Council and a Secretariat. It aims to have an important role in developing international environmental law and a number of treaties and guidelines have been concluded with its support. Conferences following on the success of the 1972 Stockholm Conference, have been held and some have resulted in the development of legal institutions and instruments such as the International Fund for Agriculture and Development and the UN Charter of Economic Rights and Duties of States.

Other UN agencies within the field of the global environment include the *International Maritime Organisation* which is concerned with maritime safety and protection of the marine environment. Thirty conventions have been adopted under the auspices of the IMO some of which are concerned with such issues as civil liability for oil pollution damage, prevention of pollution from ships and the establishment of a fund for compensation for oil pollution damage. As a number of these conventions have been adopted by national legislators, and as many of the IMO guidelines are accepted as international standards, the level of practical implementation and enforcement is, therefore, high, although this enforcement is not carried out directly by IMO but by national bodies.

The World Health Organisation

The W.H.O., a well known UN agency, promotes the highest possible level of health among people. This involves dealing with environmental factors which determine human health such as the quality of drinking water and the use of drugs. It is an important source of international standards and its guidelines on the quality of drinking water influence domestic legislation widely. Some of its notable practical successes have included the elimination of smallpox.

The International Labour Organisation

This UN agency was set up to improve the working conditions and the general welfare of workers by improving the working environment.

The Food and Agriculture Organisation

This aims to tackle problems of poverty, malnutrition and hunger. It looks at agricultural problems, desertification and deforestation and the conservation of natural resources. It has had some notable influence in the field of fisheries law in that it has prepared reports on fisheries around the world and, through recommendations, has been a major influence.

Monitoring of global warming and other climatic conditions is assisted by the *World Meteorological Organisation.*

The United Nations Educational, Scientific, and Cultural Organisation

Finally, the only UN agency to which the United Kingdom does not belong, undertakes research into the fields of natural and social science and supports technology transfer by means of technical assistance to developing countries. The United Kingdom left UNESCO on the grounds that its aims were not sufficiently specific.

Outside the UN structure, there are a number of other *non-governmental organisations* which have environmental interests. It is sometimes difficult to keep track of them, but amongst the most significant is the *International Union for the Conservation of Nature.* This body includes amongst its members, governments, government agencies and other non-governmental organisations. It has played a part in drafting treaties and contributes extensively to research and the dissemination of information through bulletins and meetings.

As international institutions, these bodies make major contributions to the development of international environmental law. They organise conferences which spawn commissions which play a role in different aspects of environmental control. They sponsor research; they develop guidelines which are acknowledged by the different nations and absorbed into domestic legislation. But do they, themselves, have a role to play in enforcing the rules they help create?

Clearly, they do not sit aside national enforcement agencies such as Her Majesty's Inspectorate of Pollution. They cannot bring enforcement proceedings before tribunals. They can cajole, warn, encourage and advise. They can produce guidelines for environmental standards which could be considered as no more than articles of faith. In short, they could be dismissed as creators of a system of law which they are incapable of enforcing. Nevertheless, they are important for a variety of reasons.[25] Many aspects of environmental pollution are global in their effect. They may also be global in their cause. The problem of the depletion of the ozone layer is a case in point. All industrialised nations, and a good many developing nations, produce the gases which are reputed to contribute to the depletion of that layer of gases in the atmosphere which filter harmful rays from the sun. One nation is unlikely to take an initiative on its own to reduce the production of these gases if it would involve a burden on industry. Even if it could be shown in the long term that these changes could benefit industry, governments in capitalist economies are obliged to take short-term views. So, an initiative to deal with the problem must be a joint initiative. All the nations must agree to reduce these gases. So, under the auspices of a supra-national body such as the United Nations a conference is organised and an agreement is entered into to reduce emissions. The agreement may be supplemented by a detailed protocol setting out precise figures and target dates. How then does the supra-national body ensure compliance? Having set the standards, the supra-national body could be involved in supervising implementation by undertaking research and inspections. If a state fails to implement according to the agreement then the body could report this fact and resulting publicity could achieve a solution. Peer pressure from other members of the group of participants to the agreement could result in compliance. It is rare for the body itself to be given further powers. One exception to this is under the 1985 Ozone Convention where there is a procedure in place to deal with recalcitrant members. If there is no formal procedure, peer pressure may not be enough. The difficulties encountered by the International Whaling Commission exemplify this. Japan and Norway both resumed whaling in the face of a majority view prevailing on the Commission

---

[25] A.E. Boyle, "Saving the World? Implementation and Enforcement of International Environmental Law through International Institutions" (1991) 3 J.E.L. (No. 2) 229.

which opposes whaling. International adverse publicity appears not to be effective in the light of a determinedly defiant nation.

SECTION 4: PRESSURE GROUPS

Mention should also be made of the vital role played in the development of environmental law, and its enforcement, by the campaigning organisations. Pressure groups have long played a role in the political world, nationally and internationally.

Some are set up to achieve narrow objectives, some have a broader ongoing remit. They exist at all levels of society from the local group set up to oppose, (or support), a particular environmental proposal to the international group campaigning on issues of global importance. A local group of residents may meet and form a group to oppose a new road and once their campaign is won, (or lost), they are disbanded.

The interplay between groups at different levels should not be ignored. For instance, a national organisation might also choose to campaign alongside a local group. This occurred in relation to the M3 extension which was proposed to bypass Winchester in Hampshire and pass through an area of special scientific interest called Twyford Down. The local residents formed an association and, together with the parish council, fought an action in the High Court, as part of their objection to the preferred route. Other organisations, such as Friends of the Earth and the Campaign for Rural England, also became involved in the campaign against this route.

The co-ordination of these campaigns can be complex. The objectives of the different groups may be different, and may, in fact, not be complementary. If a legal solution is being sought by one group, they may be concerned to keep control of the political campaign, a move which may not be met with sympathy by other activists. Nevertheless, the power of campaigns at all levels of the political spectrum, is undoubted.

Particular campaigning groups of national and international repute are Friends of the Earth and Greenpeace. They have long term objectives and can be involved in a variety of campaigns. They may choose to use legal and/or political means to achieve their objectives. They also perform an educational function in disseminating information about proposed legislative or policy changes and developments. There are many groups worthy of note, including, the Sierra Club in the United States of America, and on the national plane, the Campaign for Rural England, the Ramblers Association and the Royal Society for the Protection of Birds which have, as their names imply, more sectoral interests. The National Trust is an independent charity which purchases and manages historic properties on behalf of the nation. It has been instrumental in saving a number of properties and sites from destruction.

Other organisations operating within the environmental field include the Institution of Environmental Health Officers, a professional body, the United Kingdom Environmental Law Association which provides opportunities for the exchange of information and research for those concerned with environmental law, the Town and Country Planning Association which is concerned with promoting a better environment, and the Institute for European Environmental Policy which works closely with the European Commission.

SECTION 5: ACCESS TO ENVIRONMENTAL INFORMATION

INTRODUCTION

In an open society where environmental regulations are made by an elected body and enforced by a body which is answerable for its actions, information about sampling or monitoring results should be available to the public. If there is a limit which prescribes the amount of lead which is to be permitted in water, then, where there is a government agency responsible for monitoring the quality of that water, the results of that monitoring should be available to the public on whose behalf the regulations are made and enforced.

It is not the case in the United Kingdom that freedom of access to information has been totally denied. It has been possible to inspect local authority registers and, under the former legislation contained in Part II of the Control of Pollution Act 1974, certain registers such as water registers held by the water authorities were open to the public. It would seem, however, that there was little public awareness of the availability of this information. This may be related to such factors as the comprehensibility of the information available and the sufficiency of data included.[26]

There has, in the United Kingdom, traditionally been a tendency, within the administrative world of pollution control, towards a

---

[26] See T.P. Burton, "Access to Environmental Information: The U.K. Experience of Water Registers" (1989) 1 J.E.L. (No. 2) 192–208.

closed society peopled only by the enforcers and the enforced. This
has been justified on various grounds. Enforcement is not always a
clear cut affair. If a company is in breach of the prescribed standards
then prosecution should not automatically be the first resort of the
enforcer. If the offender voluntarily amends the fault and the
enforcer is satisfied that the pollution will not occur again, then the
regulations and the public purse are satisfied. Implicit in this justification is the premise that, within the environmental context, the
purpose of the regulatory control system is not to punish but to
rehabilitate. Although the philosophy of this assumption is seldom
addressed, a distinction is drawn in practice between environmental
crime and "mainstream" crime. If a man murders his neighbour, he
will be brought before a criminal court to answer for his deed. If he
poisons the water by allowing the factory waste pipes to overflow,
the NRA will exercise their discretion as to whether to prosecute.

There is, of course, within all enforcement systems a discretion as
to whether to prosecute. The Executive have to make decisions
which are judgmental. The police often "drop charges" or use the
mechanism of the formal caution which removes the need to prove
the crime beyond reasonable doubt to the satisfaction of a court
where the offender accepts this procedure. Nevertheless, the social
stigma of the environmental crime is significantly different from
other crimes. It falls within the administrative sphere where decision-making has rested traditionally on the exercise of discretion
which is not done within the public domain. The requirement,
therefore, to make public the information which will determine the
decision to prosecute goes counter to the tradition of administrative
decision-making in the United Kingdom.

The United States of America has the reputation for open government with laws permitting members of the public to have access to
information kept by the government. Other countries such as Australia and New Zealand likewise have such laws. As a result of a
European Directive on the freedom of access to information on the
environment,[27] the United Kingdom has been obliged to introduce
similar laws.

In the Royal Commission on Environmental Pollution's 10th
Report[28] there was a recommendation that there should be a

---

[27] Directive of 90/313, on the freedom of access to information on the environment:
[1990] O.J. L158/56. For a commentary on the government proposals to
implement this Directive see: David Hughes: (1992) L.M.E.L.R. 4(3) 73–108.

[28] Cmnd. 9194 (1984). For the government response to the Royal Commissions's
Report see Pollution Paper No. 23, an inter-departmental working party report
published by the D.O.E.

presumption in favour of unrestricted access for the public to information acquired by the pollution control authorities in the exercise of their statutory powers. Secrecy was only to be permitted where a genuine case for it could be substantiated.

The Action Programmes of the European Community called for ways to be devised to improve public access to information held by public authorities and this was highlighted as a priority issue in the fourth programme, (1987–92). The Directive which implemented this policy provides for access to any available information written, visual, aural or in database form on the state of water, air, soil, fauna, flora, land and natural sites, and on activities or measures adversely affecting or designed to protect these factors. This information is to be made available by public authorities, that is public administration at national, regional or local level. The information is to be made available to any person on request at a reasonable charge.

The Directive permits access to information to be refused where matters of confidentiality, international relations or national defence and public security are concerned. There are also broad grounds for refusal: "where the request is manifestly unreasonable or formulated in too general a manner" (Article 3.3).

This Directive was implemented in Great Britain on December 31, 1992 when the Environmental Information Regulations 1992,[29] came into force. The Regulations apply to any body with public responsibilities for the environment and the information referred to in the Regulations includes anything contained in any records. This would seem to be a narrower definition than that contained in the Directive which refers to information in any form. The Directive does not define information so it is arguable that it could include letters or memoranda which would presumably not fall within the United Kingdom classification of a "record" which is described as including "registers, reports or returns."

The Regulations permit, in addition to such matters as national security, matters affected by commercial or industrial confidentiality or which affect intellectual property to be exempted from their provisions. Information which is subject to legal proceedings is also subject to this exemption. These proceedings are broadly defined to include disciplinary hearings and any form of inquiry. It also includes information which has been subject to such proceedings and which are completed. It follows that if litigation is pending

---

[29] S.I. 1992 No. 3240. See W. Birtles, "A Right To Know: The Environmental Information Regulations 1992" [1993] J.P.E.L. 615.

neither the plaintiff nor the defendant will be able to gain access to data held by an agency which is not subject to the proceedings.

In addition to the Environmental Information Regulations 1992, there are further statutory provisions which permit access to information held by various bodies. One important provision contained in section 143 of the Environmental Protection Act 1990 which would have made registers available to the public containing information on contaminated land, has been withdrawn by the Government. Such a change in government policy indicates the difficulties inherent in the British system of administration. Significant opposition from industry which was concerned about the consequences of blight and the effect on insurance premiums, clearly influenced this governmental decision. Detailed information about the level and type of contamination of land would have informed purchasers about the potential liability they could be subject to in the future. Although the House of Lords' decision in *Cambridge Water Co.* v. *Eastern Counties Leather p.l.c.* (1994) appears to have limited the scope for litigation in respect of historical pollution, it remains the case that there may be liability under the tort of nuisance where damage was reasonably foreseeable.

As part of the open government policy, a Citizen's Charter entitled "Green Rights and Responsibilities: A Citizen's Guide to the Environment" has been published by the Department of the Environment. It reinforces three rights, the first of which is the right of access to environmental information held by public authorities. In practice, this right is circumscribed firstly by the existence of relevant data, – if the information is not recorded, (as with contaminated land) then it cannot be accessed. Secondly, if the exemptions to access are as widely drawn in practice as the Regulations appear to admit, then the limitations may severely inhibit the objectives spelled out in the European Directive.

Current government proposals suggest that the right of access to information will be extended to health and safety information held by the public sector. It is proposed that this will extend to health and safety in the workplace, in public places, transport systems, food, consumer goods and environmental health risks.[30] This, in theory, would seem to extend quite significantly the right of access to information although there are a number of exceptions. There is no official evidence, to date, however, as to how the Environmental Information Regulations, which are already up and running, are working in practice.

---

[30] White Paper on Open Government, Cmd. 2290 (1993).

Registers

A number of the enforcement agencies are required to maintain registers containing information received under their statutory obligations. This list outlines some of the registers of most significance within the environmental field.

1. National Rivers Authority (Regional Offices).

Data on consents including conditions; notices of water quality objectives; the results of monitoring and sampling of inland waterways and bathing waters and the steps taken as a result of such monitoring and sampling; particulars about authorisations under the Environmental Protection Act 1990.

2. Water Company Public Register

Quality of drinking water – summary of monitoring data for the supply zone. A water supply zone is an area designated by the undertaker with a resident population of not more than 50,000. The register contains information about any relaxations from the requirement to supply wholesome water permitted by the Secretary of State and the results of analyses of the water supply; consents given to discharge trade effluent into the sewerage system.

3. Litter authority

Litter registers kept by the principal litter authority. Record of designated litter control areas and street litter control notices.

4. Local planning authority

Planning applications; planning consents and conditions; enforcement notices; stop notices; conservation areas; contaminated land, (this is not an official register but this information is kept by some authorities).

5. Local authority environmental health department

Air pollution control registers are maintained by local authorities in relation to their duties under Part 1 of the Environmental Protection Act 1990. This will take the same form as the register maintained by Her Majesty's Inspectorate of Pollution as described in section 6 below. In addition it will contain information about authorisations made by HMIP in relation to processes operating in the area covered by the local authority. This information will be supplied by HMIP to the local authority for inclusion in the register.

6. Her Majesty's Inspectorate of Pollution

Under the Environmental Protection Act 1990, Part I, s.20, and the Environmental Protection (Application, Appeals and Registers) Regulations 1991, HMIP must keep registers containing the following information:

applications for authorisation to conduct a prescribed process, *e.g.* a waste incineration process;
authorisations which have been granted;
revocations of authorisations;
appeals;
convictions;
information relating to conditions of authorisations;
directions by Secretary of State;
other matters relating to the carrying on of a prescribed process or to the pollution of the environment.

If information is excluded as a result of a successful application to the effect that the information affects commercial confidentiality or relates to national security, then that fact must be included.

There is no prescribed form for the registers so they could be kept on computer.

New proposals contained in the Government's White Paper on Open Government[31] suggest that the principles pertaining to access to information contained in the Environmental Information Regulations 1992 should be extended to health and safety matters. This would concern the Health and Safety Executive. In addition there are proposals to extend this to food, consumer goods, safety of public places, transport systems and environmental health risks.

---

[31] Cmd. 2290 (1993).

Chapter Four

Scenario

Introduction

Environmental controls are typically dealt with according to the particular environmental medium which is being considered and this book is no exception. The reason for this ordering is primarily because of the mechanisms which are available to deal with the different forms of pollution. There is an Act of Parliament dealing with water pollution, another dealing with the control of waste, another with planning proposals and so on. Then, the enforcement agencies follow this pattern. The National Rivers Authority deals with water pollution, the Health and Safety Inspectorate deals with environmental questions relating to the work site, the local authority environmental health department deals with the control of smoke pollution. The difficulty, of course, is that a polluting event can cause problems for more than one of the environmental medium at a time. It may also be the case that, in the short term, the consequences of the polluting event may only affect one environmental medium, whereas, in the long term, the contamination may affect other environmental media.

For instance, a large industrial plant can emit fumes directly into the atmosphere and trade effluent directly into the water having an immediate impact on two environmental media. On the other hand, a large combustion plant can emit chemicals into the atmosphere which eventually come to earth, washed down by the rain. Thus, contamination of the land and water can occur as a secondary effect. A site which has been contaminated by old mine workings can leach into the groundwater drinking supply. Planning proposals for new developments can have an impact on a range of environmental concerns. They can affect the landscape, create noise, destroy natural habitats. If they involve certain prescribed processes they may be subject to the rules relating to integrated pollution control. If they involve developments concerned with waste disposal then they will fall under the waste management regime. The sources of law are manifold and frequently overlapping.

The attempt to introduce a system of integrated pollution control within the existing framework of controls only goes part of the way towards resolving some of the conflicts, and, indeed, is bound to create more. For instance, if a prescribed process falls under the integrated pollution control regime, then control over water pollution is exceptionally taken out of the hands of the agency deputed to deal with it – the NRA. But the NRA may have prescribed water quality levels for the affected river. Which enforcement agency takes precedence in the event of a conflict? This problem has been resolved administratively simply by HMIP coming to an agreement with the NRA.

The problem can be viewed from the perspective of the client. If the client is a member of the public seeking to prevent pollution or environmental damage or seeking compensation for the effect of pollution, then none of the statutory controls is likely to be appropriate. Although some of the statutory controls are available to the private individual, the subsequent difficulties of enforcement, inspection and monitoring are likely to be beyond the means and capability of an individual. There is, for example, a procedure whereby the private individual can take action to abate a statutory nuisance.[1] Where the individual is the "person aggrieved" by the nuisance, (the person suffering the effects of noise coming from a neighbour's flat, for example), and the local authority do not take action to abate it, the individual may pursue the action in the courts themselves. However, as a criminal prosecution, legal aid is not available other than for advice in the preparation of the case.[2] Reliance on the common law is likely to be the only method which will result in adequate compensation and is, therefore, usually the best or, at least, the most appropriate means available for the individual to seek redress.

The industrial client seeking advice on a development proposal will require guidance through the maze of statutory controls as well as in respect of potential civil liability. The relevant statutory controls may relate to integrated pollution control or local authority air control under the Environmental Protection Act 1990, the waste legislation and the duty of care in respect of waste might be relevant,

---

[1] Environmental Protection Act 1990, s.82.
[2] Legal Advice and Assistance Scheme, (the "Green Form Scheme"), Legal Aid Act 1974.

or water controls and the disposal of effluent involving the NRA or the water and sewerage undertaker might be appropriate.

The enforcement agency seeking advice or representation will require advice either on the interpretation of the most recent case law or statute, or will need expertise in terms of court procedure and rules of evidence. Most enforcement agencies hire lawyers to undertake the conduct of a court action. They may also seek advice on the drafting of notices or the extent of their powers in relation to the acquisition of evidence. Some of the agencies have in-house lawyers who may conduct the proceedings themselves. For example, environmental health departments within local authorities are responsible for a wide range of functions. They will usually use the services of the authority's own legal department. The council lawyers may conduct many of the magistrates' court cases themselves or may hire outside lawyers for the conduct of some proceedings. It is possible in a number of cases for officers of the agency to conduct a case themselves. Many statutes specifically provide for this. In such cases, the officer, usually well versed in the relevant legal aspects of the case, may require further expertise in the rules of evidence or procedure.

The following chapters, therefore, are in danger of creating a misleading impression of the practical application of environmental law. It might appear that subjects are discrete and a practitioner could specialise, for example, in water law to the exclusion of all other topics. While it is possible for officers of an enforcement agency to specialise within their own field, for the general environmental practitioner, nothing could be further from the truth. Even for the officer, such specialisation without some comprehension of the other parts of environmental law could be too limiting. If a problem could be more effectively dealt with under another heading and a different agency, then an officer would be advised to pass it on. Although environmental law could not be described as a seamless robe, it is certainly a patchwork quilt with each part interlocking into the next.

This chapter attempts, therefore, by the use of one scenario, to give a flavour of the practical application of environmental law by giving some examples of the overlapping jurisdictions within the field.

The scenario covers the following areas:

Public/private, (rule in *Rylands* v. *Fletcher*)/statutory nuisance. Tort of negligence.

Planning/environmental impact assessment.
Clean Air Act 1993.
Waste law.
Water law.

SCENARIO[3]

For several months the environmental health department of Cleanborough District Council has been receiving numerous complaints
from residents about smoke and noise emanating from a waste site,
comprising a disused quarry. Access is by means of a gate at the
southern end of the site. The northern side of the site is bordered by
the River Wash. The gate is controlled during the day by two men
with the help of two fierce dogs. The site is owned by a Mr. Swann
who operates the business on the site under the name of Swann Song
Enterprises.

A group of residents have formed a pressure group whose
expressed aim is to close the site. Several local councillors have
expressed warm support for the group. This group has complained
that the site is being used as an unauthorised dump by a waste
disposal business. Large lorries have been observed delivering quantities of waste materials to the site, materials that have subsequently
been observed being burned, emitting smoke and fumes. The noise
complaints are twofold. First, the dogs, which are believed to be
used as guard dogs by Mr. Swann, bark frequently and furiously,
including at night-time. Secondly, a noisy generator is used to supply
power to the cabin. Both forms of noise are amplified because of the
physical characteristics of the quarry.

Mrs. Timid, a local resident, has complained to the environmental
health department about the noise from the generator and the dogs
which disturbs her at night and during the weekends, and about the
smoke which means she cannot hang her washing out.

Last week, a lorry was seen delivering drums to the site. These
were unloaded and stacked up at the northern edge of the boundary.
The drums appeared to be rusting and one or two of them were
leaking. Some of them were labelled but in a Cyrillic script. After a
night of heavy rain on Saturday, a small landslip occurred at the
edge of the quarry site and some of the drums rolled down into the
water's edge. On Sunday, some local children pushed them into the
water for use as target practice. The drums have now sunk to the

---

[3] This scenario is based on a training programme devised by Environmental
Training Consultants for the Institution of Environmental Health Officers. Their
kind permission for its use is acknowledged here.

bottom of the river. During the following week, some dead fish have been spotted in the water and some of the local children have been taken to the doctor suffering from a skin rash. Mrs. Furious, whose two children appear badly affected by this rash, has telephoned the NRA to complain about the pollution of the River Wash. The heavy rainfall caused some flooding on the site and Mr. Swann has dug a channel through the edge of the quarry so that surplus water can flow away into the river.

Advise.

Commentary

There are various potential clients mentioned in the scenario who might seek advice; the Cleanborough environmental health department, the NRA, the pressure group, Mrs. Timid, Mrs. Furious or Mr. Swann.

There are various aspects of environmental law to be considered: the law relating to waste, planning, noise, smoke and water. The legal issues might be summarised thus:

1. Is planning permission required to use the site for the disposal of waste?
2. Is there a waste licence in force? Has an offence been committed otherwise under the waste regime?
3. Do the smoke and the noise constitute a nuisance at common law? Is there any other liability at common law?
4. Do the smoke and noise constitute a nuisance or are they prejudicial to health under the Environmental Protection Act 1990?
5. Is the smoke within the definition of dark smoke which is subject to the Clean Air Act 1993?
6. Has there been a breach of the water pollution legislation?

1. Planning controls

Planning permission would have been required to change the use of the site from a quarry to a waste disposal site. Waste disposal does not appear within a class in the Town and Country Planning (Use Classes) Order 1987, so it falls into a class of its own; it is a use *sui generis*. The deposit of waste on land is a development within the meaning of the Town and Country Planning Act 1990. Section 55(3)(b) of that Act specifically states that the deposit of waste or other refuse materials on land amounts to a material change of use where it involves an increase in the surface area of the site, or if the height is raised so as to increase it above the level of surrounding land. A relevant case for the scenario is *Alexandra Transport Co. Ltd. v. Secretary of State for Scotland*,[4] in which it was decided that the deposit of household waste in a quarry which had previously been used for the disposal of quarry waste, was development.[5] The development may amount to a change of use or, if the deposit is for the purpose of landfill, for example, then it might amount to an engineering development.

If Mr. Swann is operating without planning permission, then the local county council may consider serving an enforcement notice on him. The deposit of waste materials is a county matter.

If Mr. Swann decides to apply for planning permission, the authority may consider whether to require an environmental statement to be submitted with the application. If the waste disposal operation is being used for the disposal of special waste, then, under Schedule 1 of the Town and Country (Assessment of Environmental Effects) Regulations 1988, an environmental assessment is obligatory. If it is not special waste, then, under Schedule 2 of the Regulations, an assessment may be required where the development is likely to have significant effects on the environment. Factors such as the size of the operation, any inherently dangerous features, or the sensitivity of the location may give rise to significant environmental effects. Although neighbours are complaining about air pollution and noise, this may not be sufficient to convince the authority that an environmental assessment is called for.

Before serving an enforcement notice, the authority must consider whether they would have granted permission anyway. As the site is in a quarry it may be arguable that there are no adverse implications for the landscape. However, the effect on the local residential population is another matter. Questions of noise, vibration, and the traffic problems consequent on the movement of heavy lorries, will be considered by the authority. These factors may not be sufficient to cause an authority to reject an application. Instead, the authority may impose conditions to control these matters. These conditions could extend to aftercare of the site since, as a former quarry, the site is equivalent to a landfill site. While it is not an offence to operate without an appropriate planning permission, it is an offence not to

---

[4] (1974) 27 P. & C.R. 252.
[5] See also *R. v. Derbyshire County Council, ex p. North Derby District Council* (1979) 77 L.G.R. 389.

comply with the enforcement notice. Once served, therefore, unless Mr. Swann appeals against it, the authority may bring proceedings against him in the magistrates' court if he does not comply with it.

Another option, where the breach is very serious, would be to serve a stop notice requiring the immediate cessation of the activities. This would be subject to a right of compensation if Mr. Swann were to launch a successful appeal.

Cleanborough District Council could serve a planning contravention notice on Mr. Swann after consultation with the county council. This would require Mr. Swann to give information about his activities within 21 days.

2. Waste offences

In order to operate his site as a waste disposal site, Mr. Swann requires a waste management licence under Part II of the Environmental Protection Act 1990. It is an offence to operate a waste disposal site without a licence. Planning permission must be in force before a licence will be granted. Planning controls are concerned with land use, whereas waste controls are concerned with the operational aspects of the waste disposal business. Once planning permission is in force, the waste regulation authority should not refuse the licence except where public health will be at risk, or where there is a risk of pollution of water. Consultation with the NRA should take place. The NRA may object to the granting of the licence or they may require that certain conditions should be imposed; disagreements will be referred to the Secretary of State.

The offence of knowingly causing or knowingly permitting the deposit of controlled waste without a licence is contained in section 33(1)(a) of the Environmental Protection Act 1990. Under section 33(1)(b) it is an offence to treat, keep or dispose of controlled waste, or knowingly cause or knowingly permit it to be done, in or on any land except in accordance with a waste management licence. An offence may also have been committed under section 33(1)(c) of the Environmental Protection Act 1990 which prohibits the treating, keeping or disposing of waste in a manner likely to cause pollution of the environment or harm to human health. This would be available in appropriate circumstances even if Mr. Swann had a licence. The smoke is a substance which has come from the treatment of the waste, *i.e.* the bonfire, harm to the local people could include harm to their sense of smell as well as to their property. The consequent air pollution could amount to pollution of the environment if it were likely to do harm because of the quantity of smoke emitted, or the quality of the smoke.

The defence of due diligence is available to Mr. Swann in respect of an offence under section 33(1)(c) if he can show that he took such steps as were reasonable to prevent the emission of the smoke.

Under section 34 of the Environmental Protection Act 1990, a duty of care is imposed on producers and handlers of waste. The duty of care includes prevention of the escape of the waste. Mr. Swann may face liability under this section for the loss of the drums into the River Wash. He may also incur liability under section 33(1)(c) as the loss of the drums into the river appears to have caused harm to the environment, (loss of fish), and harm to human health, (rashes on children). It would seem unlikely that he could rely on the due diligence defence in view of his failure to store the drums properly, although he might seek to argue that the circumstances of the unusually heavy rainfall were not something he could reasonably have anticipated.

In relation to the drums, the person transferring them to Mr. Swann may also incur liability under section 34 of the Environmental Protection Act 1990, for failing to ensure their safe transfer and for failing to ensure they were adequately packed and labelled. The carrier of the waste should have been registered under the Controlled Waste (Registration of Carriers and Seizure of Vehicles) Regulations 1991, and should have provided documentation enabling Mr. Swann to take appropriate steps to deal with the waste.

The appropriate enforcement agency for offences of depositing waste without a licence or for other offences under section 33 or section 34 of the Environmental Protection Act 1990 would be the local county council.

3. Water pollution offences

The River Wash will constitute a controlled water within the meaning of the Water Resources Act 1991. Mr. Swann may have committed an offence under the general pollution offence contained within this Act. There is no indication of a discharge consent being in force from the NRA. The existence of one in the circumstances of the case is unlikely.

As a first step, the NRA could take steps to clean up the river if the effects of the pollution have not dissipated. The costs of this operation would be borne by Mr. Swann.

Mr. Swann could be prosecuted under section 85(1) of the Water Resources Act 1991 for causing or knowingly permitting any poisonous, noxious or polluting matter to enter the river. The drums and their contents would appear to fall within this category. It would be essential to establish that the presence of the drums in the river were the cause of the dead fish and the injury to the children.

This offence is an offence of strict liability. Proof of fault is not required. However, if Mr. Swann is charged with "causing" the pollution, then the NRA must show some positive act on his part. There are two possible acts which may be considered. Firstly, there is the collapse of the drums into the river. It would be necessary to show that there was some chain of operations conducted by Mr. Swann which caused the drums to end up in the river (*Alphacell v. Woodward*).[6] His action in stacking the drums at the northern edge is arguably sufficient for this. However, he might raise as a defence the fact that the drums are pushed into the river by the children, third parties for whom he is not responsible (*Impress (Worcester) Ltd. v. Rees*).[7] The action of the heavy rainwater in causing the landslip would need to amount to an intervening act breaking the chain of causation for Mr. Swann to be able to claim that it amounted to an Act of God (*Southern Water Authority v. Pegrum*).[8]

If he is charged with "knowingly permitting" the matter to enter the water, this involves some element of knowledge which may well have been lacking.

The second act is that of digging a drainage channel which allows the rainwater, and possibly polluting matter, to escape into the river. Digging the channel is a positive act on Mr. Swann's part which would amount to an act of causation (*National Rivers Authority v. Welsh Development Agency*).[9]

Under the Salmon and Freshwater Fisheries Act 1975, the NRA could bring a prosecution for the offence of causing or knowingly permitting any liquid or solid matters to flow or be put into waters containing fish so that the waters are poisonous to the fish or their spawning grounds. If there is clear proof of the presence of fish and the injury, (there are dead fish floating on the water), then a prosecution may be brought.

4. Common law liability

The potential liability of Mr. Swann at common law, may be considered under three heads: the rule in *Rylands v. Fletcher*,[10] nuisance and negligence.

---

[6] [1972] A.C. 824.
[7] [1971] 2 All E.R. 357.
[8] (1989) 153 J.P. 581.
[9] [1993] Env. L.R. 407.
[10] 1868 L.R. 3, H.L.

It has been decided that the rule in *Rylands* v. *Fletcher* is a rule within the tort of nuisance which states that occupiers are liable for the escape of something which has been brought onto the land and which is a non-natural use of the land, and which causes harm when it escapes, provided that the harm was reasonably foreseeable.

According to the speech of Lord Goff in the House of Lords in *Cambridge Water Company* v. *Eastern Counties Leather plc.*[11], the storage of the drums may amount to a non-natural use of land. Therefore, Mr. Swann's liability under this head will depend on whether the harm was reasonably foreseeable.

Otherwise, an action in private nuisance could be launched by the local residents including Mrs. Timid on the ground that the use of the site affects their enjoyment of their land or causes actual damage to the land.

The grounds for the action relate to the noise, which is concerned with personal harm, and the fact that Mrs. Timid cannot hang out her washing, presumably because of the effect of the smoke. *St. Helens Smelting Co.* v. *Tipping*[12] is authority that where physical damage occurs, in that case, damage to plants, an action in nuisance lies. In addition, in *Halsey* v. *Esso Petroleum Co. Ltd.*[13], damage caused to the plaintiff's laundry was actionable in nuisance. The action in respect of smell and noise in that case related to personal harm and, therefore, it was held, the character of the locality was relevant. As Thesiger J. said in *Sturges* v. *Bridgman*[14] "a nuisance in Belgrave Square would not necessarily be so in Bermondsey."

So, it might be held that, in respect of the noise, the locality in which the nuisance occurred was relevant. As the site is a former quarry, it could be arguable that the locality has been habitually used for industrial activities of which Mr. Swann's waste site is a typical example. Damages would reflect such a situation. In respect of damage to laundry, this limitation would not apply.

An action in nuisance in respect of the pollution to the river would lie for the riparian owners. However, it is not clear whether Mrs. Furious is a riparian owner; if not, then she would not have an action on behalf of the injury to her children.

If it can be established that a section of the community is affected by the nuisance, then it may be appropriate for an action in public nuisance to be sought. The test is whether any nuisance materially

---

[11] [1994] 1 All E.R. 53.
[12] (1865) 11 H.L.C. 642.
[13] [1961] 2 All E.R. 145.
[14] (1879) 11 Ch. D. 852 at p. 865.

affects the reasonable comfort and convenience of life of a section of Her Majesty's subjects. *Att.-Gen.* v. *P.Y.A. Quarries Ltd.*[15] The question of whether the group of local residents in the scenario who are affected by the nuisance is sufficiently large to constitute such a class, is a matter of fact to be decided. The action, which is a criminal prosecution, is brought by the Attorney-General, acting on behalf of the class. However, it is possible for it to be brought instead by the local authority acting in its own name, (section 222 of the Local Government Act 1972). Since the Cleanborough District Council are concerned with the activities of Mr. Swann, this might be appropriate in these circumstances.

An action in negligence will lie if it can be shown that Mr. Swann owed a duty to take care not to cause injury to others by his acts or omissions. The damage occurring must be foreseeable. Under the Environmental Protection Act 1990, an operator owes a duty of care. This is a statutory duty to ensure that the waste does not cause harm. It is amplified in the Code of Practice. Evidence that there has been a failure to comply with the Code would be of evidential value in an action for common law negligence. Where the elements of the tort of negligence have been established then a right to compensation for actual damage would lie. The children of Mrs. Furious may succeed in an action under this head.

5. Statutory nuisance

There are four potential statutory nuisances here: the smoke, the noise from the generator, the dogs, (section 79 of the Environmental Protection Act 1990), and the condition of the river, (section 259 of the Public Health Act 1936).

The requirement in each case is to establish that it constitutes a nuisance or that it is prejudicial to health. These are alternatives (*Betts* v. *Penge Urban District Council*).[16] There is no statutory definition of nuisance: the common law definition of private or public nuisance applies, (*National Coal Board* v. *Thorne*).[17] So, it is necessary to show that the activities constituting the alleged nuisance emanate from one site and interfere with the enjoyment of property owners on another site. It, therefore, is an aspect of a property right. "Prejudice to health" is defined within the Act. It means injurious to health or likely to cause an injury to health. It

---

[15] [1957] 2 Q.B. 169.
[16] [1942] 2 K.B. 154.
[17] [1976] 1 W.L.R. 543.

does not, therefore, have the same limitation as to property rights that the nuisance limb does.

Since the complaints arise from local residents, the action in statutory nuisance could arise from either limb of the definition. As property owners, they could allege interference with the enjoyment of their properties, or, if supported by professional evidence from a medical expert or from an environmental health officer, they could allege injury to health. They need not establish actual injury. If they can show it is likely to cause injury, this is sufficient.

The three different nuisances fall under various subsections of section 79. The noise from the dogs could be prosecuted under the same subsection, (section 79(1)(g)) as the noise from the generator. It might be possible to allege that the dogs were kept in such a way as to be prejudicial to health or a nuisance (section 79(1)(f)). It was held in *Galer* v. *Morrisey*,[18] that an animal could not fall within the section merely because it was noisy, although this was doubted in *Coventry City Council* v. *Cartwright*.[19] It may be the case that there are local bye-laws prohibiting the keeping of noisy animals which would provide an alternative cause of action.

The noise from the generator is clearly capable of falling within section 79(1)(g) provided the environmental health officers are able to provide evidence, which may include evidence of a scientific nature such as noise measurements, as to the level and quality of the noise. Vibration from machinery is also included within the definition of noise, (section 79(7)).

Smoke is covered by section 79(1)(b). It includes soot, ash, grit and gritty particles, (section 79(7)). It does not include dark smoke emitted from industrial or trade premises. Dark smoke is defined in the Clean Air Act 1993 and is to be determined by the environmental health officer by reference to a shade card known as the Ringelmann card.

Mr. Swann may seek to rely on the defence of best practicable means. This is available in respect of the alleged noise and animal nuisances as they arise on industrial, trade or business premises. It is not available in respect of the smoke nuisance as the smoke is emitted from an open site not through a chimney, (section 80(8)(b)). Best practicable means include such matters as local conditions or circumstances, the current state of technical knowledge and the financial implications. The means may include the design, installation, maintenance and operation of plants and machinery and the

---

[18] [1955] 1 All E.R. 380.
[19] [1975] 1 W.L.R. 845.

design, construction and maintenance of buildings. It is for the defendant to establish the defence. The standard of proof required for the defence is the civil standard of the balance of probabilities. The defendant must show that reasonable practicable means have been taken to deal with the nuisance. In *Chapman* v. *Gosberton Farm Produce Co. Ltd.*,[20] the defendant had sought planning permission to construct a device which would have countered the effect of the noise coming from his premises. The local planning authority had asked him for further information relating to his application. He had failed to comply with this request. When prosecuted for nuisance, he argued that his application for planning permission constituted the best practicable means to deal with the nuisance. The judge held that as he had not provided the further information he could not rely on the defence. The judge used the term "reasonable" in relation to the defendant's endeavours, rather than "best." However, this case leaves open the question as to whether the defendant could have relied on the defence if he had supplied the further information and his application had then been refused.

In the circumstances of the scenario, there is clearly the basis of an action in statutory nuisance in respect of the smoke and the noise from the generator and the dogs. The availability of the defence would depend on further information from Mr. Swann as to what steps he had taken to prevent or to counteract the noise.

The action could be brought by the environmental health officers of the local authority. The procedure would initially involve service of an abatement notice in respect of the nuisances. The authority has a duty to serve such a notice where it is satisfied of the existence of the nuisance in that it is continuing or is likely to occur or recur. There is some question as to the extent of this duty. Local authorities are faced with an increasing volume of complaints in respect of noise, for example, and their ability to bring formal action in all cases may become increasingly limited. There is no reported decision which is authority for the extent of their duty under the Environmental Protection Act 1990, although there is some evidence of attempts by local residents to oblige local authorities to act. The notice should be served on Mr. Swann as the person responsible for the nuisance. He is also the owner and occupier of the site. Mr. Swann has a right of appeal to the magistrates' court against the abatement notice, but if he does not exercise this right, and has no reasonable excuse for his failure to comply with the notice, the local

---

[20] [1993] Env. L.R.

authority may bring proceedings for breach of the notice. The maximum fine which Mr. Swann could face, as the owner of industrial, trade or business premises, is £20,000.

There is also provision for Mrs. Timid or any other affected local resident to institute private proceedings in the event that the local authority do not act, (section 82). Her application lies directly to the magistrates' court; there is no power for a private individual to serve an abatement notice. She must give Mr. Swann notice of her intention to bring proceedings. In the case of the noise nuisance, this must be three days' notice, in all other cases, 21 days.

The quality of the river, insofar as it is in a state which is prejudicial to health or a nuisance, is a statutory nuisance under section 259 of the Public Health Act 1936. Thus the local environment health department have an overlapping jurisdiction with the NRA. In practice, it would seem that local authorities do not use this provision, appearing to rely on the pollution control officers of the NRA to deal with polluted watercourses.

6. Clean Air Act 1993

If the smoke emitted from the burning of the rubbish is dark smoke, that is smoke which is as dark or darker than shade 2 on the Ringelmann Chart, then an offence has been committed under the Clean Air Act 1993. There is a defence if the emission was inadvertent or, if Mr. Swann can show that he had taken all practicable steps to prevent or minimise the emission.

SUMMARY

Agencies involved and their jurisdiction:

National Rivers Authority. Water pollution offences under the Water Resources Act 1991.

Cleanborough District Council environmental health department. Prosecution for statutory nuisances under the Environmental Protection Act 1990 and the Public Health Act 1936.

Waste regulation authority. Prosecution for failure to have licence and general pollution offence under Environmental Protection Act 1990.

Local planning authority. Enforcement notice, (query-stop notice), for breach of planning control.

Attorney-General or local authority. Public nuisance for smoke and noise.

Common law actions. Mrs. Timid for private nuisance for smoke and noise nuisance.

Mrs. Furious, on behalf of her children, in negligence and under the tort of nuisance, specifically the rule in *Rylands* v. *Fletcher*.

Chapter 5

Land

INTRODUCTION

As William Morris said in 1877; "It has been most truly said that these old buildings do not belong to us only: that they belonged to our forefathers and they will belong to our descendants unless we play false. They are not in any sense our property to do as we like with them. We are only trustees for those that come after us."

The viewpoint expressed by William Morris is based on a conviction of the need to preserve a cultural heritage; to build upon what already exists, rather than to enter upon a cycle of destruction and new growth. His ideology has much more in keeping with modern thinking than with the thinking of his own contemporary Victorians. The Victorians were prepared to sweep away the past and to put up buildings which betokened their power and their confidence in their own inviolability. A powerful thread of modern thought is concerned to preserve and conserve what is perceived as part of our history for its own sake. In fact, so attached is modern thinking to the artistic merits of the past, that present day planners and architects sometimes despair at their inability to convince people of the need to develop new ideas and new techniques.

The development of modern town and country planning law began in the Victorian era. Nowadays the control of land is a highly sophisticated feature of United Kingdom administrative law. The development of new buildings and the use to which land is put is tightly controlled. There are various reasons for this level of control.

Historical reasons relate to population growth and movement, the swift process of industrialisation in the nineteenth and twentieth centuries, and the effect of two world wars in this century. Some of these developments can be seen operating now in the developing countries.

Population growth over the last 200 years is well documented. It grew from 10 million people in 1800 to about 38 million in 1900. It now approaches 60 million. For the first time a significant change in the population trend is being observed in that the birth rate in the United Kingdom is so low that the population has stabilised. The population would be falling but for the fact that as people are living longer, the mortality rate has dropped. This trend is apparent across Europe. The trend which saw the movement of rural inhabitants into urban areas still continues, although now the trend is out of the inner cities and into suburban areas.

The developing countries are marked by their growing populations and by the huge size of their cities. Mexico City has a population of 14.2 million, Calcutta – 11 million, compared to London – 6.8 million.[1] These cities are not simply bigger, in terms of numbers, but are more densely populated; more people live per square mile of city. Population size and density is clearly linked to health and environmental questions and to educational policies. In the nineteenth century, in the United Kingdom, cholera and typhoid outbreaks were directly linked to the population growth and the movement of people into the cities. The failure of the water supply to provide clean water, and the lack of a sewerage disposal system and a basic understanding of hygiene were directly to blame for these outbreaks of disease. By comparison, in the city of Lima, Peru, today, the population of 6.4 million is served by the river network which, by the time it arrives at the city, is already heavily contaminated by the industrial processes upstream. Outbreaks of disease are being reported. It would seem that, in many of these lands, of which Africa is particularly illustrative, these issues, linked with inadequate food supplies for localities and certain social strata, will result in a severe depletion of the populations.

In the United Kingdom, the original development of planning law was closely linked to the development of laws relating to public health and housing. In many respects that original reason has been removed and economic questions are now amongst the foremost to be considered in the planning context.

When the European Community proposed a formal procedure for environmental assessment of development projects it was argued, on behalf of the United Kingdom Government, that the British planning system already took account of environmental factors. While, in principle, this is true, it is undoubtedly the case that over the last 50 years, the impact of the planning system has been as marked on such issues as land prices as on environmental questions.

---

[1] United Nations Demographic Yearbook 1991 (1993).

For instance, the policy of establishing areas known as green belts, was ostensibly to protect areas of countryside around towns so that development was not allowed to creep insidiously into the country-side. It was intended to benefit town dwellers so that they could step outside the urban environment and enjoy fresh air and green fields without too much difficulty. But, in reality, the establishment of green belts protects primarily the people already living in them and owning freehold land covered by them. Access to the English countryside is notoriously restricted compared with such systems as operate in Sweden or Norway, or even Scotland. A city dweller can drive (or take a train albeit with rather more difficulty) through acres of English countryside. In fact, this is agricultural land for the most part and access is limited. As a result of the planning restric-tions on green belts, house prices are artificially high as the poss-ibility of new building is minimal. Where planning permission is given for land within a green belt, again, its situation has a distorting effect on the price.

Other economic factors also are relevant within the planning system. The pressure to create jobs by establishing businesses and factories may be more imperative than protecting an environmental feature of the landscape. The current debate about values and the environment is pertinent. If an economic benefit to the community is greater than an environmental one, then the choice will be made in favour of the former. For instance, if a gold mine sufficient to satisfy the government's overdraft 10 times over were to be discovered under St.Paul's Cathedral, would not a compulsory purchase order be swiftly forthcoming? When the remains of the Rose Theatre were found under the excavations for the foundations of a commercial building, the commercial building went ahead. Roman and other ancient remains are frequently found when new buildings are under-way and, at best, time is given to the archaeologists to remove them before the building goes ahead.

Politics at all levels are also a powerful influence in the planning system. The initial application is usually at local level and local councils will be involved. Central government may become involved on appeal or at first instance with major projects. Europe, either through the active involvement of Members of the European Parlia-ment, or through the intervention of the Commission, is becoming increasingly active.

Planning law can be divided into those areas which apply across the spectrum of general planning developments. This covers the majority of planning issues. Then, there are those aspects of plan-ning which relate to issues which might be described as being particularly relevant to environmental control. These are special controls which apply to certain areas because of their historical interest, or because they are areas where rare plants or animals are to be found. There are a wide range of focused controls which come under this heading.

General Planning Controls

The general structure of planning law falls into two halves. Firstly, there is the development of law and policy, and, secondly, there is the regulation and enforcement of the planning controls.

Policy development. This is undertaken at all levels. At central government level, policy is developed by the Secretary of State for the Environment. As in other areas of environmental concern, planning policy is not developed as part of a national plan. Instead, it develops piece by piece and is influenced by the political and economic considerations of the day.

The Secretary of State has a variety of instruments which are available to him to supplement his legislative function in passing Acts of Parliament and regulations. Planning Policy Guidance Notes (referred to as "PPGs"), are a key method of prescribing general policy changes. There are a list of these Notes which deal with different aspects of the planning system. In addition, there are a number of circulars which provide guidance as to the implementation and interpretation of specific Acts of Parliament and regulations.

It is the local authority, however, which is critical in developing local planning policy. This is undertaken through the medium of development plans. These plans set out the manner in which the authority wishes the area for which it is responsible to develop in the future. They are based on surveys of the area which examine such matters as population size and make-up and the physical and economic characteristics of the area. So, if a survey reveals that the population is largely resident in the conurbations and is mostly made up of single households, this will determine planning policy in that it will be necessary to cater for the particular needs of that particular population. It will dictate the extent to which the authority needs to encourage the development of jobs or housing as opposed to schools and hospitals. Thus, social and economic questions are taken into account.

There are different types of development plans according to the nature of the authority. In non-metropolitan areas where there remains, for the present, a two-tier authority structure, county councils produce structure plans, and district councils produce local plans. In the metropolitan areas and in Greater London where the two-tier structure was abolished in 1986, the remaining authorities are now to produce unitary development plans which absorb some of the characteristics of development plans and some of local plans.[2] Structure plans, therefore, deal with general policy planning over a county wide area while local plans set out detailed policies and specific proposals. Unitary plans will be in two parts containing, in the first part, general policy, and, in the second part, detailed planning proposals, thus combining the characteristics of structure and local plans. The second part can be supplemented over a period of time as detailed proposals and policies are worked out.

Development plans, therefore, deal with social and economic questions. Until 1990, however, there was no specific requirement to deal with environmental issues. In 1990 the Government's White Paper on the environment[3] proposed that when development plans were being drawn up environmental considerations would be taken into account. PPG 12 now takes this into account and advocates that an environmental appraisal of policies should be undertaken. The Town and Country Planning Act 1990 requires that the authority should incorporate measures for the improvement of the physical environment and for the conservation of the natural beauty and amenity of the land.[4] The Act is supplemented by a set of rules, the Development Plans Regulations 1991, which establish a list of matters to which the authority must have regard when preparing their policies. This list gives environmental considerations the same status as social and economic considerations. It also resolves the contradiction that, while environmental questions would be considered during the determination of a planning application, the policy on which it was based would not itself have taken such matters into account. It could be argued that a formal process of environmental assessment of a development plan should be undertaken before its adoption, but such formality sits unhappily with current practice and is unlikely to be used without a formal European requirement. The Department of the Environment has issued guidelines which are intended to assist local planning authorities in carrying out environmental appraisals of plans.[5] It will, of course, be some time before it can be seen whether development plans change as a result of the new

---

[2] Town and Country Planning Act 1990, s. 12.
[3] "This Common Inheritance" Cm. 1200 (1990).
[4] Town and Country Planning Act 1990, s.31(3)(a), (b) and (c).
[5] "Environmental Appraisal of Development Plans – A Good Practice Guide" (D.O.E., 1994).

emphasis on environmental issues as plans take a considerable time to produce and have a longevity of about 15 years.

Regulation and enforcement of planning control

The responsibility for the regulation and enforcement of planning control lies at the level of local government. The regulation of land use relies on the definition of "development." Where some operation such as building or engineering or mining, or some change of use,[6] constitutes development within the legal definition, then permission is required from the local authority before that development can take place. There are, therefore, two limbs to the definition: operational developments which require some change to the physical nature of the land, and some change which involves a material change of the use to which the land is put. Operational developments will include, for example, erecting a building, constructing a road, laying sewers, open cast coal-mining and quarrying. Change of use would include changing a house from residential family use to an office, a wheat field into a caravan park or a greengrocer's shop into a factory.

The object of the planning laws is not to control every development without exception but to control those developments where there are some planning consequences. For example, the development might involve increased noise or smell or traffic in the locality, or some loss of amenity. Such developments should be reviewed and controlled by the local authority. On the other hand, if a development involves no change, then control for its own sake is undesirable.

There are specific regulations which add to the definition of development and which create specific exceptions where control is deemed unnecessary. The Town and Country Planning (Use Classes) Order 1987[7] sets out 16 classes of use. Change within a class does not require planning permission. The classifications group such uses as shops, offices and light industrial uses, restaurants and hot food takeaways in separate classes. So, a change from a shop selling shoes to a shop selling theatre tickets does not require planning permission. There is no material change in the impact of these activities on the neighbourhood and the general environment. But a change from a shop selling sandwiches to a shop selling fish and chips is not exempted from planning control. The implications of the change in

---

[6] Town and Country Planning Act 1990, s.55(1).
[7] S.I. 1987 No. 764, as amended.

terms of smell and the emission of steam are significant on the neighbourhood and, therefore, require to be subjected to the planning process.

In addition, there is a group of activities, which would otherwise fall under the general planning controls, but for the Town and Country Planning General Development Order 1988.[8] These are known as permitted developments and include a wide range of activities. Some are permitted because they are relatively small developments, for example, limited extensions to houses. In special areas of control such as conservation areas or national parks, there are greater limitations in terms of the size of the permitted extension and cladding of the exterior is not permitted. Other permitted developments include the erection of fences and gates subject to certain size limitations.

The enforcement of planning controls. This is also the task of the local authority. The procedure for enforcing control relies on an administrative procedure coupled with a criminal sanction in the event of breach of the administrative process.

The principal weapon is the *enforcement notice*. This notice can be served by the authority where there has been a development without permission or where there has been a breach of a condition. It is not a weapon to be used automatically. The authority should first consider whether they would have granted permission had they been asked. It is not designed to be wielded indiscriminately, but should be used with discretion. If the authority considers that the breach has no significant planning consequences, then it should be ignored. The notice is not to be used simply as a penalty, but should be used to achieve a planning objective.[9] Service of the enforcement notice is an administrative act, but if it is ignored, then the authority may institute criminal proceedings as contravention of the notice is a criminal offence.

In addition to the enforcement notice, the Planning and Compensation Act 1991 introduced two notices: the planning contravention notice and the breach of condition notice.

The *planning contravention notice* is something of a fishing expedition. The authority may use it where they think there has been a breach of planning control and where they are seeking further information about the use of the land or any operations carried out

---

[8] S.I. 1988 No. 1813, as amended.
[9] (1991) 18 P.P.G.

on the land. They may also seek information about the person using the land and about any other persons with interests in the land.

The *breach of condition notice* can be used where the permission has been properly implemented, but a condition has not been observed. This is an important new power introduced by the Planning and Compensation Act 1991. Conditions are an important method of controlling the exercise of a development and prior to the introduction of this notice, there was no specific way of dealing with a breach of a condition alone. This meant that an authority would be obliged to use the procedure of the enforcement notice which is fairly cumbersome.

If an appeal is brought against an enforcement notice, then the notice is suspended; the offending activity can continue. This may not be acceptable and, if that is the case, the authority are empowered to serve a *stop notice*. This requires that the activities stop forthwith even if an appeal is brought. There are limitations on the power to serve such a notice. It cannot be served in respect of the use of a building as a dwellinghouse, for example. It also may be subject to the right of compensation where an appellant appeals successfully against the enforcement proceedings.

Procedure for obtaining planning permission

Planning approval is not synonymous with environmental acceptability. The development plan, as has been shown, is not an environmental document. The control of land use in the United Kingdom is not simply an environmental activity. Economic questions or social factors may influence the judgment of the local council as much, or more, than environmental issues. The process of obtaining permission to develop land or to change its use is exercised according to the discretion of the authority. The decision lies with the authority and, although it may be judicially reviewed, a judge would only question the decision of the authority on the ground that it was a decision to which no reasonable authority could have come (*Wednesbury* principle).[10]

When an application comes before a council the formal position is that they must have regard to the provisions of the development plan and to any other material considerations.[11] A development plan is an important document for a developer in that it informs the developer of the planning policy of the authority and gives an

---

[10] *Associated Picture House* v. *Wednesbury District Council* [1948] 1 K.B. 223.
[11] Town and Country Planning Act 1990, s.70(2).

indication of what proposals an authority will support or otherwise. The question is raised as to the weight that will be attached to the development plan. Section 54(A) of the Town and Country Planning Act 1990 states that "regard is to be had to the development plan" and "the determination shall be made in accordance with the plan unless material considerations indicate otherwise." Thus a developer submitting a proposal in accordance with the policy set out in a development plan will be aware that there is a presumption in favour of the proposal. Conversely, if the proposal is in conflict with the plan, then convincing reasons would have to be shown why the plan should be overridden.[12]

Where a plan has been prepared with environmental considerations in mind, then this will ensure that all developments must take account of these issues. However, development plans will also take account of economic questions and if the plan itself has not been subjected to an assessment of its environmental effects, then proposals which accord with its policy may not themselves have taken into account their own environmental effects. For example, if a development indicates that a certain area should be marked as an area where industrial development should be allowed to grow, this may be in the light of prevailing economic factors. It may be in an area of high unemployment. If a developer then presents a proposal to build industrial units on a piece of waste land in this area, the authority would have some difficulty in rejecting such an application. Even if, at the time they make the decision, they are aware of some bad effects that the development will have on the environment, they may not be able to reject the application on this ground alone. If they do, then an appeal to the Secretary of State is likely to overturn such a decision. This problem might have been obviated if the whole plan had been subjected to an environmental assessment in the first place.

In addition to the development plan, the local authority can have regard to "other material considerations." This is a phrase which has proved ripe for judicial interpretation. A number of matters have come before the courts for determination as to whether they can legitimately be taken into account by the authority in reaching their decision. Policy guidance in the form of circulars and Planning Policy Guidance Notes clearly fall within the ambit of legitimate material considerations. Other considerations include financial questions.[13] Environmental questions could undoubtedly be taken

---

[12] [1992] 1 P.P.G.
[13] R. v. *Westminster City Council, ex p. Monahan* [1989] J.P.L. 107.

into account under this heading subject to the general principle that the consideration must relate to the general objects of planning legislation. However, such questions will be weighed in the balance against other considerations which include the presumption in favour of development.

An authority may grant permission subject to *conditions*. Such conditions must be fair and reasonable and must relate to the proposed development.[14] Sometimes conditions have been attached to achieve a compromise. For example, in *Fawcett Properties Ltd* v. *Buckingham County Council* (note 14, above), the planning application for two cottages to be built in the green belt was granted subject to the condition that they should be occupied by people employed in some capacity in the agricultural or forestry industries. Conditions could be attached relating to the appearance of the completed development, requiring landscaping, for example. In applications for mineral workings, conditions are commonly attached requiring the land to be restored after the workings are completed. Conditions can be imposed requiring the land to be restored to a certain standard. This could be to a standard enabling the land to be used for agricultural, forestry or amenity purposes. Such conditions as these can also be applied to landfill sites and other sites used for the deposit of waste.[15]

In the traditional planning structure, therefore, it can be seen that environmental issues are not central to the decision making process. Indeed, it can be argued that they are peripheral and can be ousted by the policy which supports developments which are wealth creating. It is true that environmental matters could always have been taken into account, whether in the actual decision-making stage or in the form of conditions, subject to the limitations discussed above. However, there was no objective requirement for this to happen. Local political pressure may sometimes have blocked developments on environmental grounds, but without any lobbying of this sort, local authorities could simply have ignored any adverse environmental effects of proposed developments. There was no sanction which could be taken against an authority which chose to take this path. However, in 1985, the E.C. issued a Directive which changed this traditional pattern.

---

[14] *Pyx Granite Co. Ltd.* v. *Ministry of Housing and Local Government* [1958] 1 Q.B. 554; [1958] 1 All E.R. 625; reversed in part [1960] A.C. 260; [1959] 3 All E.R. 1; *Fawcett Properties Ltd.* v. *Buckingham County Council* [1961] A.C. 636.
[15] Planning and Compensation Act 1991, Sched. 1.

The European Community's Directive on Environmental Assessment[16] required that a formal system to assess the environmental effects of particular developments be introduced. This Directive has been implemented by a number of Regulations, the key Regulations for England and Wales being the Town and Country Planning (Assessment of Environmental Effects) Regulations 1988,[17] as amended.

These Regulations provide that for certain types of project, information about environmental effects must be provided by the developer and taken into account by the local planning authority before planning permission is granted. In addition, they provide that other bodies with environmental responsibilities, such as the Nature Conservancy Council, shall be notified of the application and provide any relevant information.

The Directive did not apply solely to projects which fall under the control of the Planning Acts. Some projects which fall within the remit of the Departments of Transport and Energy, for example, will also be subject to assessment. Separate Regulations with similar procedures have been set up to deal with these.

Not all projects are required to be assessed under the Directive and the implementing Regulations. The projects which fall within the ambit of the Regulations are divided into two categories and are set out in Schedules 1 and 2. Projects which fall within Schedule 1 must be assessed. This presents no difficulty as this category includes projects of such a scale that it inevitably follows that, nowadays, an environmental assessment would be required. Ports, aerodromes, crude oil refineries, waste disposal installations, land fill sites, installations for storing or disposing of radioactive waste and power stations all fall under this category. So an authority must take an assessment into account before granting permission.

The more fluid category is contained in Schedule 2. Projects falling within Schedule 2 will be assessed where it is likely that they will have significant effects on the environment by virtue of such factors as their nature, size, or location. This might appear to be circular since it might not be apparent whether projects will have a significant effect until they are subjected to an environmental assessment. As is customary in the development of British law, a circular was issued by the Department of the Environment to provide further guidance to the Regulations. The circular issued by the Department

---

[16] Directive 85/337: [1985] O.J. L175/40.
[17] S.I. 1988 No. 1199.

of the Environment and the Welsh Office: "Environmental Assessment: Implementation of the E.C. Directive"[18]; sets out various tests to assist in deciding the question whether a Schedule 2 development is likely to have significant environmental effects. The circular indicates that there are three types of project where this is likely to be the case. These are :

1. projects of more than local importance;
2. projects on a smaller scale in particularly sensitive or vulnerable locations;
3. projects with unusually complex and potentially adverse effects.

The circular also sets out indicative thresholds and criteria for the identification of projects requiring environmental assessment, (Appendix A). For example, under the heading of agriculture, it indicates that new pig-rearing installations will not generally require assessment except where they are designed to house more than 400 sows or 5000 fattening pigs.

Schedule 2 is an extensive list which includes projects under the headings of agriculture, the extractive industry, the energy industry, the processing of metals, glass-making, the chemical industry, the food industry, textile, leather, wood and paper industries, the rubber industry, infrastructure projects including industrial estate development projects and urban development projects and other projects including holiday villages, car racing tracks, installations for waste disposal not in Schedule 1, knackers' yards, modifications of developments which fall within Schedule 1, developments within Schedule 1, where it is exclusively or mainly for development and testing of new methods or products for not longer than one year.

The Secretary of State has power to exempt any developments from the effect of the Regulations.

Procedure where a project is to be subject to an environmental assessment

It is the duty of the applicant for planning permission to produce an *environmental statement*. However, there is a duty imposed on other specified bodies to consult with an applicant, and provide any information other than confidential information, which is relevant to the preparation of the statement. These bodies are: bodies

---

[18] Circular 15/88; WO23/88.

required to be notified under article 15 of the General Development Order (amended by S.I. 1986 No. 435); any principal council for the area where the land is situated, (if not the local planning authority); the Countryside Commission; the Nature Conservancy Council; and, in certain cases involving mining, manufacturing industry, or waste disposal, HMIP.

The statement itself may comprise of a single document or a series of documents which contain an assessment of the likely impact of the development on the environment. The information required is set out in Schedule 3 to the Regulations. The statement must contain a description of the development covering site, design, and size or scale; the data necessary to identify and assess the environmental effects; a description of the likely effects by reference to the likely impact on human beings, flora, fauna, soil, water, air, climate, the landscape, the interaction between any of the foregoing, material assets, the cultural heritage. In addition, any measures to avoid, remedy or reduce the impact must be included. Finally, all this information must be summarised in non-technical language.

A variety of further information may be provided covering such matters as: the physical characteristics of the proposed development; the land use requirements during construction and operational phases; the main characteristics of the production processes involved; expected residues and emissions; the main alternatives to the proposed development and the reason for selecting this one; the likely effects on the environment resulting from the use of natural resources and emission of pollutants; the forecasting methods used to assess the impacts, and any difficulties encountered in compiling the statement. Again, any additional information must be summarised in non-technical language.

In the first instance, given the lack of precision in the Regulations and the general advice contained in the circular it might not be easy to determine whether an environmental statement is required. It is, therefore, provided, that a prospective applicant may apply to a local planning authority for a determination of this question. Such a request must be accompanied by a plan, a description of the development and the likely environmental effects, and any other information the applicant may wish to provide. The authority must reply within three weeks of the request, unless the applicant agrees to a longer period, giving full reasons if they require a statement to be submitted. Their opinion, and reasons, if any, must be made available for public inspection. The applicant has a right of appeal to the Secretary of State against an authority's opinion, or in cases where the authority fails to reply within the requisite period. Similar time periods and rules apply to the Secretary of State's reply.

A prospective applicant may notify an authority that a Schedule 1 or 2 application is to be made and that a statement is to be submitted. This notice shall identify the land and the type of development, and the main environmental consequences to be covered in the statement. Where such a notice has been given, or a direction been made, the authority must then notify the bodies referred to above.

If an application is made without a statement, the authority has three weeks in which to require one. The applicant has three weeks from the date of the authority's decision to decide whether to appeal against it or to provide a statement. If no response is made, then permission is automatically refused. The Secretary of State has general power to require environmental statements to be prepared on any appeals coming before him. In general, all developments which are, at any stage, accompanied by an environmental statement, must comply with publicity procedures and must be notified to the Secretary of State.

The time period allowed for an authority to consider an application for planning permission accompanied by an environmental statement, is 16 weeks instead of the normal eight weeks.

Where authorities are undertaking their own developments, they must, in appropriate cases, not pass a resolution without first taking the environmental information into account. They must also consult the bodies mentioned in the Regulations. If there is any doubt as to the need for environmental information to be considered they may apply to the Secretary of State for a direction.

Simplified Planning Zones and Enterprise Zones. Clearly, separate provisions were required for the application of the Regulations in simplified planning zones and enterprise zones, areas where planning controls are slacker. The position has now been clarified by a D.O.E. circular issued on November 25, 1988.[19]

In the former, (S.P.Z.s), an assessment must be made in respect of all Schedule 1 projects. Two alternative approaches are available in respect of Schedule 2 projects. Where an S.P.Z. scheme prescribes the particular types of development permitted, then the authority may either exclude all Schedule 2 type developments, or, exclude developments, which, in their opinion, would be likely to give rise to significant environmental effects. In all other S.P.Z.s, a provision

---

[19] Circular No. 24/88.

will need to be included in the scheme requiring developers to establish with the authority whether an assessment is required.

Most Enterprise Zones pre-date the implementation of the Directive, therefore the Circular states the formal position that no provision needs to be made to amend those general permissions. However, it contemplates that, in the event of any new Enterprise Zones being designated, provisions similar to those for S.P.Z.s will be implemented.

The two circulars, referred to above, provide some assistance for the developer in interpreting the Regulations. In addition to these circulars, an advisory booklet, first issued in 1986 to assist with the application of the Regulations, has been produced by the D.O.E.

This attempt to impose a formal procedure for environmental assessment has highlighted the differences in approach between the traditional manner of administrative decision-making in the United Kingdom which relies on a level of discretion and the European formal, regulatory approach. The final draft of the Directive emerged after a prolonged period of negotiations where the United Kingdom raised a number of objections. It is no coincidence that the final draft of the Directive fits into the United Kingdom planning system in the manner that it does. Even then, the United Kingdom Government sought to implement the Directive by exercising its discretion so that no projects would fall into Schedule 2. This would have meant that the only projects which were to receive a formal environmental assessment were Schedule 1 projects. This would have completely marginalised the Directive. As it is, it is estimated that only a few hundred projects are assessed per year, which means that few local authorities are gaining experience in this novel procedure.

In fact, there are considerable difficulties in the manner in which the Directive has been implemented in the United Kingdom. Although authorities have twice as long to reach their decision on an application, (16 weeks instead of eight in normal cases), they have no additional resources to conduct the assessment. The statement produced by the developer follows no specified form.

It may be one page long; it may be encyclopaedic in its scope. It is for the authority, in consultation with the other statutory bodies, to conduct the assessment. It is unlikely that the planning or the environmental health departments will have the expertise in house to review all aspects of the statement. It may, therefore, be necessary to engage external consultants to review the data. The statement may not contain all the data the authority considers necessary to conduct a proper assessment. They can call for the developer to provide more information under their general powers, or they may choose to collate the information themselves – a time-consuming and expensive process.

A further problem of implementation has arisen in relation to projects known as "pipeline" projects. Many major projects take years to come to fruition. They may be subjected to planning enquiries, held up for lack of funds or because of changing policy climates. A number of projects fell into this category, that is, they were in the "pipeline," when the Regulations implementing the Directive were passed. The view that these projects, as they received their formal approval after the implementation of the Regulations, were not subject to the formal requirement of environmental assessment, was taken by the Department of the Environment and supported by the judge in *Twyford Down and Others v. Secretary of State for Transport* (1992).[20] The notorious case of the M3 extension which cuts across Twyford Down, an area containing a number of sites of special scientific interest, plague pits, medieval holloways and other matters of cultural and scientific interest, was the subject of this case. The proposal had been a live issue for a number of years but it received formal approval shortly after implementation. The judge averred that it was not intended to be caught by the Regulations.[21]

The European Commission has disagreed with this viewpoint and had launched infringement proceedings under Article 169 of the Treaty of Rome in respect of a number of projects in the United Kingdom. In fact, the *Twyford Down* case was resolved, at least as far as this issue was concerned, when the D.O.E. sent the recommendations of the inspector at the planning inquiry to the Commission to stand as the non-technical summary. This 60 page document of considerable depth and complexity was accepted by the Commission as a non-technical summary, and the proceedings against the United Kingdom on this matter were dropped.

The decision as to whether an environmental assessment of any particular development should be undertaken rests with the local planning authority, and the courts have shown themselves reluctant to intervene. In *R. v. Poole Borough Council ex p. Beebee and others*[22] the council failed to undertake an environmental assessment of a residential development which was, in fact, their own

---

[20] [1992] 4 J.E.L. (No. 2) 274.
[21] See also *Lewin and Rowley v. Secretary of State for the Environment and the Secretary of State for Transport* (1990) 2 J.E.L. 216.
[22] (1991) 3 J.E.L. 293.

application. In fact, they failed even to consider whether they should have undertaken an environmental assessment. The judge took the view that the two conservancy bodies, the Nature Conservancy Council and the British Herpetological Society, who had been involved during the decision-making stage, would have drawn all the necessary factors to the attention of the council in any event. The judge considered that the purpose of the Regulations was to present all the relevant environmental information to the council at the appropriate stage and that this had happened. A similar approach was accepted by the Judge in the *Twyford Down* case. This approach neatly illustrates the clash between the introduction of the European model of formal regulatory procedures, and the British model of the committee-led, flexible procedure. The judge could, of course, be correct in stating that all the environmental information that would have been drawn out by a formal assessment procedure was considered in any particular case. But, the purpose of the formal procedure is to ensure that all aspects of the potential environmental effects are brought out into the light and that the opportunity is given for a careful examination of these issues. A formal assessment by an authority can provide a greater opportunity for an objective analysis of the issues in consultation with the appropriate bodies, rather than leaving it to the bodies themselves, or to local pressure groups, to front a campaign to bring these issues to the forefront.

Planning agreements .

There is a procedure which is available to developers and local authorities which permits them to enter into agreements which operate outside the general planning procedure.[23] Planning agreements have been widely criticised as a method whereby developers have been able to buy planning permission; that is, authorities which would otherwise have refused permission, have been persuaded by some inducement to grant an approval. On the other hand, the facility to enter into an agreement has enabled local authorities to make gains and to extract benefits which could not have been legitimately exacted in the form of conditions.

Section 106 has now been drawn sufficiently wide to permit agreements to be entered into which not only restrict or regulate the development or use of land, but which also allow specified operations or activities to be carried out, or which provide for land to

---

[23] Town and Country Planning Act 1990, s.106.

be used in a specified way. Any such requirements must relate to the land which is the subject of the planning application. In addition, there is power to require money to be paid to a local authority and this, unlike any other obligation, need not be limited to the land which is the subject of the application. The power to provide for a payment of money is, therefore, extensive and can relate to entirely disparate matters. In fact, it is arguable that such a payment need not be related to planning.

This clearly provides a mechanism for extracting a gain from a developer which has environmental overtones. One possibility which has been used is to require a developer to supply a piece of open land as some return for the land which is to be absorbed by the development. Major applications involving the open cast mining of areas of land which have previously been green countryside have occasionally been the subject of such an agreement. In return, the developer has acquired and made available to the local authority, land which can substitute for the land which is the subject of the application. Such an agreement has been subjected to judicial scrutiny in the first case to test the effect of section 106 as amended.

In *Wimpey Homes Holdings Ltd.* v. *Secretary of State for the Environment*,[24] the application was for a residential development with roads and the provision of open space. The application had been refused. At the planning inquiry, Wimpeys agreed unilaterally to transfer the open space land to the authority and to give a lump sum to provide for future maintenance of the open space. The authority considered that the money was not enough to maintain the open space and refused to accept the deal for that reason. The judge had to decide whether the transfer of land as part of a unilateral undertaking fell within section 106. He decided that such an undertaking was not covered by section 106 because such a transfer of title did not impose a restriction or regulation on the land which was the subject of the application. However, the agreement to pay money was not subject to this condition and therefore did fall within section 106. This leads to the absurd conclusion that an agreement to provide land for environmental purposes in exchange for the development land is not an appropriate matter for a planning agreement, but an agreement to pay for the maintenance of a piece of land is. It would seem that in these circumstances it might be appropriate for an authority to use other powers such as its powers of compulsory purchase to ensure the acquisition of such land.

---

[24] Reported in (1993) *Estates Gazette* 250, October 23.

Special planning controls

While the system of planning just described covers the whole of
the country, there are, in addition, a number of special controls
which apply to certain types of development such as mining, and
certain objects such as trees, ancient monuments and buildings.

Mining. Mining is a type of development which can have a
significant impact on the environment. The extraction of minerals is
not confined to the winning of coal. The largest form of extraction is
the quarrying of stone, gravel, (sometimes called aggregates), and
sand. These materials are used for making roads, house building and
in the making of pre-cast concrete. Although house building, and the
construction industry in general, has declined during the recession,
major projects such as the Channel Tunnel and the road building
programme, have ensured that the need for aggregates has continued to grow unabated. The coal industry has only been run down
in respect of deep mining. Open cast mining has continued to grow
and a number of new sites are opened up every year. Other mineral
extraction includes the extraction of clay. Oxford clay is extracted
for making bricks; kaolin or china clay is used in the production of
china and paper, while fuller's earth is used for the purification of
oils and in the cosmetics industry. Chalk, limestone and gypsum are
used in the production of cement and other aspects of the construction industry. Oil and gas are extensively extracted in the United
Kingdom, not just in Scotland and the North Sea, but in areas in
Dorset and the south east of England. There remain two tin mines in
Cornwall, slate quarries in Wales and a new gold mine is opening in
Scotland. In addition, there are a number of small quarries for
specialist minerals such as fluorspar which may be used for jewel-
lery, as in the form known as Blue John, mined in Castleton,
Derbyshire, or in the chemical industry once it is converted into
hydrofluoric acid.

These mining and quarrying activities in themselves have deleterious effects on the landscape, (except for the most ardent of industrial landscape admirers). They scar the landscape and dramatically
change the shape of hills and valleys. But their effects are more far
reaching than this. When mining takes place only the valuable
mineral is taken. The rest is waste. The slag heaps of the coal mining
areas have been clear evidence of this. The waste will either be piled
up or used for landfill. The minerals, once won, then need to be
transported to their place of use. This can be done by road, causing
heavy lorries to thunder through town and country. The quarrying
activities can be accompanied by processing works, causing a build-

up of industrial uses that may incrementally blight an area. These uses may cause smell, noise, dust and vibration.

The control of extraction is undertaken by the mineral planning authorities. These authorities are under a duty to produce minerals local plans which cover the county area.[25] These plans should include the provision which the authority is making for mineral working in the light of available supplies at local and national level. The potential for recycling of the waste should be addressed and other matters such as traffic volume and the noise and disruption to nearby residential areas. As in all other areas of planning, economic questions such as the necessity for industry of mineral working and the provision of local jobs, must be addressed in addition to questions of environmental impact.

Permission for mineral extraction (and for dealing with mineral waste) is controlled within the planning system but is subject to special rules. For example, there is a finite time limit on a planning permission for mineral working which is 60 years from the date of the permission. It is now standard practice for conditions to be imposed requiring the site to be restored after the minerals have been extracted. The mineral planning authority is required to conduct a periodic review about mineral working and the disposal of its waste[26] to assess whether the work should continue or otherwise. If the mineral working has been temporarily suspended, perhaps where gravel working has temporarily ceased because of lack of demand but is expected to resume, then the authority may issue a suspension order.[27] This is designed to protect the environment in that it may require that steps be taken to preserve the amenities for the time being and ensure that no deterioration in the condition of the land takes place.

Waste. Waste, (other than mineral waste), and its disposal is also a planning matter. The use of land for landfill sites, which remain the primary means of waste disposal in the United Kingdom, is a matter of increasing environmental importance. Again, there is an obligation to produce a local plan, known as a waste local plan, which covers policy on this issue at county level.[28] The plan will set out the

---

[25] Planning and Compensation Act 1991.
[26] Town and Country Planning Act 1990, s.105.
[27] Town and Country Planning Act 1990, Sched. 9, as amended.
[28] Town and Country Planning Act 1990, s.38.

criteria against which applications for planning permission to establish waste sites could be tested.[29] It might identify the general areas in which such development could take place. In general, the plan is to be concerned with the consequences for land use of the authority's policies on waste disposal.

Urban Controls

Individual buildings. These may be subject to special controls because they are of interest by reason of some architectural feature or some historic aspect. They might be the birthplace of the famous or the work of an important architect; they might sport particularly unusual features such as a wide span roof or be a fine example of a Georgian facade.[30] The term "building" is broadly defined in the Town and Country Planning Act 1990 as "any structure or erection and any part of a building so defined." So, the special controls could apply to structures such as walls or post boxes. In addition, the Planning (Listed Buildings and Conservation Areas) Act 1990 extends the category to include objects or structures fixed to a building or, otherwise, within the curtilage of a building.[31]

The importance of protecting the built heritage is recognised at national level as a priority[32] and a department, the Department of National Heritage, was specifically created with conservation policy as part of its remit. It would seem, however, that the Minister has some considerable latitude for overriding the presumption in favour of the listed building and permitting development. In the House of Lords' decision in *Save Britain's Heritage* v. *Secretary of State for the Environment and others*[33] they upheld the decision of the Secretary of State to demolish eight Grade II listed buildings where they were still of economic use. The new development was vaunted as being an important design by a prestigious architect.

The Secretary of State is responsible for the listing of special buildings in consultation with English Heritage. This can be done

---

[29] See the D.O.E. Consultation Paper, "*Waste Disposal and Development Plans*" (1990).

[30] Circular 8/87, Appendix I.

[31] s.1(5). For a definition of structure see *Debenhams plc* v. *Westminster City Council* [1987] A.C. 396; [1987] 1 All E.R. 51, HL, and *Att.-Gen (ex rel. Sutcliffe)* v. *Calderdale Borough Council* (1982) 46 P. & C.R. 339; [1983] J.P.L. 310, CA.

[32] PPG 12 "Development Plans and Regional Planning guidance" P.P.G. 12 gives "high priority to conserving the built and archaeological heritage."

[33] (1991) T.L.R., March 1.

without informing the owner in advance. This is desirable in some cases where an owner might take drastic action in respect of a building which is known to be under consideration for listing. However, now that there are more stringent controls on the demolition of buildings, it seems somewhat unnecessary, in many cases, to list first and notify afterwards.

There is an emergency procedure which can be used where a building which has not yet been listed but is considered to be of special interest is about to be demolished or altered.[34] A local planning authority can serve a *building preservation notice* which is valid for six months and gives the Secretary of State time to consider listing.[35] If the Secretary of State decides not to list, compensation may be payable.

Listed buildings are graded according to their importance and interest. Grade I is top of the list as a building of "exceptional interest," Grade II* are "particularly important buildings of more than special interest" and Grade III are "buildings of special interest which warrant every effort being made to preserve them." These listings do not come from the statutes but are adopted as a matter of practice,[36] and are used to inform local authorities when deciding on planning policy in relation to the buildings and the area around them.

Once a building is listed then it is subject to more stringent controls than other buildings. Permission, known as listed building consent, must be obtained from the local planning authority and English Heritage must be notified before any works are undertaken to demolish or alter or extend the building so as to alter its character. If listed building consent is not first obtained, then an offence is committed. This applies to works inside the building if they will affect the character and to works which would otherwise be permitted by the General Development Order. The penalty for this offence, which is an offence of strict liability,[37] has been increased, in line with other environmental offences, to £20,000.

Where listed buildings are not kept in repair, then, in certain circumstances, the Secretary of State and local planning authority can take steps to repair them or to acquire them compulsorily.

---

[34] Planning (Listed Buildings and Conservation Areas) Act 1990, s.3(1).
[35] s.3(3).
[36] Circular 8/87, Appendix 1.
[37] R. v. *Wells Street Metropolitan Magistrate, ex p. Westminster City Council* [1986] 1 W.L.R. 1046.

Conservation areas. There are in many towns whole areas, as opposed to individual buildings, which retain qualities worth preserving; areas where there are a number of buildings of historic or architectural interest which have character. Since 1967, it has been possible for local planning authorities to take steps to protect such areas from the ravages of development control. If one building in such an area is demolished and replaced by a modern office block, the character of the whole area can be lost. It is, of course, possible for a local planning authority to take such questions as the character of the neighbourhood into account when considering any planning application, but the designation of an area as a conservation area, gives the authority greater scope to protect it.

Under the Planning (Listed Buildings and Conservation Areas) Act 1990, the authority have a duty to consider whether any areas in their locality should be designated as conservation areas. Where they do decide to designate an area then special controls apply. Trees, often an important feature of a conservation area are subject to such a control: they may not be chopped down or damaged in any way without the authority first being given the opportunity to consider whether they should be preserved. Advertisements, often the bane of an otherwise attractive high street, may be subjected to special controls at the authority's discretion. During the housing boom of the late 1980s, a number of London boroughs exercised their discretion to prohibit the display of the many "For Sale" boards which had appeared, like a forest, in many streets within conservation areas destroying their character. Demolition is also prohibited without special consent known as conservation area consent.

When a planning application is received for development in a conservation area, the authority conduct the normal procedure for all planning applications in that they will take into account the development plan and any other material considerations. The fact that an area is a conservation area does not have the automatic effect of stifling all development. Properties can be demolished and new properties built. However, the authority has a particular duty to give special consideration to the desirability of preserving or enhancing the area. This raises certain questions as to the nature of this duty. Should the authority only give consent to developments which have a positive and beneficial effect on the area, or should they give consent to all developments except those which have a negative or harmful effect on the area? The issue is whether the duty is to continue to improve the area, or simply to maintain the status quo. It would seem that the duty is the lower of the two – that an authority need do no more than keep the area at its existing standard, provided that a development has no adverse effect, then there is no obligation to show that it will have a positive effect – a neutral development will be permitted, (*South Lakeland District Council* v. *Secretary of State for the Environment*).[38]

Conservation areas have proved a popular method of control. There are now 7,500 conservation areas in existence which cover 4 per cent. of the national building stock.

Hazardous Substances. The storage of hazardous substances on land can cause particular problems. They may be explosive or highly flammable, such as propane gas, or toxic, such as ammonia. The control of these substances on land has been assigned to the local planning authority under the Planning (Hazardous Substances) Act 1990.[39]

Between Town and Country

Green Belt. In between the urban and the rural environment are the green belts. Designed to check urban sprawl and restrain development encroaching on the countryside, green belts operate as a buffer zone. Within the green belt, designated by the local planning authority, development is restricted and has a consequent effect in making existing developments within green belts of a high value.

Advertisements. Adverts can be unattractive and detrimental to the amenity of an area. There are general provisions to control all forms of outdoor advertising contained in the Control of Advertisements Regulations 1992.[40] There is also power to define areas of special control,[41] which can include rural areas and areas which require special protection for the amenities. So, the purpose of these special controls is to protect the quality of the environment, not for other reasons such as public safety. Where such an area is designated, then there are only narrow classes of adverts which may be displayed without consent. These include adverts placed in moving vehicles – taxis and buses for example, traffic signs, and election posters.

---

[38] [1992] 2 A.C. 141.
[39] This Act came into force on June 1, 1992 after being amended by the E.P.A. 1990 and the Planning and Compensation Act 1991. See also the Planning (Hazardous Substances) Regulations 1992.
[40] S.I. 1992 No. 666.
[41] Town and Country Planning Act 1990, s.221.

Countryside controls

While conservation areas and listed buildings deal with the urban environment, there are also a number of methods which use the same principle of designating an area of land, but which are designed to preserve aspects of the countryside. They are now covered by the Countryside Act 1968 and the Wildlife and Countryside Act 1981. The authorities mainly responsible for them are the Countryside Commission (for England), and the Countryside Council for Wales[42] and local planning authorities. The reasons for the designation differ. National parks and country parks have, amongst their objectives, the need to provide recreational areas for the enjoyment of the public. Other designations may be for the preservation of particular flora and fauna.

National parks. One of the earliest forms of control, they were established in 1949.[43] They may be designated because of their natural beauty or because of their flora, fauna or particular geological features. The object of the designation is to preserve and enhance them. Development is strictly controlled and the local planning authority can take positive steps to develop the area for the enhancement of its recreational facilities. They can, for example, build picnic sites or camping sites, and can acquire land compulsorily for these purposes.

A national park encompasses an area which may include areas of moorland, the farms in the area and even the towns. For example, in the Peak District National Park, the area includes, not only the Peaks but also the town of Bakewell. Thus, industrial areas could also fall within the national park. It is an ordinary area of land where, because of some special features, such as the Peaks in Derbyshire, or the Lakes in Cumbria, special controls are considered necessary.

There are 10 national parks in all covering 9 per cent. of the total land in England and Wales.

Areas of outstanding natural beauty. These are a separate designation. A national park may also, in ordinary terms, be an area of natural beauty. However, they are large tracts of land, whereas an area of outstanding natural beauty is normally a smaller area, such as a hill or a range of downs, which requires some special controls for its preservation or enhancement. The emphasis is not on preservation for the purposes of public enjoyment or recreation.

---

[42] Established under the E.P.A. 1990, s.130.
[43] National Parks and Countryside Act 1949.

Country parks. These, on the other hand, are areas specifically designated for public enjoyment. They are municipal parks which are set aside purely for recreational purposes. There is no combined use in a country park, it will not include areas of agriculture, for instance. The emphasis in the modern country park tends to be on activity sports, such as boating, rather than on immaculate flower beds.

National nature reserves. These can be established by the relevant Nature Conservancy Council[44] where land needs to be managed specially for the study of flora and fauna and their habitats or for the study of the physical characteristics of the land. An agreement will be entered into with the owner of the land as to the way in which the land should be managed, or, the Nature Conservancy Council may acquire the land compulsorily.

A local authority may designate a local area as a nature reserve in the same way as the Nature Conservancy Council with whom they should consult.

Sites of special scientific interest. As the title implies these sites are concerned to protect scientific aspects not to conserve nature or to promote recreation. The scientific aspect may be biological, (concerned with flora or fauna) or geological, (concerned with geological or physiographical matters).

The boundaries of a site may be drawn sufficiently wide to permit the creation of a buffer zone around the area which includes land of less scientific importance provided this creates a single environment.[45]

The Nature Conservancy Council informs the owners of the site as to the features which are of special interest and which operations will be potentially damaging.[46] Cultivation of the site could be classified as a potentially damaging operation so a farmer would be restricted from ploughing and sowing a field without notifying the Nature Conservancy Council. The operations which can be notified are quite extensive.[47] There is then a four-month waiting period which is designed to promote an opportunity for the owner to enter into a management agreement with the Nature Conservancy

---

[44] Under the E.P.A. 1990, there are separate councils for England, Scotland and Wales.
[45] *Sweet v. Secretary of State for the Environment* (1989) 1 J.E.L. 245.
[46] Wildlife and Countryside Act 1981, s.28.
[47] *Sweet v. Secretary of State for the Environment and the Nature Conservancy Council* (above).

Council. If the site is deemed to be of national importance or the survival of a species is threatened then a *nature conservation order*[48] can be imposed and more stringent safeguards apply including the power of compulsory purchase where a person gives notice that he intends to carry out a potentially damaging operation.

The efficacy of the provisions in protecting these sites is best expressed by Lord Mustill in *Southern Water Authority v. Nature Conservancy Council*[49]:

> "It needs only a moment to see that this regime is toothless, for it demands no more from the owner or occupier of an SSSI than a little patience. Unless the council (*the Nature Conservancy Council*) can convince the Secretary of State that the site is of sufficient importance to justify an order under s.29 – as we have seen, a task rarely accomplished – the owner will within months be free to regard the notification and carry out the proscribed operations, no matter what the cost to the flora etc. on the site. In truth the Act does no more in the great majority of cases than give the council a breathing space within which to apply moral pressure, with a view to persuading the owner or occupier to make a voluntary agreement."

The case decided that a person who has no connection with the land before starting a proscribed operation on it, is not an "occupier" within the meaning of section 28 of the Act. They do not, therefore commit an offence if they do not observe the waiting period specified in that section. This would also include the fly-tipper who dumps rubbish on land and then departs. Such a person dumping rubbish on an SSSI does not commit an offence under the Act.

There are now over 5,000 SSSIs in England and Wales but only about 30 nature conservation orders, which impose a stricter regime, have been made. The efficacy of this method of zoning an area of land which is of special interest because of some scientific feature is clearly in doubt.

SSSIs are also the method used in the United Kingdom of implementing its obligations under both European and international law in respect of the protection of birds.

Under the European Wild Birds Directive of 1979[50] there is a provision for the establishment of *special protection areas* to ensure the survival and reproduction of certain species of birds. This, in relation to migratory birds, applies in particular to wetlands. These

---

[48] Wildlife and Countryside Act 1981, s.29.
[49] (1993) 5 J.E.L. 109 at p. 110.
[50] Directive 79/409: [1979] O.J. L103/1.

special areas, once designated, must be notified to the Commission and steps must be taken to avoid pollution or deterioration of these habitats so as to affect the birds.

In the United Kingdom, this Directive is implemented through the system of SSSIs and through the planning system. The Directive is vague in respect of the obligations it imposes on Member States but it has been subject to a decision of the European Court of Justice – *Commission of the European Communities* v. *Federal Republic of Germany*, supported by the United Kingdom.[51] The case concerned an area known as Leybucht Dykes, a coastal wetland area in north-west Germany. The area is part of a national park and was listed as a special protection area under the Birds Directive. The site was noted particularly for its population of avocets, a rare bird, (used by the Royal Society for the Protection of Birds as its emblem). The work undertaken by the German Government was designed to protect the coast and it was shown that the work on the dyke would result in an improved habitat for the birds, albeit they would be disturbed during the course of the work. The work involved moving the dyke seawards which reduced the area of wetlands available to the birds and therefore reduced the size of the special protection area. The court held that the size of a special protection area could only be reduced in "exceptional circumstances." Unfortunately the court failed to define what it meant by this phrase except to say that the public interest would have to outweigh the ecological interests of the birds. However, the court did state that this would not include economic or recreational interests. In the particular circumstances of the case, the court did find in favour of the German Government in that the danger of floods and the need to protect the coastline were sufficiently genuine reasons to justify the work provided it was kept to a minimum and the special protection area was only subject to the smallest possible reduction. The court was also influenced by the fact that the Government had promised that compensatory measures would be taken in that new salt water meadows would be created and two navigation channels which crossed the area would be closed, leaving the area in complete peace. Although the court found against the Commission which was arguing that a special protection area should be protected in all circumstances except where human life was at risk, it raised the level of protection of

---

[51] Case 57/89R, *Commission* v. *Federal Republic of Germany*: [1991] I E.C.R. 883; [1989] E.C.R. 2849 February 28, 1991, (Lexis). For a case analysis see: D. Baldock, "The Status of Special Protection Areas for the Protection of Wild Birds" 4 *Journal of Environmental Law* (No. 1) 139–144.

special protection areas to a higher degree than many Member States have accorded them.

The next step forward at European level in relation to the designation of areas for the protection of species, is the Habitats Directive.[52] This Directive extends similar protection to that provided under the Wild Birds Directive to other endangered or rare species of animals. The text of this Directive has already been watered down to enable Member States to interfere with special protection areas where the public interest in relation to matters of a social or economic nature warrant such interference.

There is also an international convention in this field known as the Ramsar Convention which covers the conservation of wetlands and waterfowl by the designation of sites. Contracting parties, of which the United Kingdom is one, are under a duty to compile a list of such sites and to promote their conservation. This is undertaken in the United Kingdom, as with the Wild Birds Directive and Habitats Directive, by means of the designation, in the first instance, of Sites of Special Scientific Intererst.

The status of SSSIs has been tested in the British courts. In *R. v. Poole Borough Council ex p. Beebee and others*[53] the council proposed building housing on land which was designated as an SSSI. In fact, the building proposal came first and the designation came second. The Nature Conservancy Council extended an existing SSSI to include the building land. This was because the land, (part of Thomas Hardy's Wessex), supported a number of protected species, including smooth snakes, sand lizards, the Dartford Warbler, the Nightjar and the Hobby. The SSSI was extended in particular because of the presence of the reptiles in that part. The whole area had been made a candidate for a special protection area under the Wild Birds Directive. In accordance with procedure, the council notified the Nature Conservancy Council (NCC) of their decision to build. The NCC objected and asked the Secretary of State to call in the application which he refused to do. The council went ahead and gave themselves planning permission to build. Applicants representing the Worldwide Fund for Nature and the British Herpetological Society applied for a judicial review of the council's decision.

The judge dismissed the claim to quash the council's decision. This raised the question of the status of SSSIs in the face of a presumption in favour of development. The site had been subject to

---

[52] Directive on the Protection of Natural and Semi-natural Habitats and of Wild Flora and Fauna: Directive 92/43; [1992] O.J. L206/7.

[53] [1991] 2 P.L.R. 27.

an outline planning permission for development for residential purposes. There were historical reasons, therefore, and social reasons to support development. On the other hand, there were also ecological reasons accepted by all parties as to the need to conserve the site. The Nature Conservancy Council had stepped into the picture at a late stage in order to protect the area, but, nevertheless, the council accepted that there were sound ecological reasons for conserving the site. The planning committee weighed the competing claims and found in favour of development. This exemplifies the process of planning decision-making in the United Kingdom and the manner in which environmental issues are weighed in the balance against all other considerations and may, in the end, be discounted. The judge found that there was nothing in this decision-making process exercised by Poole Borough Council which indicated a failure to take any significant matter into account. He did not, therefore, see fit to interfere with their decision.

Ancient monuments and archaeological areas. Stonehenge, Avebury Circle and Verulamium are all well known sites of great antiquity and importance. They are part of the national and cultural heritage. There are thousands of such sites, however, across the country, which are also part of the cultural heritage but are not so well known and which may not be receiving adequate protection.

Under the Ancient Monuments and Archaeological Areas Act 1979 (as amended) the Secretary of State has a duty to compile and maintain a list of monuments which are considered to be of national importance. English Heritage must be consulted before a decision on scheduling is taken. Once a monument has been scheduled, then it is an offence to demolish, destroy or damage it without permission. The offence is absolute although the level of fine will reflect the degree of negligence on the part of the defendant. In *R. v. J.O. Sims Ltd.*,[54] the Court of Appeal substituted a fine of £15,000 where a developer inadvertently destroyed part of the remains of Winchester Palace in Southwark, London. The provisions operate to some extent like the provisions applying to listed buildings although there are significant differences.[55] Compensation is payable if expenditure is caused by the refusal of a scheduled monument consent.

---

[54] [1993] Env. L.R. 323.

[55] For a critique of the system of protection for the historic environment see, "Archaeology and Planning – A Case for Full Integration" [1991] J.P.L. 1103 and P. Jewkes, "Protecting the Historic Built Environment" [1993] J.P.L. 417.

The issue of the Secretary of State's power to schedule monuments arose in the discovery of the remains of the Rose Theatre on the south side of the Thames on a site which was about to be developed. The Rose Theatre was the playhouse where most of Marlowe's plays were performed and two of Shakespeare's plays staged their first night. When the importance of the site was realised a campaign was launched to preserve it. English Heritage entered into discussions with the developers and an informal agreement was entered into in which the developers promised to revise their plans so as to protect the site and to make access to it possible. As a result the Secretary of State decided not to schedule the site, thus avoiding the payment of compensation and any further delay in development. His decision was upheld in the Queen's Bench Divisional Court.[56]

Apart from the obligation to consult English Heritage, the Secretary of State is not required to consult the local planning authority or hold an inquiry when considering whether to schedule an ancient monument or not. As in the example of the Rose Theatre, he can act on his own initiative. This leaves the public without any forum for representations or objections other than to use the measure undertaken by the campaigners in the Rose Theatre case – to apply to the Divisional Court for a judicial review of the Minister's decision. Likewise, if an owner of a scheduled monument applies for consent to carry out work on it, then this is not a public procedure unless the Secretary of State deems that other people should be consulted. This state of the law leaves the cultural heritage in a vulnerable position.

Trees. There are special measures for preserving trees where it is considered desirable.[57] An individual tree can be protected, or a group of trees or woodland. The local planning authority can impose a tree preservation order which prevents a tree being felled or damaged in any way. It would seem that the ordinary understanding of what is meant by a "tree" is to be adopted in deciding whether a control is appropriate.[58]

Contaminated Land. This issue has become a cause *célèbre* in the Government's environmental policy. A major proposal was drafted into the Environmental Protection Act 1990[59] which provided for

---

[56] R. v. *Secretary of State for the Environment ex p. Rose Theatre Trust Company.* (1990) 1 W.L.R. 193; (1990) 2 J.E.L. 231.
[57] Town and Country Planning Act 1990, s.198.
[58] See *Kent County Council* v. *Batchelor* (1976) 33 P. & C.R.; *Bullock* v. *Secretary of State for the Environment* (1980) 40 P. & C.R.
[59] s.143.

registers to be maintained by local authorities containing details of land which was contaminated. It was intended that registers should contain information about the investigations and treatments which land had received. The general principle was to be that, once on the register, always on the register.[60] This was because it was acknowledged that treatment would rarely be successful in completely removing contamination. It was anticipated that the register would provide a useful source of information for purchasers and developers. It was also intended that the registers could be used by those seeking to trace the source of contamination affecting neighbouring land.

Land may be contaminated because of previous industrial uses. Leakages from chemical works can contaminate the soil beneath the works and can leach into the groundwater system thus polluting the drinking water supply. Landfill sites can produce methane gas. Contamination can be ancient. The Romans worked copper and lead mines and metal mining and processing can go back for centuries in certain areas.[61]

The recognition of the problems posed by contaminated land is relatively new compared to the problems of air and water pollution. The cause and effect of problems associated with contaminated land are not as immediate as with the other media. The problems created by landfill gases caused by the decaying of organic waste, can be demonstrated in dramatic form. The explosion in Nottinghamshire which destroyed a bungalow, (although the occupants miraculously escaped), is a case in point. What to do about such contamination is another matter. The practice now at such sites is to monitor the escape of gas. Heavy metals in land can be taken up by plants and grazing animals and, thus, enter the human food chain. The dust from asbestos, used for industrial and construction purposes, can be inhaled and cause serious lung diseases. But the effect of contamination will depend on the subsequent use to which land is put. If it is not used for agricultural purposes then the metals may not enter the food chain. An office block on the site of a former scrapyard which is likely to contain metals such as cadmium and lead would not present a hazard. Such metals are unlikely to migrate into surrounding land.

---

[60] See *Hansard*, H.C. Vol. 202, col. 414 WA, (February 6, 1992) (Minister for the Environment), and the written answer reprinted in (1992) J.P.L. 331–332.
[61] For a detailed discussion of the legal and technical problems arising in relation to contaminated land, see T. Cairney (ed.), "Contaminated Land" (1993).

The issue, then, is not simply to assess whether a site is contaminated, but to devise an appropriate land use policy in relation to such a site.

The proposal to establish these registers of contaminated land caused a concerted campaign of opposition to be launched by the property industry. The industry saw the registers as having the effect of devaluing industrial land and causing insurance premiums to rise or simply not to be available. The problem arises from the manner in which conveyancing is conducted in this country. If I buy a house then I must look out for myself and inspect it to discover any faults. Provided that the vendor answers my questions carefully and honestly then I have no redress if the property subsequently turns out to be disappearing into a waste tip. The same applies if a developer buys land that was previously used for processing chemicals. The likelihood is that there will be some historical contamination. It is for the purchaser to find it out or to take the risk. The property industry was alarmed at the prospect of information relating to the existence of contamination being publicly available. They perceived it as a blight on land and an unwarranted shift of the risk from purchaser to vendor. As a result, the government has not implemented this proposal and has indicated that further consultations will take place. It seems unlikely that this section will be implemented in its present form in the near future, if at all.

In fact, an open assessment of potentially contaminated sites need not be perceived as a blight. A contaminated site which is developed without such an assessment may ultimately have deleterious effects on the environment in that dangerous substances may leach into the water table and enter the drinking water supply. Legal liability may arise in the future in respect of such pollution. If the contamination is dealt with before it causes pollution, it may prevent such liability and the consequent damages payable. Insurance companies may be more ready to insure a treated site where the risk has been assessed than the unknown quantity of an unassessed site. Contamination is not synonymous with pollution[62] unless the extreme view is taken that any alteration with the earth involves a polluting activity.

---

[62] Royal Commission on Environmental Pollution, Tenth Report, *Tackling Pollution – Experience and Prospects*, Cmnd. 9194 (1984).

Chapter Six

Air

INTRODUCTION

In urban areas, the motor car and other traffic have made the problem of air pollution particularly acute. Various cities such as Rome, San Francisco and Los Angeles have acquired reputations for appalling smog conditions. In heavily-trafficked areas the concentrations of nitrogen dioxide and carbon monoxide can exceed international health guidelines. Some cities have attempted to take radical solutions to deal with the problem of pollution and traffic jams at the same time. In Athens, the Government introduced a system where car drivers took it in turns to have access to the city. In Oslo, tolls have been introduced in an attempt to reduce car use in the city. Such measures have not been altogether successful, creating inequalities and other difficulties of enforcement.

In the 1950s the problem of urban air pollution was made worse by the burning of coal in domestic fireplaces. So-called pea-soupers, which adequately describe the conditions, were notorious in London, and caused many deaths. Such problems of low-lying pollution can be made worse by particular climatic conditions.

Various measures have been taken at European and international level to deal with the problems of traffic pollution, but the growth in the use of cars, which is not expected to diminish in the foreseeable future, seems destined to negate the impact of these measures. Cleaner technology has been one attempt to deal with the problem, for example. Yet, it would seem that while governments on the one hand appear to support measures to encourage a reduction in pollution, such as encouraging, by tax incentives, the use of unleaded petrol, on the other hand, they continue to build roads. It has become a truism amongst environmentalists that lack of investment in a public transport system and an emphasis on the use of personal transport, has been a major factor in the increase of environmental pollution and damage.

In the nineteenth century the problem of industrial air pollution became evident. Coal was the major source of energy with its consequent pollution problems. The development of the alkali works were another significant factor in the production of acidic emissions. The alkali works produced different forms of soda. Soda is an alkali which is used, in its different forms, in numerous industrial processes. During the production of soda, acid is released. This, when released into the atmosphere, causes pollution problems. As a result, a series of Alkali Acts were passed controlling these processes under the aegis of an Alkali Inspectorate. These acts are the forerunners of modern air pollution control.

One of the features of the alkali works was the production of acid rain. This problem is notable today with the production and emission of sulphur dioxide by coal-fired power stations. The acid rain is blown westwards from the United Kingdom and is alleged to be a factor in serious damage to some forested regions and salmon hatcheries in Scandinavia.

The production and emission into the atmosphere of chlorofluorocarbons by refrigerants and aerosols is a factor which, it is claimed by one school of scientific thought, contributes to the reduction in the concentration of ozone around the earth.

However, the polluting effects on the atmosphere of natural occurrences on the earth should not be overlooked. The eruption of the volcano on the Philippines in 1991 is said to have had the effect of lowering the earth's temperature by one degree centigrade at the time and is thought to have done serious damage to the ozone layer by emitting a plume of gas 20,000 feet into the air. Such natural activity is not created by man nor, for the present, is it controllable.

Today air pollution control in the United Kingdom is conducted at two levels. The more serious sources of air pollution are controlled by the central inspectorate, HMIP, as part of a system of control called integrated pollution control. Less serious sources of air pollution are controlled at local government level by local authority environmental health officers. There are a number of parallels between the two systems. However, it is less confusing to deal with them in two separate parts.

SECTION 1: UNITED KINGDOM LEGISLATION

INTEGRATED POLLUTION CONTROL

Much criticism has been directed at the range of environmental controls for their fragmentation. It is apparent from the way it is necessary to structure this book, that the controls are disparate. There is one system for controlling land use, one for water pollution, another for waste, and so on. The difficulty is then compounded by the multiplicity of bodies dealing with the authorisation of different processes or land uses, and then dealing with the enforcement of the environmental controls and breaches thereof.

The absurdity of the situation stems from the fact that the same process can cause pollution of a number of different environmental media. For example, a waste tip which is not properly managed, can blight an area of land, it can pollute the groundwater system, it can contaminate the soil and it can emit harmful gases into the air. If a company is to be allowed to construct a landfill site on a piece of land then the offices of the local planning authority, the waste disposal authority, the local authority environmental health department, Her Majesty's Inspectorate of Pollution and the National Rivers Authority could all be involved.

The system of integrated pollution control is an attempt to come to terms with problems of this sort. It was introduced by Part I of the Environmental Protection Act 1990. It applies to a list of different processes and substances which are particularly hostile to the environment. It is subject to the control of HMIP which authorises the processes and regulates them subsequently. HMIP is not just concerned with the emission into the atmosphere of harmful gases but is also concerned with pollution of the water supply.

Integrated pollution control and water

This leads to the unsatisfactory situation that there are now two bodies which have controls over water pollution – HMIP and the NRA. In practice this did originally cause certain difficulties, although it would seem that these two bodies have now come to a working arrangement in terms of their administrative responsibilities. This arrangement is contained in a document called a "Memorandum of Understanding." Where an application to HMIP involves a release of a prescribed substance into water, then HMIP must consult the National Rivers Authority. The NRA can then insist on specific conditions relating to the authorisation to maintain its water quality objectives. This does not prevent HMIP from setting tougher conditions than those required by the NRA. The NRA can block an authorisation if they are prepared to certify that an authorisation will cause the water to fail the water quality objectives.

Thus, where a process is subject to Part I of the Environmental Protection Act 1990, then HMIP is responsible for any consequent pollution problems into the media of the air and water.

Integrated pollution control and waste

The processes which are subject to IPC will inevitably produce waste. HMIP can attach conditions relating to the way in which this waste is to be managed. However, HMIP's control stops short of the act of disposal of the waste. This then falls under the control of the Waste Regulation Authority. There must be liaison between HMIP and the Waste Regulation Authority in relation to any waste that is destined for landfill.

Integrated pollution control and planning

Planning controls remain separate. It is likely that such a process will have fallen within the requirements of the environmental assessment regulations. This means that the applicant will have been required to produce a statement of the environmental effects of the project as well as having to make a detailed application to HMIP for approval. This overlap has been examined by a working party formed from a committee of the United Kingdom Environmental Law Association and Institute of Environmental Assessment which made three recommendations. These were: to make an optional tandem procedure with one assessment; to permit the environmental statement, produced for planning purposes, to serve in the integrated pollution control procedure; to examine further ways of reducing conflict.

Such a streamlining of procedures makes eminent sense in that it reduces the amount of bureaucracy. One major complaint of industrialists has been the increase in bureaucratic procedures which lead to increased costs and expensive delays in construction timetables. There is nothing to be gained in environmental terms by creating duplicitous procedures. In fact, to the extent that environmental controls can be more easily enforced where industry is a consenting partner, then there is much to be lost. If it is the case that two procedures are effectively looking at the same issues, then they should be streamlined providing the resulting procedure is sufficiently broad to accommodate the different angles and implications of the environmental effects of the project. It may be the case that such a streamlining is not as easily accomplished as might appear at first sight. It may still be necessary for a number of different officers and experts to examine a complex proposal. The issues surrounding a new incineration plant for instance include questions relating to land use, waste disposal and air, ground and water pollution. While different bodies deal with these different aspects of environmental control a streamlined approach is a long way off. The establishment of some co-ordinating agency is increasingly needed.

Integrated pollution control and worker protection

The system of integrated pollution control is aimed exclusively at the protection of the environment. The controls relating to the protection and the health and safety of the work force remain separate. These controls are maintained under the Health and Safety at Work Act 1974 by the Health and Safety Executive. There needs to be liaison between H.M.I.P and the H. & S.E. to ensure that the different controls are compatible. There is also a Memorandum of Understanding agreed between HMIP and the Health and Safety Executive.

Introduction of integrated pollution control

The introduction of the system of integrated pollution control is still underway. The previous regime was based on the Alkali, etc., Works Regulation Act 1906. In fact, the need for air pollution control was first perceived as a result of the pollution from alkali works. The 1906 Act will eventually be repealed but presently these works remain registered and subject to control under that Act. HMIP is the enforcing agency in respect of their activities. It would have been an impossible task to require these works to re-register under the integrated pollution control system overnight. Apart from all other complications, HMIP, which is still barely staffed up to its full complement, would not have been able to cope. So, the system is being phased in. A timetable set out in the Environmental Protection (Prescribed Processes and Substances) Regulations 1991[1] shows that all works will be subject to the new system by 1996. New applications will be dealt with straightaway and should be made once the

---

[1] S.I. 1991 No. 472, as amended by the Environmental Protection (Amendment of Regulations) Regulations 1991, S.I. 1991 No. 836 and the Environmental Protection (Prescribed Processes and Substances) (Amendment) Regulations 1992, S.I. 1992 No. 614.

design stage has been drawn up but before construction has begun. Applications to make substantial variations to existing processes will also be dealt with immediately.

How integrated pollution control works

The system applies to the "most potentially polluting or technologically complex industrial processes" and to the substances which are "the most harmful or potentially polluting when released into the environment whether air, water or land."[2] So, the system controls substances and processes. These are listed in the Environmental Protection (Prescribed Processes and Substances) Regulations 1991.

The substances are grouped into three lists according to whether they are to be controlled in respect of their effect on water, air or land. For instance, the release of pesticides onto land, mercury into water and asbestos into the air are all prescribed. Permission to release these prescribed substances into any environmental media is subject to a test as to whether the best available techniques have been used which do not entail excessive cost. This is known as the BATNEEC principle.

Processes which are to fall under the system of integrated pollution control are listed under Part A of these Regulations. (Those processes under Part B are subject to local authority air pollution control.) These processes are listed under six different headings known as chapters. These are:

fuel production processes, combustion processes (including power generation);
metal production and processing;
mineral industries;
the chemical industry;
waste disposal and recycling; and
other industries.

These general headings are then broken down into further subdivisions setting out more detailed descriptions of the processes. For example under waste disposal and recycling the first section deals with incineration. This is then divided into two parts: Part A and

---

[2] "Integrated Pollution Control: A Practical Guide." Guidance issued by the D.O.E. and the Welsh Office.

Part B. Part A includes the processes to be subject to integrated pollution control which fall under the aegis of HMIP. These include the incineration of waste chemicals which is a process which is potentially polluting. The list under Part B includes human cremation which is less hazardous and therefore falls subject to local authority control in respect of the emissions into the air.

A process will not be prescribed where it does not release any of the listed substances or where the release will be so trivial that it will not cause any harm. There is thus a de minimis rule. Working museums which may well demonstrate extremely polluting processes, are exempt from the regulations on the ground that they are of historical or educational interest.

Procedure for granting authorisation

The familiar system of control by means of authorisation is applied under the system of integrated pollution control. No prescribed process may be carried out without authorisation from HMIP. In addition, HMIP must review the authorisation at least once every four years. The Environmental Protection (Applications, Appeals and Registers) Regulations 1991[3] prescribe in detail the procedure for an application for authorisation to conduct a prescribed process. The application is to be made in writing to HMIP and must contain a considerable amount of information relating to the process, substances resulting from the process, the techniques employed to prevent or reduce the release of these substances, and an assessment of the consequences of such a release into the environment. There are special forms available from HMIP.

Consultation is to take place with the Health and Safety Executive and, in appropriate cases, the Minister of Agriculture, Fisheries and Food and the Secretaries of State for Wales or Scotland. Where the release of the prescribed substance will be into water, the NRA is the body to be consulted; where release is into a sewer – the sewerage undertaker; where a release may be into a site of special scientific interest – the Nature Conservancy Council.

The application for authorisation must be advertised in one or more newspapers circulating in the locality where the process is to be carried on. A notable feature of the system of integrated

---

[3] S.I. 1991 No. 507, as amended by the Environmental Protection (Amendment of Regulations) Regulations 1991, S.I. 1991 No. 836.

pollution control is that it is a public procedure. The public are to be informed and are to be enabled to make representations about the process. In addition, registers are to be kept by HMIP. These registers are to include information about the application, the authorisation, any convictions held by the person relating to the carrying on of a prescribed process, particulars of monitoring information and reports relating to an environmental assessment of the process. However, the process may be one involving questions of national security, or it may give rise to questions of commercial confidentiality. There are provisions for such information to be excluded. In cases of alleged commercial confidentiality, applicants must show that their commercial interests would be prejudiced to an unreasonable degree; they must show that they would be disadvantaged financially. HMIP will determine whether it is an appropriate case to exclude the information from the register. If the applicant disagrees with the decision, there is a right of appeal to the Secretary of State.

The time-limit for considering these applications is four months except in cases involving commercial confidentiality or national security when there are provisions for a longer time limit. The four-month deadline may be impossible in certain cases. For example, some processes may be very new and complex. In these cases, a staged application is permitted lasting throughout the design and construction stages. HMIP are encouraged to become involved in the earlier stages of design to ensure that the best practicable environmental option is considered. This clearly raises difficulties in terms of HMIP's ability, at a later stage in the process, to refuse permission to proceed. Their position might be compromised by their earlier involvement in the process. This raises the conflict which becomes apparent when the regulatory body must move from a position where compliance through co-operation is the guiding philosophy, to a position where prosecution for failure to comply becomes the norm.

Conditions. The authorisation may be granted subject to conditions.[4] A fundamental condition relates to the BATNEEC principle. There are, in fact, two principles: BATNEEC and BPEO (the best practicable environmental option). These two principles are interlocking. BATNEEC is described as a minimum objective. HMIP may set more stringent requirements than implied by this principle if that is necessary to achieve other objectives. The obligation to comply

---

[4] E.P.A. 1990, s.7.

with the BATNEEC principle is basic, and, in the event of a prosecution, it is for the operator to prove compliance with this condition.

What is BATNEEC? It is for the individual inspector to fix conditions which will ensure that the BATNEEC principle is satisfied. There are a number of guidance notes issued by the Secretary of State dealing with specific classes of processes which provide guidance on this issue. BATNEEC might be expressed as a performance standard. In other words, if the appropriate techniques are used, then an emission level of x may be achievable. The inspector could, therefore, set a specific emission level as part of the BATNEEC philosophy.

Conditions could also relate to the number, qualifications, training and supervision of the employees and the design, construction, layout and maintenance of the buildings.

BATNEEC replaces the former principle of "best practicable means" which was applied under the Alkali and, etc, Works Regulation Act 1906 and the Control of Pollution Act 1974 and which remains part of the Health and Safety at Work Act 1974. There is some debate as to whether the new principle represents a stricter approach or otherwise. There is some case law on the interpretation of the term "practicable" which indicates that questions of cost and risk are taken into account.[5]

D.O.E. guidance[6] explains that the term "techniques" embraces both the process and the operation of the process. It includes the design and its components.

"Available" means that the technique is generally accessible and has been developed or proven within the business context. This appears to exclude novel processes, particularly if they have not been extensively used within the particular industrial field in question.

"Best" means most effective in achieving the objectives.

"Not entailing excessive cost" is considered in relation to new processes and existing processes. A balance is suggested in respect of new processes to the effect that economic considerations can outweigh environmental protection. If the cost is too high in relation

[5] See, e.g. Adsett v. K. and L. Steelfounders and Engineers [1953] 1 W.L.R. 773; Edwards v. National Coal Board [1949] 1 K.B. 704; Coltness Iron Co. v. Sharp [1938] A.C. 90. See also HMIP Note, "Best Practicable Means: General Principles and Practice" (BPM 1/88, January 1988).
[6] General Guidance Note 1 (G.G.1), E.P.A. 1990, Pt. 1, Secretary of State's Guidance, Introduction to Pt. 1 of the Act.

to the economic advantage to be gained then the presumption in favour of best available techniques will be displaced. This approach typifies the cost benefit analysis approach to environmental questions. It also reflects some of the issues which were taken into account in assessing "best practicable means." The guidance note does not elaborate on this aspect but gives more information in respect of existing processes. Reference is made to the detailed process guidance notes which require gradual updating of techniques and to the E.C. Air Framework Directive. This Directive also takes into account economic considerations and the desirability of avoiding excessive costs. Factors such as the length of productive life left to the plant and the nature and volume of polluting emissions are to be taken into account.

The BPEO principle is to be considered when prescribed substances are to be released into more than one environmental medium. Where a release of this nature is to take place, then BATNEEC is to be used to minimise the pollution to the environment taken as a whole not just to the environmental medium into which the substance is to be discharged.

The principle of the best environmental option was considered in detail by the Royal Commission on Environmental Pollution in their twelfth report[7] although it was first considered in their fifth report, *"Air Pollution Control: An Integrated Approach."*[8]

BPEO is described in the twelfth report as a "procedure that would lead to reductions in environmental pollution and to improvements in the quality of the environment as a whole." It was envisaged as part of a co-ordinated system of pollution control in which environmental impact was a major factor. Alternatives should be sought to achieve the desired environmental result and the search for these alternatives should include something akin to a life cycle analysis of the product. Options such as the introduction of clean technologies or the elimination of waste as a by-product should be considered. These options should be evaluated at an early stage for their environmental impacts since the further a project passes beyond the design stage, the more difficult it becomes to consider a range of options.

The report accepts that "practicable" must include an assessment of the financial implications of the options. However, it rejects a consideration of local conditions and circumstances on the ground

---

[7] "Best Practicable Environmental Option", (Cmnd. 310) 1988.
[8] Cmnd. 6371 (1976).

that that might lead to lower standards in certain areas because of such factors as political and social pressures.

"Best" is to be interpreted in the light of the prevailing evaluation of the predicted impacts at the time. What is best may change as a result of scientific knowledge or popular attitudes.

Thus, the report envisages that the evaluation of the best practicable environmental option will entail a rigorous examination of the very basis of the proposal. It will challenge the principles on which a process is based and will cause a critical examination to take place. It cites as an example a proposal for a waste incineration plant. The application of BPEO would not be confined to such questions as the siting of the plant or the technologies to control emissions from it. Instead, the very need for the process would be considered and relevant options to consider would include the use of alternative processes to eliminate the need for the plant in the first place.

There are some similarities to the procedures that could be applied within the land use planning system where the application of the rules relating to the assessment of environmental effects are involved. In these circumstances, a consideration of the alternatives is supposed to take place. Frequently, alternatives are dispensed with at an early stage and all efforts are concentrated on justifying one proposal. By the time a proposal reaches the stage of a planning inquiry any possible alternatives have usually been cut off. An effective application of both BPEO and environmental impact assessment means that a rigorous analysis of several proposals should take place at a stage when the options remain open. In the context of the system of integrated pollution control, when the application is before HMIP, the planning stage has already passed. Therefore, only one proposal will stand before HMIP and the effectiveness of a procedure which is designed to test the *best* environmental option which is practicable in the circumstances, must, as a result, be flawed.

In addition to the conditions which HMIP may impose, the Secretary of State may give directions specifying which conditions may or may not be imposed. These directions may relate to individual authorisations or to all authorisations. However, the Secretary of State may not interfere with the BATNEEC principle.

The power of HMIP to impose conditions relates, therefore, to the attainment of specific objectives. In particular, the attainment of the objective that the best available techniques not entailing excessive cost should be utilised. This is to achieve the prevention or the reduction of prescribed substances into any of the environmental media, and, where they are released, to render them harmless.

Where any substances are to be released into more than one of the environmental media, then the objective is broader. The environment as a whole is to be considered. In these circumstances, the best environmental option should be used.

The validity of conditions will, no doubt, in due course be tested from time to time, by the judiciary. It can be anticipated that the usual administrative principles derived from the application of the doctrine of *ultra vires* and the *Wednesbury* case[9] will apply.

Variations. Technology is constantly developing as a result of pressures to compete more effectively and also as a result of environmental and political pressures. An authorisation granted this year may be out of date in two years time. With the pressure to develop cleaner technologies it is important that HMIP has the power to initiate changes within industry. There is, therefore, provision for HMIP to review conditions and authorisations every four years. It is also possible for the operator to initiate the review procedure. The *Environmental Protection (Applications, Appeals and Registers) Regulations 1991*[10] prescribe the procedure for variations.

If a proposed change is to be substantial, then it is necessary for the public to have the opportunity to be consulted and to participate. This will apply where the substances to be released change, or where the amounts released change. Detailed information on what constitutes a substantial change is contained in the HMIP Guidance Notes.

Costs. The cost of running the regulatory body, HMIP, is clearly substantial. They must consider applications, inspect, monitor and enforce authorisations and conditions. There is a charging scheme which aims to recover the cost from the operators who are subject to the control of HMIP. Operators must pay a fee when making an application; they must pay an annual fee in respect of each authorisation; and, they must pay a fee when an application for a substantial variation takes place. This is some attempt to enforce the policy that the polluter should pay.

---

[9] *Associated Picture House* v. *Wednesbury District Council* [1948] 1 K.B. 223.
[10] S.I. 1991 No. 507.

Enforcement

The enforcement powers of HMIP follow the pattern of enforcement in other regulatory fields, notably food safety law and health and safety provisions.

There are two notices that can be served: enforcement and prohibition notices. An enforcement notice can be served where there is a breach of a condition or an anticipated breach. Broader controls are available under a prohibition notice. This can be served even where there is no breach of an authorisation or a condition. In other words, the operator can be complying with the provisions of the permission in all respects but still be subject to a notice prohibiting the carrying on of the part of the process in question. The conditions for service of such a notice are that the process involves an imminent risk of serious pollution of the environment. It may relate to the manner in which the process is being carried or the process itself.

The key to the service of a prohibition notice is the determination of what constitutes an imminent risk and what amounts to serious pollution. Pollution is defined within the Act as harm to man or living organisms which means harm to health or interference with the ecological systems. It also includes offence to man's senses or harm to his property. Guidance as to what would constitute "serious" pollution is not forthcoming. Some discussion as to this question took place in the debate in Parliament, which, since the decision in *Pepper* v. *Hart*[11] may be called in aid in interpreting the meaning of the section. It would seem that the key to use of the prohibition notice is the need for speedy and decisive action. An example is given of an accident at one plant which releases substances which could react with substances released from another plant. A notice should be served on the other plant to prohibit the release of the substance until the danger has passed.[12]

There is a right of appeal against these notices to the Secretary of State. Failure to comply with the notices constitutes a criminal offence.

Powers of the inspectors. The powers of enforcement officers in any regulatory field are critical in the execution of the control envisaged. If officers have insufficient powers of investigation, then enforcement of the law is undermined. Yet, a balance has to be maintained between the enforcement of the law and the rights of

---

[11] [1993] 1 All E.R. 42 (H.L.).
[12] *Hansard*, H.L., Vol. 520, col. 897.

individuals to go about their business without undue pressure or harassment. Since environmental controls are criminal in nature, albeit they fall into the category of administrative regulatory crimes rather than "mainstream" crime, the powers of officers must be curtailed by proper procedures to ensure fairness. After all, a conviction under an environmental regulation can result in extensive fines and even imprisonment. It may also affect the future operation of a business and, thus, a person's livelihood.

An officer must, just as is a policeman, be subject to the criminal codes of practice and, therefore, must be familiar with the Police and Criminal Evidence Act 1974 and the Codes of Practice made thereunder. These prescribe rules and guidance for the conduct of interviews with witnesses and suspects, cautioning and the taking of evidence. If the codes are not adhered to and this causes prejudice to the accused, then this could give rise to an acquittal.

All statutes creating criminal regulatory offences prescribe the powers of the enforcing officers. The Environmental Protection Act 1990 is no exception to this and, indeed, is particularly detailed and extensive in terms of the powers given to the inspectors.[13]

A power of entry is a basic power and is provided in cases where the inspector has reasonable grounds for believing that a prescribed process is being carried out, and to premises where a prescribed process has been carried out and where the condition of the premises gives rise to the risk of serious pollution of the environment. The introduction of the words "on reasonable grounds" means that an inspector must exercise professional judgment as to whether a prescribed process is being carried out in the specified circumstances. Speculation or a fishing expedition would not be sufficient.

Detailed powers in relation to the taking of photographs, measurements and samples are included. The inspector also has power to interview a person where there is reasonable cause to believe that that person has relevant information. This person may be required to sign a declaration averring the truth of the answers given. There are also powers for dealing with emergencies. That is, where an inspector finds that something is a cause of imminent danger of serious harm then it may be seized and destroyed subject to certain safeguards.

Many of these powers are consistent with powers in other enactments, in particular, the Health and Safety at Work Act 1974. They do, however, extend them and are, in many respects, more detailed.

---

[13] s.17.

For example, the power to take photographs is not expressed in other statutes such as, for example, the Food Safety Act 1990, although it was clearly intended to apply from a reading of the *Hansard* debates. This omission has been addressed in the Environmental Protection Act 1990.

Registers. In keeping with the ethos of public control, the Environmental Protection Act 1990 allows for registers to be maintained. These will contain information about applications, authorisations, notices, appeals, convictions, etc. For further details on the content of these registers see Chapter 3, page 94.

LOCAL AUTHORITY AIR POLLUTION CONTROL

In practice, this remains far more extensive than the integrated pollution control exercised by HMIP. Although it covers types of pollution which are not as serious by definition as that which is subject to integrated pollution control, yet it relates to many instances of pollution which affect people in their daily lives and which can be detrimental to the environment.

The first point of distinction between local authority control and HMIP control, is that local authorities in this sphere of their activities, are exclusively concerned with *air* pollution. The concept of the integration of controls over the different media has not been applied to the local sector. It is only available and exercisable by the central agency.

Secondly, local authorities control air pollution in a number of different ways and under different enactments and statutory powers. They have similar powers to HMIP under Part I of the Environmental Protection Act 1990. They also have controls over smoke pollution.

Local authority air pollution control under Part I of the Environmental Protection Act 1990.

The system parallels that exercised by HMIP. Prescribed processes must not be operated without an authorisation by the local authority. They must impose conditions which ensure that the best available techniques are used which do not entail excessive cost. The best practicable environmental option is not relevant to local authorities because it only applies where a discharge is taking place into more than one of the environmental media. Since local authorities are only concerned with discharges into one of the media – air – then this will never apply to them.

Local authories have identical powers of enforcement to ensure that appropriate standards are being met.

Local authorities must also maintain registers. These are different from the registers maintained by HMIP in that they contain information not only about local authority authorisations but also about HMIP's authorisations of processes which are operating in their local area. Thus, the local authority register will be comprehensive in relation to all authorisations under Part I of the Act in their locality.

The Environmental Protection (Prescribed Processes and Substances) Regulations 1991[14] list the processes which are subject to local authority air pollution control in Schedule I, Part B. There may be cases where there is some doubt as to whether a process is Part A, and therefore subject to central control under HMIP, or, whether it is Part B, and subject to local authority control. In the first instance, the operators are recommended to approach the agency they consider the most likely to be the relevant body. If the local authority is approached and is uncertain then they are recommended to approach HMIP for a discussion about the matter.[15]

The Regulations also prescribe a timetable for the application of the authorisation procedure under Part I of the Environmental Protection Act 1990 to existing processes. This should have been completed by September 1992.

The problem of duplication of controls is again addressed in relation to local authority air pollution control. In particular, special provisions are made to avoid the duplication of controls over waste.[16] Liaison is also recommended between the local authority and the Health and Safety Executive particularly in relation to the exercise of enforcement powers.

Government guidance is available to local authorities in respect of their powers under Part I of the Environmental Protection Act 1990, in General Guidance Note 2.[17] It covers the matters required to be covered in authorisations and deals in detail with the application of conditions to authorisations. BATNEEC, as for all authorisations, is

[14] S.I. 1991 No. 472.
[15] General Guidance Note 1 (G.G.1) (April 1991), issued by the D.O.E., the Scottish Office and the Welsh Office.
[16] Environmental Protection (Prescribed Processes and Substances) Regulations 1991, Sched. 2, r.5.
[17] General Guidance Note 2 (G.G.2) (April 1991), issued by the D.O.E., the Scottish Office, the Welsh Office.

the general condition. Specific conditions are to be designed to make it clear to the operator what the obligations are in maintaining standards. They can be imposed in relation to emission limits and the monitoring of emissions and exhausts, amongst others. They are also intended to provide more comprehensive information for the public when they consult the register. Conditions should be enforceable, clear for both industry and the public, relevant to air pollution control and workable. It is permitted to impose a condition which requires an operator to monitor the processes from a point outside the boundary of the premises. These guidelines are comprehensive and will undoubtedly limit the opportunity for judicial challenge if local authorities adhere to them.

Local authority air pollution control under Part III of the Environmental Protection Act 1990.

Air pollution control is now included as a statutory nuisance under section 79 of the Environmental Protection Act 1990.[18]

Smoke emitted from premises so as to be prejudicial to health or a nuisance constitutes a statutory nuisance.[19] Smoke includes soot, ash, grit and gritty particles emitted in smoke. The defence that the defendant used the best practicable means to prevent, or counteract the effects of the nuisance, is available where the smoke is emitted from a chimney. Premises includes land and vessels. This could, therefore, include a street.[20]

Fumes or gases emitted from premises so as to be prejudicial to health or a nuisance are a statutory nuisance.[21] Fumes means any airborne solid matter smaller than dust, and gas includes vapour and moisture precipitated from vapour. This only applies to private dwellings which means a building or part of a building used as a dwelling. So, it would not include fumes coming from another part of the property such as the driveway. The defence of best practicable means is not available under this subsection.

---

[18] Smoke pollution was formerly covered under s. 16 of the Clean Air Act 1956 which is now replaced by the relevant subss. of s. 79 of the E.P.A. 1990.
[19] s. 79(b).
[20] *Att.-Gen.* v. *Kirk* (1896) 12 T.L.R. 514.
[21] s. 79(c).

Dust, steam, smell or other effluvia arising on industrial, trade or business premises and being prejudicial to health or a nuisance is also a statutory nuisance.[22] Dust does not include dust emitted from a chimney as an ingredient of smoke as this would be dealt with under subsection (b). This subsection is limited to industrial, trade or business premises and it is a defence if the best practicable means have been used to prevent, or counteract the effects of, a nuisance.

The defence of best practicable means is available in limited circumstances as described above. The existence of a trade practice may be called in aid to support this defence. Such evidence will only be successful if the trade practice is itself applying the best practicable means to avoid or mitigate the pollution. A bad practice will not be upheld by the courts simply because it is the custom of the trade.[23]

Economic questions are frequently raised in relation to this defence. It may be argued that the best means are not practicable on the grounds that they would make the operation uneconomic. The defence includes the word "practicable" and economic factors may be taken into account in determining this aspect of the defence. However, it would seem that the fact that use of the best practicable means would cost money or cause the operation to be unprofitable would not nessarily mean that the defence would be available.[24] In any event, it is for the defendant to establish the defence on the balance of probabilities.

The procedure to be adopted by the local authority was strengthened in the Environmental Protection Act 1990.[25] In the first place, the authority may anticipate the commission of a statutory nuisance and take steps to prevent it occurring. Secondly, the authority may initiate their proceedings by serving an abatement notice.

An abatement notice is a notice which is usually to be served on the person causing the nuisance. It will require the abatement of the nuisance and can require that certain steps should be taken to achieve this. There is a right of appeal against an abatement notice to the magistrates' court which must be exercised within 21 days from

---

[22] s. 79(d).
[23] See *Scholefield* v. *Schunck* (1855) 19 J.P. 84.
[24] See *Wivenhoe Port* v. *Colchester Borough Council* [1985] J.P.L. 175.
[25] s. 80.

the date of service of the notice. If the recipient does not appeal but does not comply with the abatement notice, then an offence has been committed. This is a streamlining of the previous procedure which required the authority to seek a nuisance order in the court before a prosecution could be brought. So, the procedure now is, that once the authority are satisfied that a nuisance has been committed, they should serve an abatement notice. There is a right of appeal by the person served to the magistrates' court within 21 days. Failure to comply with the notice is an offence.

Where the person causing the nuisance fails to comply with the notice then the authority does not need to prosecute automatically. They have power to abate the nuisance and do whatever is necessary to achieve compliance. For example, in *Liverpool City Council* v. *Mawdsley*[25] the local authority were dealing with a noise nuisance caused by the loud playing of a radio. They applied successfully to the court for an order to search the flat and seize the radio. Where the authority incur expenses in seeking to achieve compliance with the abatement notice, these can be recovered from the defendant or charged on the property to which they relate.[27]

There is also provision within the Environmental Protection Act 1990, s.82, for an individual aggrieved by a statutory nuisance to make a complaint to a magistrates' court.

This new system of air pollution control by local authorities has been the subject of two reports by the National Society for Clean Air and the Association of Metropolitan Authorities. The second report, in January 1993, was critical of the implementation of Part I of the Environmental Protection Act 1990. A survey was undertaken which indicated that many operators are continuing to operate without authorisation and are, therefore, breaking the law. By that date, 12,100 processes were subject to the local authority system of air pollution control and 40 prosecutions were pending for failure to apply. Local authorities had found themselves under huge pressure to process applications by the due date and considered that they were inadequately supplied with technical resources and trained staff to deal with the system.

---

[25] (1992) 4 Land Management and Env. L.R. 51.
[27] See s. 81A Environmental Protection Act 1990, inserted by the Noise and Statutory Nuisance Act 1993.

Local authority air control under the Clean Air Act 1993.

This Act consolidates the Clean Air Acts 1956–68 and Part IV of the Control of Pollution Act 1974 and only contains minor technical amendments. It gives effect to the recommendations of the Law Commission and the Scottish Law Commission.[28] It is important to remember that the provisions relating to statutory nuisances caused by smoke have been moved into the Environmental Protection Act 1990. There are a number of D.O.E. circulars under the earlier legislation which remain useful, subject to this caveat. Some of the provisions, notably those relating to chimney heights, have of late, been the subject of adverse comment by the government. It has been proposed that, as part of the Government's policy on minimising regulations, some of these regulations should be repealed further to the provisions in the Deregulation and Contracting Out Bill.

The Clean Air Act 1993 deals with controls on dark smoke from chimneys and from industrial or trade premises, smoke, dust and grit from furnaces, etc., smoke control areas and the collection of information.

There is a specific provision which prevents overlaps with the integrated pollution control regime under the Environmental Protection Act 1990.[29] This prevents any processes which are classified as prescribed processes under integrated pollution control from being subject to the Clean Air Act 1993, thus avoiding duplication of controls.

Part I of the Clean Air Act 1993 deals with the prohibition of dark smoke from chimneys of any building, or from chimneys which serve furnaces of fixed boilers or industrial plants, or from any industrial or trade premises. So, an emission of dark smoke from debris burned on a demolition site is covered by this part of the Act.[30] Dark smoke is classified according to a shade card known as the Ringelmann chart. This is a chart which environmental health officers can use to assess the type of smoke emitted from a chimney. In fact, environmental health officers often tend to rely on their own professional judgment in making this assessment. The officers may choose to use photographic or video evidence which may be more effective when used in evidence in the magistrates' court.

---

[28] Report on the Consolidation of Certain Enactments relating to Clean Air (1992) Law. Comm. No. 209; Scot. Law Comm. No. 138.
[29] Clean Air Act 1993, s. 41.
[30] *Sheffield City Council* v. *A.D.H. Demolition* (1984) 82 L.G.R. 177.

There are certain defences available in this Part. In particular, where the defendant acted inadvertently or used all practicable steps to minimise the pollution.

Part II deals with the emission of smoke, dust or grit from the chimneys of industrial furnaces and provides that the local authority may prescribe emission limits. This part also deals with the regulations for the height of chimneys.

Part III gives local authorities power to declare areas as smoke control areas. Local authorities have power to do this without reference to the Secretary of State, although the Secretary of State has power to order an authority to designate an area. The designation of a smoke control area is to abate smoke pollution. The original provisions in the 1956 Act came about as a result of the problems of smoke pollution caused by the burning of domestic fuel. The Secretary of State's power to require the designation of a smoke control area allows for the implementation of European Directives which specify certain limit values for emissions into the atmosphere. This part also provides for the adaptation of fireplaces to accommodate the burning of smokeless fuel.

Part IV deals with controls on the content of fuels and Part V provides for the publication of information by local authorities and for research and education on problems of air pollution.

As part of the Government's declared aim to reduce "red tape," many of the provisions have been targetted for reform or abolition, once the Deregulation and Contracting Out Bill has been passed.

SECTION 2: EUROPEAN LEGISLATION

European measures can be classified into different categories: emissions from motor vehicles and diesel engines; protection of the ozone layer; lead in air and petrol and sulphur emissions.

The measures are either directed at controlling individual substances, or are aimed at the control of emissions from industrial plants.

Controls on industrial plants

In 1984, a framework Directive was passed which dealt with air pollution from industrial plants.[31] This introduced the concept of authorisations for industrial plants – a system already in operation

---

[31] Directive 84/360: [1984] O.J. L188/20.

in the United Kingdom. Similarly, the 1988 Council Directive on the limitation of emissions of certain pollutants into the air from large combustion plants[32] set out to control emissions by setting emission limits for new plants based on the principle of the best available techniques not entailing excessive cost. This Directive was developed in part as a result of the international convention on long range transboundary pollution originally agreed in Geneva in 1979 and subsequently amended by protocol.

In addition, there are two Directives dealing with emissions from new and existing waste incineration plants.[33]

Controls on substances

Gases from engines. There are Directives which control emissions from engines. They deal with emissions from motor vehicles, tractors and diesel engines.[34] These Directives adopt the technical requirements laid down by the United Nations Economic Commission for Europe. These requirements relate to such matters as the approval of vehicles and the adoption of uniform conditions for the approval of motor vehicle parts and equipment. The Directives are highly technical. For example, there are tests relating to the emission of carbon dioxide at idling speed and the durability of anti-pollution devices.

The Directives do not impose binding requirements on the Member States. The Member States need not adapt their own legislation to take account of the measures in the directives. However, what they may not do, is ban the import of cars and other specified vehicles from other Member States which comply with the requirements of the Directives. Thus, if a vehicle is manufactured which complies with the requirements of the Directives, then it is guaranteed freedom of movement throughout the Community. If it does not comply, another Member State can refuse to import it.

---

[32] Directive 88/609: [1988] O.J. L336/1.

[33] Directive on the prevention of air pollution from new municipal waste incineration plants, Directive 89/369: [1989] O.J. L163/32 and Council Directive on the prevention of air pollution from existing municipal waste incineration plants, Directive 89/429: [1989] O.J. L203/50.

[34] For example, Directive on the approximation of laws of the Member States relating to measure to be taken against air pollution by gases from engines of motor vehicles, Directive 70/220: [1970] O.J. L76, implemented under the Road Vehicles (Construction and Use) Regulations 1986 and the Motor Vehicle (Type Approval) Regulations 1980. Directive relating to the measures to be taken against the emission of pollutants from diesel engines for use in vehicles, Directive 72/306: [1972] O.J. L190, as amended.

This, therefore, is an effective measure for achieving compliance with an environmental standard.

Sulphur in the air. There are various measures to control the presence of sulphur in the atmosphere. The object of the Directive on the sulphur content of liquid fuels is to reduce the amount of sulphur emitted from fuel by the expedient of reducing the amount contained in fuel in the first place.[35] Almost all organic fuels contain some sulphur. When the fuel is burned it converts the sulphur into sulphur dioxide which in turn, when it gets into the atmosphere, is transformed into sulphuric acid. This is a basic cause of acid rain.

Sulphur dioxide in the atmosphere is further controlled along with smoke in Directive 80/779[36] which prescribes air limit values. It would seem that the combination of sulphur dioxide and smoke at low levels in the atmosphere is particularly dangerous for people breathing it and can cause bronchitis and other lung related diseases including lung cancer. The scientific community, however, is not clear as to whether these two substances are synergistic, that is, whether the combined effect of the two is more serious than the effect of each of them taken separately.[37] Nevertheless, this is implemented in the United Kingdom by the Air Quality Standards Regulations 1989 although further regulations to take account of the latest amendments to the Directive are awaited.

Lead in the air. Lead is controlled in a similar way to sulphur. Limit values are imposed for the amount of lead detected in air,[38] and in petrol.[39] The former measure is implemented by the Air Quality Standards Regulations 1989, and the latter by the Motor Fuel (Lead Content of Petrol) Regulations 1981, as amended. The Directive on lead in petrol was amended to introduce the requirement that unleaded petrol should be available on the market.

---

[35] Directive on the approximation of laws relating to the sulphur content of certain liquid fuels, Directive 75/716: [1975], (O.J. L307/22) as amended. This Directive will be replaced by Directive 93/12: [1993] O.J. which sets stricter limits as from October 1, 1994.

[36] Directive 80/779: [1980] O.J. L229/30.

[37] See for example the evidence of Professor Lawther to the House of Lords' Scrutiny Committee on this Directive.

[38] Directive on limit value for lead in air, Directive 82/884: [1982] O.J. L378/15, as amended by Directive 91/692: [1991] O.J. L377/48.

[39] Directive 85/210: [1985] O.J. L96/25, as amended.

A controversial proposal was the Directive on the biological screening for lead.[40] The object of the proposal was to screen the population every two years and to set mandatory standards for lead levels in the human body. This proposal was watered down and the present Directive effected two screenings of the population for reference purposes only. In the United Kingdom, these took place in 1979 and 1981. Most of the groups sampled met the reference levels in the Directive.[41] These are not the only surveys undertaken in the United Kingdom for this purpose, but have provided significantly wider information on the subject.

There are further measures at European level controlling the presence of nitrogen dioxide[42] in the air, and preventing and reducing asbestos.[43]

Chlorofluorocarbons in the atmosphere. There have been various measures seeking to control the presence of chlorofluorocarbons, (CFCs), in the atmosphere. CFCs became widely used in aerosols, refrigerants and air conditioning because they are safer gases than those previously used. They are also used in the manufacture of polyurethane foam. CFCs are non-flammable and are effective as propellants. However, they are alleged to be one of the culprits in the deterioration of the ozone layer, and, as such, have been subjected to international and European controls. The drift of the controls has been to limit the use of CFCs in the manufacturing industries. In 1980, the Community passed a decision which sought to reduce the levels of two particular types of CFCs used in aerosol cans to the levels used in 1976.[44] This was followed by a further decision in 1982,[45] which provided a precise definition of production capacity for the whole Community and a co-operation procedure between the Member States and the Commission in terms of information gathering and evaluation. At this point, concern about the ozone

---

[40] Directive on biological screening of the population for lead, Directive 77/312: O.J. L105/10.
[41] Quinn M.J. 1982, 'The Findings of the EC Blood Lead Survey," Paper given to the 49th Annual Conference of the National Society for Clean Air.
[42] Directive on air quality standards for nitrogen dioxide, Directive 85/203: [1985] O.J. L87/1.
[43] Directive on the prevention and reduction of pollution by asbestos, Directive 87/217: [1987] O.J. L85/40.
[44] Council decision concerning chlorofluorocarbons in the environment, (80/372/EEC): [1980] O.J. L90/45.
[45] Council decision of November 15, 1982 on the consolidation of precautionary measures concerning chlorofluorocarbons in the environment, (82/795/EEC): [1982] O.J. L329/29.

layer was becoming a matter of international concern and in 1985, the Vienna Convention for the Ozone Layer was negotiated. The difficulties of seeking to operate at international level are plain in the development of this convention. On the one hand, the Third World was concerned that its developing industrial economies should not be stifled and, while the industrialised countries had the research and development facilities to develop alternative technologies, this was not available to them. The European Community was concerned at the cost to industry of requiring new processes to be developed. The USA supported a reduction of CFCs on the ground that they had taken unilateral action already and did not wish to be disadvantaged in commercial terms. As a result the convention did very little other than urge that something should be done. In 1987, a protocol to the convention was agreed. This is the 1987 Montreal Protocol on substances that deplete the ozone layer. This protocol set firm targets for the reduction and eventual elimination of ozone depleting substances. It also sets out provisions for enabling the transfer of technology between the industrialized countries and the developing countries and delimits some controls on the trade of ozone depleting substances.

The European Community, along with about 50 other parties, agreed the protocol which has subsequently been amended in the light of advancements in technology. In 1988, the E.C. adopted a Regulation on the depletion of the ozone layer[46] which was replaced and strengthened in 1991 by a further Regulation.[47]

In some respects, this Regulation introduces measures that are more severe than those agreed in the protocol. This latest Regulation controls the import and export of CFCs and other ozone depleting substances; it controls production and consumption in order to phase out these substances; it deals with management, data reporting and inspection. The 1991 Regulation was amended in 1992.[48] There are also two Council Decisions which allocate import quotas for CFCs and other ozone depleting substances.[49]

Finally, there is a Directive which deals with the presence of ozone at low levels in the atmosphere which can be a hazard to human

---

[46] Regulation 3322/88: [1988] O.J. L297/1.
[47] Regulation on substances that deplete the ozone layer, 91/594: [1991] O.J. L67/1.
[48] Regulation 92/3952: [1993] O.J. L405/41.
[49] Council decision of July 15, 1991, (91/359/EEC): [1991] O.J. L193/42, and Council decision of February 5, 1992, (92/94/EEC): [1992] O.J. L35/31.

health and the environment. The Directive deals with the provision of measuring stations and the exchange of information between Member States to enable the public to take precautionary measures.

Chapter Seven

Water

INTRODUCTION

Apart from being an essential of life, water has many uses in our society. We drink it, we bathe in it, we wash and cook our food in it, we clean our cars and water our plants with it.[1] Industry cools its machinery in it, uses it as part of its production processes and transports its goods on it. We all tip our waste into it.

Water has different forms. There is sea water, rivers and streams, lakes, glaciers, ice and underground water. Some comes with salt, some without. Water is a transportation medium. Just as it might carry a tree after a flood, so does it carry minerals, nutrients, bacteria and chemicals.

Water has different qualities depending on its source. It may be soft or hard in quality. This depends on how much magnesium or calcium salts water contains. For those living on the chalk downs of southern England, the calcium levels are high. Therefore, the water is hard. But a trip to a granite area, where the water has drained off the rock without absorbing these chemicals, will find water that is soft. When hard water is boiled, it leaves behind the calcium; a look inside a kettle is evidence enough. Bottled water is sold for the particular quality of the water. It may be from a source where the water has drained off land, absorbing certain minerals in the process. Bottled water is not "pure" water. Pure water consists of two hydrogen atoms and one oxygen atom and is only obtainable under laboratory conditions. All water is contaminated, that is, it contains other elements apart from the strict chemical constituents which make up pure water. Some of the contaminants are good, some are

---

[1] "Around a quarter of all water put into the public supply is used for flushing toilets and one-fifth is used for personal washing. Only about 3 per cent. of water is used for things like washing cars and watering gardens" Ruth Evans, Director of the National Consumer Council.

not. Some are deliberately added during the various processes which end up producing tap water.

The drinking water supply comes from several sources. Some of it comes from wells or boreholes. This is known as ground water and it is pumped out from underground. The difficulty in pumping it depends on the depth of the water. Water has a natural level underground known as the water table. In droughts the water table drops; in heavy rain it rises and is drained away by rivers into the sea. So, there is a natural reservoir of water under our feet.

Because of the heavy and constant demand for water, it has proved necessary to store it at times of excess. Thus, around the countryside are man-made dams and reservoirs built for this purpose. The water is piped from these reservoirs into the drinking water supply. The other source of drinking water is straight from the rivers and canals.

The water is then treated by the water companies. They filter it to remove soil and other matter by passing it through such materials as sand and gravel. Sometimes aluminium sulphate is added although aluminium is naturally present in some water. This chemical causes particles in the water to collect together so they are easier to remove. This is a dangerous compound if used improperly. If added directly to the drinking water supply it would form sulphuric acid. This is what occurred at the Camelford pumping station pollution incident when the aluminium sulphate was pumped into the wrong pipe and mistakenly entered the drinking water supply direct causing a number of health problems. Chlorine is usually added. This is a powerful chemical which kills many bacteria which would otherwise be harmful to humans. It is added in varying quantities depending on the state of the water. Sometimes it can be detected in tap water by the smell which is reminiscent of the public swimming pool. Another chemical which is usually added, although it may already be present, is fluoride, instrumental in preventing tooth decay, although its other health effects are debatable. Not all the water companies add this; they only do so where it has been requested by the district health authority.

These chemicals are deliberately added. Others appear in the water by other means and their presence may be undesirable. In many instances, their presence is subject to controls.

Lead and water pollution

Lead is probably among the most serious of pollutants found in water. Its presence in water is largely man-made and occurs where the water supply passes through old lead pipes and tanks. This is particularly a problem in soft water areas such as Glasgow. Lead pipes have not been permitted since 1976, but may still be present in some areas or in older houses. Grants are sometimes available to replace them. Lead, if absorbed in sufficiently high doses, can cause mental retardation in children, and can affect the brain and nervous system. Lead is, however, more likely to be absorbed through atmospheric pollution.

Nitrates and water pollution

The presence of nitrates in water has been the cause of much concern and has also been the subject of enforcement proceedings brought by the Commission against the United Kingdom, under Article 169, for failure to implement the Drinking Water Directive. In certain parts of the United Kingdom, the level of nitrates in the drinking water exceeds the EC guidelines and a complaint in respect of this breach was made to the Commission by Friends of the Earth.

Nitrates come mainly from the use by farmers of fertilisers. These, if used in large quantities, flush down into the groundwater system and into the rivers and drinking water supply. The production of food is without question a matter of critical importance for any country. In the United Kingdom, farming practice has been a phenomenal success in terms of its productivity. Since the Second World War, when the need for a degree of self-sufficiency was very apparent, government policies on the production of food have ensured that farming techniques have become very sophisticated. The essence of the success has been intensive farming techniques both in respect of cereal and livestock farming. Much of this is achieved by the increased use of nitrogen containing fertilisers and manures. So successful has this been that the problems of agriculture across Europe relate largely to over-production. Europe produces more food than it can consume.

The issue of nitrate pollution of the water supply has been addressed at European level. The Common Agricultural Policy is a European plan on agricultural practices across Europe. In common with other European initiatives, it was originally an economic plan. It is still largely concerned with protecting farmers against economic adversity and ensuring the production of a plentiful supply of food. To that end, it exempts agriculture from the general rules on competition, fixing prices for food and granting subsidies to farmers to ensure their continuing existence. Recent discussions on the

Common Agricultural Policy have included references to environmental issues and the view has been expressed that agricultural policy must take greater account of environmental policy.[2]

The European Commission has issued a Directive on the protection of waters against pollution caused by nitrates from agricultural sources.[3] This Directive recognises the need for good agricultural practices and recommends the creation of areas designated for particular protection because of their vulnerability. In response to this Directive the Ministry of Agriculture, Fisheries and Food declared the first group of Nitrate Sensitive Areas in 1990 and now proposes to increase this number by up to 30.[4] The proposal contains a financial incentive for farmers who agree voluntarily to reduce the amount of nitrates leaching from their land thereby protecting groundwater sources. The approach of using financial inducements to change farming practices is typical. It has been used extensively in areas outside water protection such as the protection of meadows and the set aside policy of taking land out of production is based entirely on this method. However, even where farmers are now using less of these chemicals and are replacing them with different types of products, it can take many years for a chemical to work its way through the chain.

The health effect of nitrates on humans is not altogether clear. There have been some very rare cases where they have led to a blood disorder in babies known as blue baby syndrome. When nitrates enter the infant body, they can be converted into nitrites. Animal experiments have shown some link between the presence of nitrites and cancer. There is no scientific evidence, however, that clearly links this with cancer in humans.

This raises the question of the link between the proof necessary to satisfy the scientific community, and the standard of proof necessary in a court of law. Under the present state of scientific understanding, what would be the remedy available to a person living in a high nitrate area who contracted cancer? Possible causes of action might lie against the water company for failing to implement European parameters. Apart from the legal difficulty of founding such a claim, the major stumbling block would be in establishing a causal link between the presence of nitrates in the water and the presence of cancer in the plaintiff. If the claim were a civil action for damages,

---

[2] Commission's Green Paper, *Perspectives for the Common Agricultural Policy.*
[3] Directive 91/676: O.J. L375/1.
[4] Nitrate Sensitive Areas (Designation) Order 1990, (S.I. 1990 No. 1013); "Agriculture and England's Environment: new Nitrate Sensitive Areas."

then the standard demanded by the law is the balance of probabilities. An expert witness would not be able to make such a commitment on the basis of the scientific evidence available.

Sewage and water pollution

Pollution may occur through the presence of sewage effluent in water. Sewage effluent is what is discharged by sewage treatment works. These works treat matter from both domestic and industrial sources. Domestic sewage is mostly organic and in the process of decomposing it requires dissolved oxygen. If it enters water in an untreated state, therefore, it consumes a great deal of oxygen in the course of its decaying process. The same effect is achieved when leaves fall in autumn into a fish pond. As the leaves decay, they use up the oxygen, there may then not be enough for the fish who are competing with the decaying leaves and they may die. This is one of the reasons why, when pollution of a river occurs, the fish are subsequently found floating on the surface. The amount of oxygen that the decaying matter requires is called the biochemical oxygen demand, (BOD), and this is a scientific measurement used to express the polluting power of materials thrown into the water. Different materials have a different biochemical oxygen demand and therefore have varying effects when they enter water. Clearly, a certain amount of organic material is bound to enter water and, provided it is not too much, the water can cope with it. Oxygen enters the water from the air and by the effect of some plants. In normal circumstances this means that a balance can be maintained. In fact, some decaying material in water is necessary to provide a balance of nutrients.

At the sewage treatment works the sewage is first screened, (filtered), and the solid matter, (*sewage sludge*), is then settled. This sludge may then be burned, buried or, in the past, it used to be dumped into the North Sea. It may also be sprayed on farmers' fields.

The potential problem with sewage sludge is that it will contain residual matter which might be harmful to living things. Sewage treatment works deal with domestic sewage, (everything flushed down the lavatory) and the effluent from industry. When the bulk of the liquid is taken out, leaving the sludge, it will contain the residues from the industries. So, it could contain parasites and pathogens, such as salmonella, from an abattoir, or heavy metals such as cadmium and lead from battery factories, or chrome and nickel from electroplating plants. If the sludge is then sprayed on agricultural land, these residues will eventually end up back in the drinking water system.

Sewage sludge, however, is rich in organic matter, nitrogen and phosphorus, and very beneficial for agricultural purposes. It can improve plant growth, the ability of soil to retain water, and the structure of the soil. It is desirable, therefore, that it should be recycled rather than dumped or buried, provided it is adequately treated to remove the potential hazards.

The problem was recognised at European level and the Directive providing for the protection of the environment and in particular of the soil, when sewage sludge is used in agriculture, was passed in 1986.[5] The Department of the Environment issued regulations[6] in 1989 and a Code of Practice.[7] These provide for the testing of sludge and of the soil where it is being used. They prescribe certain parameters for the amount of metals acceptable in the sludge. If certain organisms or metals are found then specific treatments are recommended. They also state that sludge should not be applied to growing fruit or vegetables otherwise they would take up unacceptable levels of metals which would then be eaten by the consumer. If the sludge is not reused by agriculture, then it will be treated as waste and either buried in landfill sites or incinerated.[8]

The *liquid effluent* which remains after the sludge is removed should be treated so that the breakdown process is complete. It is then normally discharged into a river or the sea. It may be that the river into which the liquid is discharged is a source of drinking water. The liquid effluent should, in that case, be treated to a high standard. In some cases the liquid effluent is only lightly treated or not at all depending on where it is being dumped. There is no doubt that the action of the sea rapidly disperses this effluent. The difficulty arises where the sewage is not adequately screened in the first place, or where the action of the tides brings it quickly into shore, or where it is not discharged at a distance into the sea. This is one of the areas where Europe has been active. The Bathing Water Directive examines the quality of bathing water and the presence of sewage is one of the features which has caused a number of bathing areas to fall below the standards. The Directive on urban waste water treatment[9] is concerned with the treatment of sewage and industrial

---

[5] Directive 86/278: [1986] O.J. L181/6.
[6] Sludge (Use in Agricultural) Regulations 1989, (S.I. 1989 No. 1263).
[7] Code of Practice for Agricultural Use of Sewage Sludge, D.O.E. (1989).
[8] See Chap. 8 on Waste.
[9] Directive 91/27: [1991] O.J. L16/29.

effluent. The objective of the Directive is to safeguard the environment from the adverse effects of discharges of waste water. The Directive prescribes a programme of treatment for sewage and industrial effluent over a specified period of time.

Where the treatment plants are situated in sensitive areas, the Directive recommends a more stringent method of treatment and prescribes a shorter period of time for compliance – by December 31, 1998. The criteria for designating a sensitive area include the possibility of eutrophication of freshwater lakes and other waters and estuaries. This means the process whereby, if nutrients are added to water in large quantities, they cause excessive growth of algae and other plants which use up the oxygen supply to the detriment of the natural balance of the water. After all, nitrogen and phosphorus are added by the farmer to the field to make the plants grow better. They have the same effect if put into water – they make the underwater plant life grow better. Nutrients might be deliberately added to the water in a watercress farm to get a bigger crop of cress. The principle is the same. It becomes a problem when the plant life becomes excessive. When it dies and starts decaying, there is then insufficient dissolved oxygen in the water for fish to live. If the fish cannot live in it, then the water is also unhealthy for humans to drink, because it would have a high level of bacteria in it. A lake or estuary may be more sensitive than the open sea because there is less movement of the water. In the open sea the tides sweep away the nitrates and disperse them over a large area. In a lake the water is not exchanged for new water over a large area in the same way. Thus a build up of nutrients – the process of eutrophication – may occur. So, special measures need to be taken in these areas. The problem was encountered recently in some of the inland reservoirs. With a number of consecutive seasons of low rainfall, the water in the reservoirs was not exchanged and concentration of nutrients increased causing the growth of a particularly poisonous form of blue algae.

Another criterion for designating an area as sensitive is because it is an area where the surface freshwaters are taken for drinking water purposes. Other areas may be less sensitive where there are particular conditions present which prevent the discharge of waste water from causing these difficulties.

Provision is made in the Water Resources Act 1991 for the designation of water protection zones[10] and nitrate sensitive areas.[11]

---

[10] Water Resources Act 1991, s.93 and Sched. 11.
[11] Water Resources Act 1991, s.94 and Sched. 12.

Agriculture and water pollution

The main form of pollution from agriculture – the use of nitrates – has already been discussed, as has the use of sewage sludge as a fertiliser. There is also a Code of Practice issued by the Ministry of Agriculture, Food and Fisheries which prescribes good agricultural practice for the protection of water.[12] This Code of Practice is very extensive and, in common with the normal principles governing such codes, failure to follow the Code would be taken into account in any legal proceedings. Consideration to the terms of the Code should therefore be given when acting in prosecutions relating to farmers. Further Codes on the protection of soil and air are also being prepared. The Code covers the storage and application of livestock wastes, the use of slurry, irrigation, solid manure, silage effluent, fertilisers, fuel oil, pesticides, disposal of animal carcases and the use of nitrates.

Controls on water

Controls on water can take two forms. It can be controlled according to its use, so, water destined for drinking and water in which people will bathe are subject to controls. The other set of controls relates to the limitation of certain substances which can enter water. So, a river in which people go swimming, could be tested according to the rules pertinent to determine the quality of bathing water, or it could be tested to ascertain the presence of prohibited chemicals.

There is another dichotomy present in the choice of methods to be adopted to control the quality of water. If a factory discharges effluent into a river, the amount of effluent which is permitted could be controlled at source. That is, the factory could be permitted to emit a certain amount of effluent containing specific levels of chemicals, known as an emission limit or limit value. Alternatively, the amount the factory is permitted to emit could be determined by testing the quality of the water in the river into which the effluent is discharged, (the receiving waters), known as a quality objective or standard. There are arguments on either side. The purpose of the legislation is to improve the quality of water up to a certain standard. The quality of the water differs according to the river. Fast flowing rivers move and break up contaminants quicker than slow moving rivers and take in more oxygen. The River Thames has

---

[12] Water (Prevention of Pollution) (Code of Practice) Order 1991 (S.I. 1991 No. 2285).

oxygen artificially pumped into it in order to improve its BOD. Rivers which run through heavily industrialised countries will end up carrying a higher accumulation of contaminants than rivers in different situations. Therefore, regulations which are flexible according to the quality of the receiving water, will more accurately implement the spirit of the legislation. However, this means that some factories will have stricter controls than others. They will, therefore, have to operate at greater cost than others which will affect their comparative profitability. In addition, a system which sets individual emission limits according to the quality of the receiving water will require an extensive system of monitoring and enforcement. A blanket limit is simpler to enforce.

The argument is compounded at European level by geographical differences between Member States. The United Kingdom has traditionally favoured the use of quality objectives. The rest of Europe prefers limit values. The United Kingdom is a group of islands and the rivers flow fast dispersing contaminants quickly. Rivers on continental Europe tend to be longer and more sluggish, accumulating greater concentrations of chemicals which disperse less quickly. Difficulties have been encountered at European level in establishing which test to use, although something of a compromise has been hammered out.[13]

Control of Substances in Water

The first group of regulatory controls, therefore, relates to the control of specified substances in water. At European level, there is an extensive framework in place. Firstly, there is the Directive on pollution caused by certain dangerous substances discharged into the aquatic environment.[14] This Directive establishes a framework for future action. Such a Directive is roughly equivalent to a broadly framed Act of Parliament which requires the detail to be filled in subsequently by ministerial regulation. This dangerous substances Directive is followed by a series of further Directives, charmingly referred to as daughter Directives, which deal with individual substances.

The Dangerous Substances Directive classifies substances into two lists. The first list contains substances which are particularly unpleasant and therefore should be eliminated. The second list contains a group of substances which should be reduced. The difference

---

[13] For a detailed description of the negotiations on this matter at European level, see, Haigh, *EEC Environmental Policy & Britain* (2nd. revised ed., 1989), p. 71.
[14] Directive 76/464: [1976] O.J. L129/23.

between the two lists reflects the scientific understanding of the difference in effect between the groups of chemicals. List I contains such substances which are particularly toxic, or which persist over a long period of time without breaking down, or which have the effect of causing a build-up of harmful substances – known as bioaccumulation. Substances which may cause cancers are included in List I, as are mercury and cadmium and mineral and petroleum oils, (fossil fuels). Organohalogen and organophosphorus compounds are also included.

List II includes a number of metals such as lead and silver, substances which affect the smell or taste of drinking water or fish, and substances which affect the balance of oxygen in water such as ammonia and nitrites. The controls on these substances can be confined to particular localities according to the quality of the receiving waters.

The Directive does not fix the limit values for these substances. This is done through the series of daughter Directives. However, it is a basic requirement of the Directive that discharges to the aquatic environment must be authorised and emission standards laid down. The aquatic environment includes most types of surface waters within the territory of the State: inland surface waters, territorial waters and internal coastal waters. Groundwaters were originally included but are now covered by a separate Directive.[15]

The clash between the two different systems of testing the presence of dangerous substances in water is highlighted in Article 6 of the Directive which provides that quality objectives can be laid down in addition to limit values:

> "The limit values established . . . shall apply except in cases where a member state can prove to the Commission . . . that the quality objectives established . . . are being met and continuously maintained."

The United Kingdom Government has declared its intention to make full use of the provisions of Article 6 which permit use of quality objectives.[16] The Government's view is that the standards to which the individual discharges are required to conform, should be set so as to ensure that a prescribed level of water quality is achieved and maintained in the receiving water. However, there is an acceptance

---

[15] Directive on the Protection of Groundwater against Pollution caused by Certain Dangerous Substances, Directive 80/68: [1980] O.J. L20/43.
[16] *Water and the Environment. The Implementation of European Community Directive on Pollution Caused by certain dangerous substances discharged into the Aquatic Environment*, D.O.E. Circular 7/89; Welsh Office Circular 16/89.

of the view that there is a need to reduce the overall level of discharges of the most dangerous substances.

In the United Kingdom the Directives are being implemented by regulations under the Water Resources Act 1991 and the Water Industry Act 1991. The Surface Waters (Dangerous Substances) Regulations 1991, establishes a system of classification for the relevant waters and prescribes concentrations for certain listed substances. The Trade Effluents (Prescribed Processes and Substances) Regulations 1992, and earlier regulations, prescribe certain substances which may only be discharged into the public sewers with an authorisation from HMIP. These substances are commonly known as "red list" substances.

Control of water for specific purposes

There are controls in respect of water which is used for bathing, drinking and for rearing fish and shellfish. There are comprehensive European Directives in this field and, indeed, it is an area where the Commission has been particularly active in bringing successful enforcement proceedings.

Drinking water. There are three European Directives which control the quality of drinking water. The first Directive was passed in 1975 and relates to the quality of surface water for drinking.[17] The surface water was divided into three categories. The categories represent different levels of quality for water and, therefore, the treatment prescribed for purification varies. Surface water falling in category A1, therefore, requires simple treatment and disinfection, category A2 requires normal physical and chemical treatment and disinfection, while category A3 requires intensive treatment.

In the United Kingdom, the water companies have a statutory duty to supply water that is "wholesome," and it was felt by the Government that this requirement was sufficient to implement the Directive. In fact, the Directive only requires that 95 per cent. of samples need to comply with the mandatory levels for substances in the water prescribed in the Directive.

The 1979 Directive on the sampling and analysis of surface water for drinking[18] prescribes the sampling procedures to be carried out to ensure that water complies with the requirements in the 1975 Directive.

---

[17] Directive concerning the quality required of surface water intended for the abstraction of drinking water in the Member States, 75/440: [1975] O.J. L194/26.
[18] Directive 79/869: [1979] O.J. L271/44.

The 1980 Directive relating to the quality of water intended for human consumption[19] is more extensive than the 1975 Directive which was limited to surface water. The 1980 Directive relates to all water intended for human consumption and includes water used during food processing operations. So, it would apply to frozen chickens, for example, which are passed through several changes of water, absorbing a good deal of it in the process. This water, which is consumed along with the chicken, is subject to the same controls as water drunk from the kitchen tap.

The Directive contains three Annexes which contain a great deal of scientific information against which the water is to be tested. Values are then set which are either Guide levels, set at the discretion of the Member State, or maximum admissible concentrations where values must be set and met. These levels are called parameters. In this context, this refers to the figure which has been set by the scientists to determine the amount of any substance permitted in water for drinking purposes. These figures are arbitrary to the extent that they can be changed if scientific understanding develops or, if for some other reason, it is considered necessary to change these figures.

The parameters set relate to a number of factors affecting the quality of the drinking water. These concern such matters as taste, smell, transparency as well as the presence of a number of substances such as copper, aluminium, lead and bacteria including those related to the presence of faeces. In fact, there are 62 different standards specified. In addition, the Directive provides that regular monitoring of the drinking water must take place.

There are grounds within the Directive for a Member State to derogate from the requirements. This means that a Member State may not be required to comply with it. However, such derogations are limited and would not be allowed where public health would be put at risk.

Implementation of this Directive in the United Kingdom has not been without problems. These problems have not been unrelated to the administrative changes occurring to the water industry as a result of the privatisation policy of the Government. The Directive had to be implemented by July 1982, and the quality of drinking water had to comply with the requirements of the Directive by July 1985. It was not until 1989, that the Water Supply (Water Quality) Regulations were passed. By this time, the Commission had started enforcement proceedings against the United Kingdom for failure to

---

[19] Directive 80/778: [1980] O.J. L229/11.

implement the Directive. The Commission continued its enforcement proceedings in the European Court of Justice on the ground
that the Regulations did not apply to Scotland and Northern
Ireland, nor to the food industry, and that nitrate levels in 28 supply
zones exceeded the maximum admissible concentrations prescribed
in the Directive, as did lead levels in 17 supply zones. The Commission won all the points in the European Court of Justice except in
relation to lead levels in Scotland. In particular the Court held that
the maximum admissible concentrations were legally enforceable,
thus enabling potential litigants to rely directly on the terms of the
Directive.[20]

The water undertakers in the United Kingdom, now the water
companies, have a duty to supply water which is wholesome.[21]
Wholesomeness is defined in the Water Supply (Water Quality)
Regulations 1989. These Regulations contain scientific tables listing
substances and parameters in the same manner as the Directive.
They also prescribe requirements for the monitoring, sampling and
analysis of water supplies. These requirements are imposed on the
water undertakers, not on the regulatory bodies. The Drinking
Water Inspectorate only has the resources to check that the water
companies are carrying out proper monitoring and sampling
procedures. The Inspectorate monitors the monitors. Drinking
water supplies from private sources are governed by the Private
Water Supplies Regulations 1991.[22] These seek to ensure that such
water is controlled so as to satisfy the requirements of the Drinking
Water Directive.

Bathing Water. Bathing water, particularly around the coastal
areas, can contain bacteria and other micro-biological organisms
which are harmful to people. When poliomyelitis was endemic in the
population it was possible to contract it from bathing water. Nowadays, throat infections and stomach disorders may result after
bathing in the sea. A recent claim has been that hepatitis A was
contracted by a wind surfer who was surfing near to an outlet
discharging raw sewage into the sea. The organisms which cause
these illnesses are most likely to come from poorly treated or
untreated sewage which is swept back into shore by the action of the
tides. However, it is also possible that it could have been discharged
from a passing ship. Apart from health questions relating to the

---

[20] See *Friends of the Earth* v. *United Kingdom*, No. Co. 1905/89, High Court.
[21] Water Industry Act 1991, s.67.
[22] S.I. 1991 No. 2790.

presence of sewage, it is not a pretty sight, and the amenity value of bathing water can be marred in this way.

This is an area of water quality control which, again, has been the subject of concern at European level. The Bathing Water Directive, passed in 1975,[23] provides for the reduction of pollution of bathing water. The same mechanism for control as in the Drinking Water Directive is prescribed, that is, the use of limit values within certain parameters which are flexible and subject to determination. It specifies I values and G values. I values are imperative and must be followed. Member States are to use best endeavours to follow G values which are guides. Member States are to test the bathing water for the presence of certain substances which are unacceptable and potentially dangerous to human health.

Bathing water is defined as fresh and sea waters in which bathing is explicitly authorised or where bathing is not prohibited and is traditionally practised by a large number of bathers. It does not include artificial areas such as swimming pools. Thus, round the coasts of the United Kingdom, a number of areas are classifiable as bathing areas. Sampling of bathing waters is also required which should take place where the daily average density of bathers is highest. It should begin two weeks before the beginning of the season.

In the United Kingdom the provisions of this Directive have been implemented by the Bathing Waters (Classification) Regulations 1991. These Regulations adopt the classification method and the sampling requirements for the monitoring of standards set out in the Directive.

But what if the analysis of the samples shows that the value limits are exceeded? There is, in fact, no control on the future use of the bathing area if this happens. People would not automatically be prohibited from using a bathing area which does not comply with the Regulations. All that happens is that a system of identification is used which classifies those beaches which fall foul of the standards.

Fish. Controlling the quality of water in which fish live is important as fish can absorb substances which are then eaten with the fish. There are two European Directives aimed at water standards for freshwater fish[24] and for shellfish waters.[25] Under the Salmon and

---

[23] Directive 78/160: [1976] O.J. L31/1.

[24] Directive on the quality of fresh waters needing protection or improvement in order to support fish life, Directive 78/659: [1978] O.J. L222/1.

[25] Directive on the quality required for shellfish waters, Directive 79/923: [1979] O.J. L281/47.

Freshwater Fisheries Act 1975, there is an offence of causing or knowingly permitting matter, which is poisonous or injurious to fish or to their spawning grounds, to enter water.[26]

The future for European water legislation

In December 1993, a European Council decision endorsed a Commission Report which set out proposals for future changes in the European régime on water. Much pressure has been brought by some of the member states for European water law to conform to the principle of subsidiarity. The proposals suggest, firstly, that the existing Directives on Drinking and Bathing Water will be replaced by framework directives. Secondly, it is proposed that the Urban Waste Water Treatment Directive and the Nitrates Directive will be retained on the ground that they already conform with the subsidiarity principle in that they simply define objectives leaving member states free to achieve them in their own way.

Thus, future changes at European level may be expected.

The organisation of the water supply and the disposal of sewage in the United Kingdom

The responsibility for water has included the supply of drinking water, provision for sewerage, land drainage and flood prevention. Until 1989, these functions were part of the public sector and were performed by the water authorities and local authorities. Functions relating to land drainage and flood prevention remain within the control of local authorities. The water authorities were organised on a geographical basis according to the principal river basins. They had been established by the Water Act 1973 and took over the responsibility for the supply of water, sewage treatment and quality control from a diverse collection of authorities, including the river authorities which numbered 27 in all. Prior to the 1973 Act, local authorities had been responsible for sewage collection and treatment. Thus, the 10 regional water authorities acquired their responsibilities from different sources. The reform represented a logical reorganisation of the water services.

In 1986, the Government announced radical plans to remove the responsibility for the supply and quality control of water and for sewage collection and treatment from the public sector and pass it into the hands of companies with limited liability constituted under

[26] s.4

the Companies Acts. This proposal was particularly controversial in that the water companies were also to be in charge of controlling the quality of water. Thus, a company, whose objective would be to make profits for its shareholders, would be responsible for monitoring environmental standards. This presented a potential conflict of interests. This aspect of the proposals was rethought, and it was concluded that a separate body should be created to take on this role which was previously undertaken by the water authorities. Thus, the Water Act 1989 established the 10 water companies which are quoted on the stock exchange, and the National Rivers Authority, which is the regulatory body.

The water companies are now subject to the control of the Water Industry Act 1991. This Act imposes duties on the companies which can be enforced by the Secretary of State or the Director-General of Water Services. The status and functions of the Director-General demonstrate the peculiar effect of the privatisation of a public utility in that a company which has a profit-making function is subject to controls which limit its freedom of action in the market place. The water companies, where they are statutory sewerage undertakers, have authority to give consents to trade premises to discharge trade effluent into the public sewers.

The Director-General of Water Services is head of OFWAT, the independent regulator.[27] His functions are defined by the Water Industry Act 1991. His role is to ensure that the water industry in England and Wales operates a fair and efficient service. This means that he must control price increases for the water companies' services and oversee their investment programme. He is, therefore, an economic, as opposed to an environmental, regulator. The Director-General's role, however, has implications for water quality and environmental protection. Major investment is mainly concerned with environmental improvements required to meet European standards. The cost of environmental improvements is met by the charges paid by the consumer. So, price fixing determines the facility of the water companies to invest. While it is the responsibility of the Secretary of State to define water quality, it is the responsibility of OFWAT to ensure that the water companies can finance their activities. To this end, the Director General enforces a

---

[27] For a discussion of the role of the Director General of Water services, see "Profile" (1992) *Journal of Water Law* 193–195, November.

formula set by the Secretary of State which limits the charges which the water companies can make.

The environmental regulators are the Drinking Water Inspectorate and the NRA.

The National Rivers Authority

The NRA was originally set up in 1989 and is now constituted under the Water Resources Act 1991 with extensive powers and responsibilities. The foremost duties of the NRA are to control pollution and to improve the quality of the river systems and coastal waters of England and Wales. It also has a role to play, in conjunction with local authorities, in undertaking flood prevention works.

Abstraction licences. Water can, in general, only be abstracted for domestic, agricultural or industrial purposes under licence. The NRA is responsible for issuing licences[28] to abstract and these licences state how much can be taken over a specified period. The application for a licence is publicised and individuals may make representations or object to a licence being granted. There is a right of appeal to the Secretary of State from decisions of the NRA. The NRA is resourced in part by charging for the grant of licences and for the actual process of abstraction.

Discharge consents.[29] The other licensing control which the NRA has, is the power to issue consents to discharge trade or sewage effluent into certain waters known as *controlled waters*.

These include[30] coastal waters extending out three miles, inland waters such as rivers, lakes, reservoirs or ponds and ground waters. In fact, the definition includes all inland and coastal waters with the exception of some inland waters which do not drain into other waters, that is, they are land locked. The procedure for applying for a discharge consent is, again, a public procedure. Members of the public may make written representations which must be considered by the NRA.

The NRA may attach such conditions as they think fit to the grant of a discharge consent. These conditions may relate to the quality, quantity, nature, composition or temperature of the discharge.

---

[28] Water Resources (Licences) Regulations 1965 (S.I. 1965 No. 534).
[29] Water Resources Act 1991, Sched. 10.
[30] Water Resources Act 1991, s.104.

Deposit of waste. The NRA also has certain functions under the Environmental Protection Act 1990 in relation to the deposit of waste into controlled waters. Where an authorisation is sought under this Act to discharge waste into controlled waters, if the NRA certify that, in its opinion, the discharge will cause the quality of the water to fall below the standards, then the authorisation must be refused. The NRA also has a right to attach conditions to the grant of such an authorisation.

Anti-pollution works. The NRA has an important role to play in carrying out the preventive principle.[31] If a spillage has occurred which threatens to pollute the waterways, then it can carry out preventive work or work that will limit the damage or remedy any damage that has already occurred. They can undertake work to restore the water to the condition it was in before the pollution occurred. This could include replacing plant and fish life.

Such an operation is likely to be very expensive, and the NRA accordingly have power to recover the cost from the polluter – a case of the "polluter pays."[32] They are not prevented from subsequently pursuing a prosecution against the polluter. The polluter may, therefore, be subject both to a court fine and also for the clean up costs reasonably incurred by the NRA.

The NRA is the primary body for law enforcement in relation to the water pollution offences under the Water Resources Act 1991.

The water pollution offences in the United Kingdom

The principal water pollution offences are now contained in the Water Resources Act 1991. The first group of offences relate to polluting controlled waters.

The offences fall into four categories. One is a general pollution offence. It is broadly defined, creating an offence where any poisonous, noxious or polluting matter or any other solid waste matter enters controlled water.[33] The other category deals with the emission of effluents into controlled waters.

There is no definition of what constitutes "poisonous, noxious or polluting matter" in the Act. This leaves it open to the courts to interpret the section. The Act does not require that the matter should only be poisonous to humans. Accordingly in *National Rivers*

---

[31] Water Resources Act 1991, s.161.
[32] Water Resources Act 1991, s.161(3).
[33] Water Resources Act 1991, s.85(1).

Authority v. *Egger (U.K.)*,[34] the Crown Court interpreted polluting matter to include matter which is "capable of causing harm in that it may damage a river's potential usefulness." The Court said that, in this context, "damage" meant "harm to animal, vegetable or other life in a river and/or aesthetic damage." This is evidence of the Act's flexible definition. According to this decision, the court was prepared to accept that aesthetic damage on its own would be enough to found a prosecution under s.85(1).

In considering the meaning of the word "poisonous," the Divisional Court in *Schulmans Inc* v. *NRA*[35] highlighted the difficulty of the need for scientific proof in achieving a successful prosecution. The matter which entered the river was fuel oil. The court found that there was no evidence to establish how much fuel oil was necessary to make the water "poisonous" for fish.

"Any other solid waste matter" presents less difficulties in interpretation. It clearly applies to the sort of discarded waste matter which can be seen floating in rivers or which fishermen catch believing they have hooked a 20 pounder. Abandoned shopping trolleys and old boots fall in this category. Such items may not be poisonous; that is not required by the offence. It would seem possible to commit this offence where the major damage relates to the aesthetic appearance of the water.

The second category of offences under section 85 relates to the emission of matter from a sewer or drain in breach of a prohibition notice,[36] or the emission of sewage or trade effluent from a building or fixed plant onto land or lakes or ponds which are not inland freshwaters in breach of a prohibition notice.[37] The NRA has power to issue notices prohibiting discharges in these circumstances. It is, therefore, an offence to discharge in breach of a prohibition notice.

The third category of offences relates to the discharge of sewage or trade effluent into controlled waters,[38] and the fourth category relates to the obstruction of waters so as to cause or worsen pollution.[39]

All these offences are subject to maximum penalties of £20,000 fine and/or three months imprisonment on summary conviction, and an unlimited fine and/or 2 years imprisonment on conviction on indictment.

---

[34] (1992) 4 Land Management and Env.L.R. 130, 209 ENDS Report.
[35] (1992) 4 Land Management and Env.L.R. 130; 3 *Water Law* 72.
[36] s.85(2).
[37] s.85(4).
[38] s.85(3).
[39] s.85(5).

All of the offences have a common factor. They are committed when a person "causes or knowingly permits" the pollution to occur. These offences fall into the classic model of the regulatory criminal offence of strict liability. Proof of negligence or fault is not required. There are two separate offences here; one of "causing" and one of "knowingly permitting." Most of the case law is concerned with the offence of "causing" pollution.

The leading House of Lords decision on the offence of "causing" pollution is *Alphacell* v. *Woodward*.[40] In this case, an overflow of polluting matter into a stream was caused when the pumps leading from a settling tank became blocked by brambles, ferns and leaves. The pumps had been installed in the settling tanks in order to prevent an overflow. Normally, the liquid, once purified in the tanks, would be pumped back into the factory for reuse in their production processes. However, if the pumps failed to operate, a channel, which had been provided for the purpose, took the liquid straight into the river. The appellants were convicted of causing polluted matter to enter a river. Their appeal was dismissed by the House of Lords on the grounds that their positive and deliberate acts in building and operating the settling tanks with an overflow channel leading directly into the river, and in failing to install tanks which were an effective safeguard against overflow, had led directly to the overflow and pollution of the river.

Lord Wilberforce held that the offence of causing pollution must involve some active operation or chain of operations which involve, as a result, pollution of the water. It involved more than mere tacit standing by and looking on. On the other hand, he considered that knowingly permitting involved a failure to prevent the pollution which must be accompanied by some knowledge. The offence of causing, therefore, involves a positive act, although that positive act does not need to be negligent.

This part of the water pollution legislation has recently been subject to a considerable amount of judicial analysis, largely because of the diligence of the NRA in prosecuting polluters. In *NRA* v. *Welsh Development Agency*[41] the respondent created factory units on its land which it leased to tenants. A clause in each lease stated that the tenant would not discharge effluent into an adjacent stream. One of the tenants *did* discharge effluent into the stream through a drainage channel which had been designed and constructed by the respondent. The NRA chose to prosecute the landlord for the

---

[40] [1972] A.C. 824; [1972] 2 W.L.R. 1320; [1972] 2 All E.R. 475.
[41] [1993] Env. L.R. 407.

offence of causing the pollution, rather than the tenant; a decision which caused some comment in the court.

The facts were, therefore, materially different from *Alphacell* v. *Woodward*. In that case, there was no question that the appellants had not been actively involved in the polluting act. In *NRA* v. *Welsh Development Agency*, the respondent was not directly involved in the emission. Its involvement rested on its act of designing and installing the drainage system through which the effluent was discharged. The Divisional Court held that the respondent's act was not a positive or deliberate act which caused the pollution. There was nothing in the design or construction of the drainage system which played a part in the discharge of the effluent.

A similar decision was reached in *Wychavon District Council* v. *NRA*[42] by the Divisional Court. In this case sewage flowed into the River Avon because of a blockage in the sewer pipe situated between Evesham Hospital and the river. The council had responsibility for the day-to-day operation of the sewage system and within a couple of days cleared the blockage so that the discharge did not occur again. The argument put by the NRA was that the council had failed to prevent the overflow, and, on being told of it by NRA's pollution control officers, they failed to find the cause promptly and therefore, caused the discharge to continue for two days. This argument was rejected by the Court who considered that the council performed no positive or active operation which interfered with the continuing flow of sewage into the river.

The Court did consider that the failure of the council to act promptly in halting the flow of sewage could have amounted to negligence. They also indicated that there were facts which could have amounted to the commission of the offence of "knowingly permitting" the pollution to occur. However, they had not been charged with that limb of the offence.

These decisions follow the earlier decision in *Price* v. *Cromack*[43] where the appellant had entered into an agreement with a neighbour to allow two lagoons to be built on his land which would carry effluent from the neighbour's industrial premises. A crack in the lagoons permitted effluent to leak into the nearby river. The Divisional Court held that there had been no positive act which could be said to have caused the pollution.

It is clear that the judges in these cases are looking at the last act which occurred in the chain of events leading up to the act of

---

[42] [1993] Env.L.R. 330.
[43] [1975] 1 W.L.R. 988; [1975] 1 All E.R. 113.

pollution to determine whether the defendant "caused" the pollution. In fact, a number of events lead up to the final act of pollution. In *Price*, if the lagoons had not been built with the agreement of the defendant, the pollution would not have occurred. In *NRA* v. *Welsh Development Agency*, if the defendant had not developed the land and built the drainage system, the pollution would not have occurred. In *Wychavon District Council*, if the council had acted quickly, the discharge would have been stopped within hours rather than days. However, by examining the last act, the courts are taking a narrow view of the meaning of "cause." It might be asked whether this interpretation is strictly in line with the authority of *Alphacell* v. *Woodward*. In *Impress (Worcester) Limited* v. *Rees*[44] the judge expressed the issue in the following manner:

> "On general principles of causation, the question . . . was whether that intervening cause was of so powerful a nature that the conduct of the appellants was not a cause at all but was merely part of the surrounding circumstances. If the justices had asked themselves that question, it seems to me that it would have been susceptible of only one answer, namely that it was not the conduct of the appellants but the intervening act of the unauthorised person which caused the oil to enter the river."

This was a case where a trespasser had entered the premises of the defendant and released a tap which allowed fuel oil to enter the River Severn. The defendants were acquitted of causing the pollution.

The NRA appear, through their prosecuting policy, to be intent on widening the judicial interpretation. However, it would seem that no widening will occur without an appeal to the House of Lords. An alternative measure, speculated upon by the judges in the cited cases, would seem to be to use the other limb of the offence in these cases; that is, the offence of "knowingly permitting" the pollution to occur. The courts would have less difficulty in convicting where no positive act is required. However, it may be that the difficulty of establishing knowledge might prove something of a hurdle in practice.

Defences. There are various defences available to these charges. Statutory permission such as discharge consents from the NRA, authorisations from HMIP, or licences from a waste regulation authority fall into this category. Otherwise, if the discharge is made

---

[44] [1971] 2 All E.R. 357.

as a result of an emergency to avoid danger to life or health and all such steps as are reasonably practicable are taken to minimise the discharge and its polluting effects, this will constitute a defence. The NRA must be notified of such an event and, it would seem that they are only prepared to accept as an emergency situation, one which is beyond the defendant's control.[45]

There is also some protection for the owners of abandoned mines where the water from such mines enters controlled waters. When a mine is working, a major part of the operation is to keep it free from flooding. When mine shafts are opened up underground, the groundwaters would naturally flow into them. Action must, therefore, be taken to keep them clear. One of the reasons why a decision to close a mine has tremendous economic and practical consequences is because of the problem of flooding. Once an abandoned mine has flooded, it would be phenomenally expensive to reopen it. The decision is, therefore, usually perceived as irrevocable. With the projected closure of most of the United Kingdom's deep pits, this issue will become more prominent.

Water pollution and the common law

The impact of the common law on cases concerning water pollution was discussed in Chapter 2. The most recent case of *Cambridge Water Co. v. Eastern Counties Leather plc.*[46] delimits the right of a property owner to an unpolluted flow of groundwater.

Property owners, in the form of riparian owners, also have rights to receive water in an unpolluted state. Actions for compensation for nuisance and an injunction are well established forms of action in this field. An action in trespass may also be a possibility where waste material is deposited on the river bank.

Protection of the sea and international waters

A consideration of water pollution necessarily involves a consideration of pollution of the sea and other international waters, such as lakes and rivers. Major pollution incidents such as oil spillages have made such issues a matter of public interest. Such incidents not only affect the quality of the water but also affect the marine life. The seas and oceans are used in common as a means of transport and this includes transport of huge quantities of oil. Disaster at sea for

---

[45] (1992) 4 *Land Management and Env.L.R.* 131.
[46] [1994] 1 All E.R. 53.

these vast tankers may mean extensive pollution incidents. In fact, while the immediate impact of an oil spill may be obvious, the ability of the sea to break up and dissipate the spillage may vary considerably. For instance, the oil spillage by the Braer, in 1992, at the Shetland Islands, was rapidly dissipated by the action of the tides and currents which are among the most powerful in the world.

This is an area where an international legal regime has developed to control such incidences of pollution. The International Maritime Organisation has been at the forefront of this development. The 1982 UNCLOS (United Nations Convention on the Law of the Sea), seeks to provide a global framework for the law of the sea and has, among its objectives, the promotion of the peaceful use of the sea, the conservation of marine resources, the equitable use of its resources and the protection and preservation of the marine environment. In addition the 1973/1978 MARPOL Convention aims to protect the marine environment.

In the United Kingdom, the key statutes control the prevention of pollution by oil and other substances by discharges into the territorial waters and emergency measures to deal with pollution incidents such as the Torrey Canyon disaster of 1967.[47] There is also strict liability on shipowners for the persistent escape of oil[48] although there may be a financial limit on the amount of damages payable in the absence of fault. There is an international fund supported by levies from importers of oil to bridge any gaps this policy of limiting the availability of damages may incur.[49]

The process of dumping at sea, in the past, a popular way of disposing of anything unwanted from radioactive waste to sewage sludge, is now only permitted by licence. Such a licence will only be granted after due consideration has been given to the effect of the dumping on the marine environment and human health.[50] The dumping of radioactive waste at sea has been halted by voluntary agreement for a decade.

---

[47] Prevention of Oil Pollution Act 1971; Merchant Shipping (Control of Pollution by Noxious Liquid Substances in Bulk) Regulations 1987; Merchant Shipping (Prevention of Pollution by Garbage) (Amendment) Regulations 1993; Merchant Shipping (Prevention of Oil Pollution) (Amendment) Regulations 1993.
[48] Merchant Shipping (Oil Pollution) Act 1971.
[49] Merchant Shipping Act 1974 and the 1971 International Convention on the Establishment of an International Fund for Compensation for Oil Pollution Damage.
[50] Food and Environment Protection Act 1985.

Chapter Eight

Waste

INTRODUCTION

What is waste?

Every time we shop at the superstore, we contribute to the mountain of waste. It is possible to quote figures which show that the production of waste amounts to millions of tons; but such figures are meaningless except to the statistician. If, however, the accumulation of waste by the ordinary shopper is considered, some comprehension of the problem is soon at hand. Each week, the householder fills a dustbin full of waste material.[1] Visits to the municipal tip and to the local recycling centres may also have taken place. Move back one pace in the life cycle of the product purchased from the shop, to the packaging waste which the retailer had to deal with. Then step back again to the manufacturer and the waste products of the manufacturing process; one step further to the extractive industry for the raw materials used in the manufacture. A consideration of the waste produced in this context indicates the extent of the problem. Waste is produced at each stage: by the consumer, by the retailer and by the manufacturer.

In the industrial context, waste is produced at every stage. When coal is mined, as much or more material that is unwanted is disposed of. When chemicals are processed, the residues form waste.

Waste can be classified in different ways. It can be defined according to its source. It either comes out of the home – household waste, or, out of the shop or office – commercial waste, or out of the factory – industrial waste. Waste comes in different forms. It can be organic or non-organic. Organic waste can decay. Waste food from the household can be composted and returned the soil. Household

---

[1] The Recycling Plan for Erewash Borough Council quotes a figure of 6.6 kilogrammes per person of household rubbish produced each week.

waste such as tin cans and plastic is inorganic and cannot be treated in the same way. Waste can be solid, such as the householder's empty bottle, or the slag heap from the coal mine, or the packaging material from the superstore. It might be in liquid form such as sewage effluent. It could be in the form of a gas, such as sulphur dioxide from the coal generated power station, or CFCs from the aerosol or refrigerator, or methane from the herds of domestic cattle grazing on the green fields of England.

Waste can be defined according to the potential harm that it can do. Some waste can be inherently dangerous. This danger can affect humans directly. Radioactive waste is dangerous in this way. Exposure to the radioactive waste products of the nuclear power or weapon making industries can cause death or serious injury to humans. Toxic chemicals from the chemical processing plant can be dangerous if they come into contact with the skin or are swallowed or inhaled.

Waste can pollute the environment and be indirectly dangerous to humans. It can enter the atmosphere or the water supplies causing damage to plants and animals or affecting the climate. Other forms of waste can, in themselves, be harmless. Packaging waste is not poisonous if touched and does not enter the atmosphere or water supply. A pile of cardboard boxes outside a shop can be unattractive to look at and may attract rats if it contains food waste, thus constituting a hazard to human health. But, in its original condition, a piece of cardboard is not dangerous. The slag-heap from a coal-mine is not dangerous. People may walk on it or live by it without coming to harm. Its method of storage may be hazardous as was demonstrated by the appalling Aberfan disaster of 1966, when the slag-heap slipped and buried part of the village including the school and its occupants.

Waste may acquire dangerous properties. It may react with other substances thus becoming dangerous. For example, petrol fumes and smoke react with sunlight and produce carcinogenic chemicals.

Waste may be corrosive, that is, it may eat away or destroy solid materials. Acids may be capable of this action.

The classification of waste is important in determining the controls which are appropriate to deal with it. The more hazardous the waste, whether directly or potentially, the more stringent the controls which are required. Waste which is deadly on contact needs to be more rigorously controlled than waste which is stable and harmless. Dangerous waste should be distinguished from other types of waste.

It is also important to make the distinction as there is an international market for waste. Waste is an economic good and is bought and sold on the international markets. It is transported across land and sea and, if hazardous, needs particular care. There is, therefore, a need to have an internationally agreed definition of what constitutes waste which is particularly dangerous. Such a definition would be the basis for agreed protocols on packing and management of such waste.

Dangerous waste is variously described in different legal régimes as special waste, hazardous waste and toxic waste, as well as dangerous waste. In the United States of America such waste is listed by the Environmental Protection Agency and is characterised by such features as its potential to catch fire, its corrosiveness, its reactivity or its toxicity.[2] Such wastes are then subject to a particular form of management. The effect of this method of listing is extremely wide. As no thresholds are specified, any form of waste containing a listed substance is classified as hazardous waste and treated accordingly, even if the quantity of the proscribed substance is small and causes no problem.

In 1989 an international convention on the control of the transboundary movements of hazardous wastes and their disposal was agreed at Basel. This convention adopts a similar approach to the principles adopted in the U.S.A. for the definition of hazardous waste. Annex I of the Convention lists categories of waste which are deemed to be hazardous unless they do not contain any of the characteristics contained in Annex II. There are 18 "waste streams" in Annex I, which include, for example, clinical waste from hospitals, waste from the manufacture of wood preserving chemicals, and waste oils. It also includes a list of constituents, for example, mercury, lead and asbestos. These items must then possess one of the characteristics contained in Annex III, such as being flammable, explosive, toxic or ecotoxic. Toxic is defined as having effects if breathed in, eaten or absorbed by the skin, and includes carcinogenicity. Ecotoxic is defined as having an adverse effect on the environment by means of bioaccumulation or by having a toxic effect on biotic systems. These definitions appear to be detailed and profound. However, the gap between scientific knowledge and environmental regulation is acknowledged in the Convention itself. Not all hazards from waste are fully understood. In many fields tests

---

[2] See J.T. Smith II, "The Challenges of Environmentally Sound and Efficient Regulation of Waste – The Need for Enhanced International Understanding" (1993) 5 J.E.L. 91.

do not exist to assess the potential hazards. Ecotoxicity is a particularly undefined area which depends to a considerable degree not on scientifically valid tests, but on political pressure.

The Convention also accepts wastes which are not mentioned in the document, but which are accepted as hazardous at national level, as being covered by the provisions of the Convention.

At European level, the definition of hazardous waste follows much of the pattern set in the Basel Convention. The latest directive on hazardous waste,[3] effective from December 31, 1993, replaces the original 1978 Directive.[4] It expresses the necessity of establishing a precise and uniform definition of hazardous waste based on experience. It, as in the Basel Convention, cites a list of different categories of waste and wastes with certain constituents, which, if they have certain properties, will be defined as hazardous. The list is more detailed than in the Basel Convention. A list is to be drawn up which will take further matters into account in order to provide more detail on the question of determining which waste is hazardous. This will provide further detail on the origin and composition of the waste and limit values for the concentration of the constituents. This will prevent waste being classified as hazardous where there is only a small amount of the proscribed constituents present. The question of scientific verification remains open, however. There are no agreed tests for a number of the listed characteristics. What makes a waste ecotoxic, for example? It is tempting to assume that the answer will depend on political prejudice rather than scientific precepts.

In the United Kingdom dangerous waste is described, somewhat euphemistically, as "special waste." Special waste is waste which "may be so dangerous or difficult to treat, keep or dispose of that special provision is required for dealing with it."[5] The current definition of which types of waste fall within this category is set out in the Control Of Pollution (Special Waste) Regulations 1980. A list of substances such as acids and alkalis, lead and mercury compounds and laboratory chemicals appears in Schedule 1. This list appears to be very broad. However, in order to be classified as special waste, any of the substances must satisfy other specific tests. These tests relate to the effect of the substances on human health. They must be either "dangerous to life," or have a flash point, (catch fire or explode), of 21 degrees Celsius or less. Dangerous to life

---

[3] Directive on hazardous waste, 91/689: [1991] O.J. L377/20.
[4] Directive on Toxic and Dangerous Waste, 78/319: [1978] O.J. L84/43.
[5] E.P.A. 1990, s.62.

clearly means human life.[6] These regulations were drafted in 1980 and the reference to human life alone is indicative of the changes that have occurred in the last decade. Thus special waste in the United Kingdom is currently defined by reference to its effect on humans and not to the wider environment. The effect on humans is also defined as a direct effect as it is to be tested by its effect if certain quantities are swallowed, inhaled or come into contact with skin or eyes. This definition is narrower than the definitions at European and international level and awaits amendment.

Radioactive waste is, by all definitions, hazardous to humans and the wider environment. It is, however, mostly excluded from the definitions and controls of dangerous waste as it is covered by its own special provisions, (see Chapter 9).[7]

Mining and Quarry waste is also dealt with mainly under other areas of legislation, in particular land use planning, (see Chapter 5). The Secretary of State does have power, however, to make this type of waste and agricultural waste subject to the provisions applicable for dealing with general waste.

Other waste is referred to, in the United Kingdom, as "*controlled waste*," in other words, that waste which is subject to controls apart from special waste. This includes household, industrial and commercial waste.[8]

Household waste includes waste from domestic premises, caravan sites, residential homes, educational establishments and nursing homes.

Industrial waste includes waste from factories, public transport facilities such as airports and bus stations, and premises used for the provision of public utilities.

Commercial waste means waste from premises used for a trade or business or for recreational purposes.

These definition may be subject to interpretation by the courts. In the recent judgment of the Divisional Court in *Thanet District Council* v. *Kent County Council*[9] it was held that seaweed which was collected from the beach by the authority in order to enhance

---

[6] Pt. II, Sched. II of the Regulations.
[7] See the Radioactive Substances Act 1993.
[8] E.P.A. 1990, s.75; the Controlled Waste Regulations 1992, (S.I. 1992 No. 558.) For licensing matters only the definitions under the former law apply and are to be found in Control of Pollution Act 1974, s.30 and the Collection and Disposal of Waste Regulations, (S.I. 1988 No. 819.)
[9] [1993] Env.L.R. 391.

the amenity of the area, and which was dumped on other land, was not controlled waste.

These definitions provide a classification of different types of waste and form the basis for the legislation relating to the duty to collect waste and the licensing obligations. However, there is an initial and fundamental question which must be answered before different types of waste can be classified – what is waste?

The government took the view that a single definition of waste should be adopted throughout the European Community. The definition of waste in the 1975 Framework Directive has, therefore, been adopted. This is implemented through the Waste Management Licensing Regulations 1994 which establishes a list of categories[9A]. Waste is defined as any substance or object in these categories "which the producer or the person in possession of it discards or intends or is required to discard." This supersedes the definition in section 75(2) of the Environmental Protection Act 1990.

One person, having no further use for an item may throw it away. Another person may have a use for it and retrieve it. Is it waste? The many charity shops which fill the high streets sell clothes and other items which have, for the most part been discarded by their former owners. Is that waste? Food waste was collected during the Second World War to feed the pigs – was that waste? A glass bottle can be reused, as can aluminium cans and foil – are they waste? Scrap metal merchants and rag and bone men operate on the basis of collecting other people's waste. The issue is critical for if an item is to be defined as waste, it then falls subject to the waste regime which involves the obligation to have a license to operate, and the statutory duty of care.

A High Court judge has given a definition of waste:

"It is, of course, a truism that one man's waste is another man's raw material. The fact that a price is paid by the collector of material to its originator is, no doubt, relevant; but I do not regard it as crucial. If I have an old fireplace to dispose of to a passing rag and bone man, its character as waste is not affected by whether or not I can persuade the latter to pay me 50 pence for it. In my judgment, the correct approach is to regard the material from the point of view of the person who produces it. Is it something which is produced as a product, or even as a by-product of his business, or is it something to be disposed of as useless?" (*Berridge Incinerators Ltd.* v. *Nottinghamshire County Council*.)[10]

[9A] Pt. II of Sched. 4 of the Waste Management Licensing Regulations 1994.
[10] This case is unreported but is cited in the D.O.E. Circular 13/88 on the "Control of Pollution Act 1974, The Collection and Disposal of Waste Regulations" at para. 2.7.

This case related to a planning matter as does *R. v. Rotherham Metropolitan Borough Council ex p. Rankin.*[11]

In this case planning permission was given to construct a waste recycling centre. Buildings which are to be used for the treatment of trade waste are subject to special provisions requiring the application to be advertised to enable the public to be informed of the planning proposal. This application was not advertised and a local resident challenged the local planning authority's decision on the ground that the development was for the treatment of trade waste. The centre was to collect used solvents from its customers, purify them and make them available for reuse. The judge held that it was wrong, under the relevant planning provisions, not to consider this process as involving the treatment of waste. He did not consider it essential to show that the item had no further use for it to constitute waste.

In the judgment in the *Rankin* decision, reference was made to an unreported case, *Charles Neil Ashcroft* v. *Michael McErlain Ltd.*[12] This case was concerned with the definition of waste under the Control of Pollution Act 1974 now repealed in respect of licensing matters. Again, the case involved material which was to be reused. Soil was taken from one field so that a road could be constructed. It was replaced on a paddock to raise the level. The approach taken by the court was to take, as a starting point, the ordinary everyday meaning of the word. For this, they looked to the Oxford English dictionary which included within the definition of waste: materials eliminated or thrown aside as worthless after the completion of a process. The court decided that excavated soil was capable of being waste although, in any particular case, it was a question for the justices to decide.

In *Kent County Council* v. *Queenborough Rolling Mill Company Limited,*[13] the site of a former pottery was being cleared of material which included ballast, china clay and pieces of china and pottery. The contractor clearing the site offered to supply the material to the owner of a site on the edge of an estuary which was particularly prone to subsidence. The arrangement was for the mutual convenience of the parties and no money changed hands. If the material fell within the definition of controlled waste then, when it was deposited on the estuary site a licence was required. The court held that it did constitute waste. The purpose to which the substance was

---

[11] (1990) 2 J.E.L. 250.
[12] (Decided on January 30, 1985.)
[13] (1990) 2 J.E.L. 257.

put was of no relevance. The nature of the material had to be considered at the time of its removal from the pottery site. If it was waste then, it remained waste when it was deposited, even if it at that point fulfilled a useful function.

This, therefore, indicates that the material is to be examined from the viewpoint of the person discarding it. This was also applied in the case of *Long* v. *Brook*.[14] The effect of this was to give the broadest interpretation to the meaning of waste. When the owner of an item no longer has a use for it, it becomes waste. The old fridge handed to the rag and bone man is waste; the glass bottle put in the recycling bin is waste, and so on.

There are many implications from this approach. Recycling is, currently, a predominant issue for environmentalists and governments have responded by adopting policies which encourage this as a method of waste disposal. If waste which is to be recycled is to be subject to the strict controls of the waste régime, then this is a disincentive. The test currently being applied by the British judiciary is clearly not based on value. This contrasts with the definition of waste posed by the World Health Organisation: "something which the owner no longer wants at a given place and time and which has no current or perceived market value."

However, the consideration of the value of the material may be entirely misplaced in environmental terms. The controls imposed by the waste régimes at all levels – national, European and international – are designed to prevent harm being caused by waste. Harm can be caused to human health or the wider environment. If a material is to be discarded by one person, then it has the capacity to cause harm whether it is to be reused by another person or to be buried in a landfill site. The ballast in the *Queenborough* decision had the same potential for harm wherever it was deposited. The contaminated solvents in the *Rankin* decision were as risky whether they were to be recycled or dumped. The determination of environmental hazard relies on the nature of the material, not its economic worth.

This definition tallies with the definition in the 1975 European Directive on waste[15] which defines it as any substance or object which the holder disposes of or is required to dispose of. The amended Directive lists categories of waste, disposal operations and operations which may lead to recovery. These lists are to be subject

---

[14] [1980] Crim.L.R. 109.
[15] Directive on waste, 75/442: [1975] (O.J. L194/39), as amended by Directive 91/156: [1991] O.J. L78/32.

to controls. The emphasis is on the quality of the material in the hands of the holder.[16] This definition has been upheld in two cases appearing before the European Court of Justice: *Vasseso* and *Zanetti*.[17] This definition is also reflected in the eleventh report of the Royal Commission on Environmental Pollution: "Managing Waste: the Duty of Care"[18] where waste is defined by reference to the person who wishes to dispose of it. However, the report continues to mix the concept of value into the definition when it states that matter is waste when somebody regards it as valueless and wants to get rid of it. It is arguable that this definition would not cover the contaminated solvents in the *Rankin* decision since the whole process was part of an operation which involved the collection of the dirty solvents, their clean up and their return. The holders of the contaminated solvents could not be said to regard them as valueless since the whole commercial arrangement was one operation. Waste paper and scrap cars can be sold. They must still constitute waste because of their potential to cause harm.

The United Kingdom Government responded to this debate with a paper issued in December 1993 entitled: "*The Definition of Waste*". It proposed that the original definition in the Environmental Protection Act 1990 should be replaced by the definition in the 1975 European Directive on Waste. This was effected by the Waste Management Licensing Regulations issued on May 1, 1994 which are supported by a Circular[18A]. In essence, the effect of this change is that only "those substances or objects which fall out of the commercial cycle or out of the chain of utility" will be subject to the controls which apply to the collection, transport, storage, recovery and disposal of waste.

Controls on waste

The waste régime in the United Kingdom. The régime distinguishes between controlled waste and special waste. The régime itself was in a state of flux pending the full implementation of the Environmental Protection Act 1990. Part II of that Act deals with the control of waste on land. The provisions in that Part relating to licensing were originally expected to be implemented by June 1, 1993, but were finally implemented on May 1, 1994. Virtually

---

[16] See the case analysis by Michael Purdue, (1990) 2 J.E.L. 259.
[17] Case 359/88, *Zanetti and Others*: [1990] I E.C.R. 1509, Lexis transcript.
[18] Cmnd. 9675 (1985).
[18A] D.O.E. Circular 11/94 "*Environmental Protection Act 1990: Part II Waste Management Licensing. The Framework Directive a Waste.*" See Addendum.

all of Part II of the Environmental Protection Act 1990 has now been implemented.

The administration of waste was altered by the Environmental Protection Act 1990, s.30. The functions of authorities are divided into three parts: regulation, collection and disposal. Much of the change is to do with the introduction of competitive tendering. Waste disposal authorities are to award waste disposal contracts through competitive tendering and are to make contracts with waste disposal contractors who may be private sector companies or companies set up by the local authority. A local authority waste disposal company must be at arm's length from the waste disposal authority.[19]

The licensing system was originally introduced by the Control of Pollution Act (C.O.P.A.) 1974 and licenses to deposit waste were available from the disposal authorities subject to a prior grant of planning permission. Under the Environmental Protection Act 1990, s.35, it is the waste regulation authority which is responsible for the issuing of a waste management licence. Conditions could be attached to the disposal licence under the Control of Pollution Act 1974, but the effect of these conditions was limited by the courts. In *Leigh Land Reclamation Ltd.* v. *Walsall M.B.C.*[20] it was held that the only time when breach of a condition constituted an offence was when it related to a *deposit* undertaken in breach of a condition. In other words, a breach of a condition relating to some other matter, such as the provision of eating facilities or sign boards, was not actionable.[21]

It has, however, been held in the Divisional Court decision of *R.* v. *Metropolitan Stipendiary Magistrate, ex p. the London Waste Regulation Authority and others* and the *County Council of the Royal County of Berkshire, ex p. Scott and another*,[22] that the necessity to obtain a licence under the C.O.P.A. 1974 applied to cases where waste was being held on a temporary basis at transfer stations, not

---

[19] D.O.E. Circular 8/91, Welsh Office Circular 24/9: "Competition for local authority waste disposal contracts and new arrangements for disposal operations," and see also *R* v. *Avon County Council ex parte Terry Adams Limited, The Times,* January 20, 1994.

[20] [1992] Env.L.R. 16.

[21] The *Leigh Land* case was held to have been wrongly decided on another point (see note 22).

[22] [1993] Env.L.R. 417. The Divisional Court decided that the earlier decision of the Divisional Court in *Leigh Land Reclamation Ltd. and Others* v. *Walsall Metropolitan Borough Council* was wrongly decided.

just to situations where waste had reached its final resting place. The Divisional Court considered that the policy of the C.O.P.A. 1974 was to regulate operations having substantial consequences for the local environment.

Controlled waste may not be deposited, treated, kept, or disposed of without a licence. The licensing method is used as a means of controlling waste. This method has not been changed by the Environmental Protection Act (E.P.A.).

There will, however, be changes in the nature of the offence which can be committed when waste is deposited, etc., without a licence once the E.P.A. is fully implemented.

The general offence of depositing waste is contained in section 33 of the E.P.A. Section 33(1)(c) provides that it is an offence to "treat, keep or dispose of controlled waste in a manner likely to cause pollution of the environment or harm to human health." A due diligence defence is available to the commission of this offence as well as the emergency defence and the defence of acting on employer's instructions. Thus, the Act does not follow the precedent for regulatory offences of creating a strict liability offence.

The offence created under section 33(1)(c) is notable for its breadth. "Pollution of the environment" is defined in section 29 to mean the release or escape of the waste into any medium so as to cause harm to man or any other living organisms supported by the environment. "Harm" is further defined to mean "harm to the health of living organisms or other interference with the ecological systems of which they form part and in the case of man includes offence to any of his senses or harm to his property." Thus, the offensive smell of a waste tip would be covered, as presumably would its unattractive appearance.

This offence can be committed whether or not the offender has a licence. The other parts of the section deal with the situation where waste is handled in some way without a licence or in breach of a condition in a licence. Section 33(1)(c) creates a new offence that is concerned with environmental protection not with enforcing the licensing regime.

The new offences in section 33(1)(a) and (b) replace the previous offences in section 3, Control of Pollution Act 1974. These deal with the liability for the deposit of waste without a licence. The offence in section 3(1)(a) of the C.O.P.A. 1974 was of causing or knowingly permitting the deposit of controlled waste on land or using plant or equipment for the deposit of waste. In the E.P.A. the offences have similarities except for one important difference; section 33 refers to *knowingly* causing or knowingly permitting such deposit. The new offence seems, therefore, to incorporate an element of knowledge which was lacking in the former offence under the C.O.P.A. 1974.[23]

In *Kent County Council* v. *Beaney*[24] the meaning of "knowingly permitting" under the Control of Pollution Act 1974 was considered and it was held that an inference could be drawn from the particular facts of the case that the respondent knew of the tipping that was taking place on his land.

The penalties have been substantially increased; six months imprisonment and/or a fine up to £20,000 in the magistrates' court, two years and/or an unlimited fine in the Crown Court. (In the case of special waste – controlled waste which is dangerous or difficult to treat – the penalty is the same except that the maximum sentence on indictment is five years imprisonment.)

The Duty of care, introduced by the Environmental Protection Act 1990, and in force from April 1, 1992, is an important and novel form of liability on producers and handlers of waste. Liability ceased, under the previous legislation, the moment the waste left their hands. Their liability will now extend beyond the moment the waste leaves their control. There are implications for insurance valuations and civil liability in this new duty of care.

The term "duty of care" is a familiar term derived from the law of tort and the famous case of *Donoghue* v. *Stevenson.* It is a common law principle which has been adopted by Parliament on previous occasions, (for example, in the duty owed by an occupier of land to visitors to that land.[25]) The central idea of the common law principle is that a person owes a duty to take care not to injure others by his acts or omissions. The duty extends down the chain of consumers who do not necessarily need to be connected by contract.

When the duty of care principle was first introduced it was understood as extending liability from "cradle to grave." In fact, the duty of the waste producer is not as extensive as that. Instead, it is designed to satisfy the European ideology on the environment that the polluter pays. The producer of waste is responsible for the proper disposal of the waste. This means that the producer must ensure it is transferred to a responsible carrier. The producer can no longer escape liability simply by passing the waste onto anyone else who could include the fly-tipper.

The duty as spelled out in the E.P.A. 1990, s.34, is:

[23] See J. Bates, *UK Waste Law* (1992).
[24] [1993] Env.L.R. 225.
[25] Occupiers' Liability Act 1957.

1. to prevent the commission of one of the statutory offences, (see above);
2. to prevent the escape of waste;
3. on transfer to make sure it is transferred to an authorised person;
4. to ensure that a written description goes with the waste so that others can comply with the duty.

So, the provisions focus on the control of waste prior to disposal and the steps to be taken on disposal. Liability after transfer will be limited to failing to take reasonable steps to detect and prevent breaches by the next person in the chain. It is likely, therefore, that a waste producer who complies with the rules of guidance on transferring waste, will be considered to have taken such reasonable steps.

This duty is imposed on all those who import, produce, carry, keep, treat or dispose of controlled waste, (E.P.A. 1990, s.34). This includes special waste. It was implemented by the Environmental Protection (Duty of Care) Regulations 1991,[26] which are supported by a Code of Practice, "Waste Management: the Duty of Care," and a circular issued jointly by the Department of the Environment, the Scottish Office and the Welsh Office, "The Duty of Care."[27] The only exception is in respect of the householder who produces domestic waste from the home. When we fill our dustbins with household rubbish, we are not "holders of waste" under the Act, and are not subject to the duty of care.

The Circular is directed at waste disposal authorities and offers advice and interpretation of the duty of care. Local authorities are also waste producers and are also subject to the duty of care. In their capacity as waste collection authorities they collect, carry or transfer waste through direct labour organisations. Where they award contracts to the private sector they will not be waste holders. However, they will be subject to the duty of care as brokers. This means that when an authority arranges for the transfer of waste the correct documentation will have to be produced. The circular contains a suggested transfer form for this purpose and urges authorities to produce standard documentation.

The Code of Practice provides guidance on how to discharge the duty of care imposed by section 34, Environmental Protection Act 1990. If a waste producer is taken to court for failing to comply with

---

[26] S.I. 199 No. 2839.
[27] 19/91, 63/91, 25/91.

the duty of care, the Code can be used in evidence. It has the same status as the Highway Code in a traffic case. So its contents are critical to the waste industry. If waste producers fail to follow the guidelines, they are exposing themselves to prosecution.

The Code gives step by step advice and is divided into six sections:

1. Waste producer to identify waste

Every person who handles the waste must be provided with a description of the waste so they know how to handle it. They should know its components in enough detail to know, for example, whether it can be safely transferred from one vehicle to another, what containers are appropriate and whether it can be mixed with other waste.

2. Duty to hold waste carefully

All holders of waste must keep it safely while it is under their control. They must also ensure it is in a fit state to travel. Under the new system the holder has responsibility for seeing the waste safely on its journey. The liability may not be "cradle to grave" but is more extensive than before when it ceased once physical possession had passed.

3. Check the transferee

Under the Controlled Waste (Registration of Carriers and Seizure of Vehicles) Regulations 1991, a comprehensive system of registration of carriers of waste was introduced from April 1, 1992. Registration may be refused if the carrier has been convicted of an offence connected with waste management and the authority think it would be undesirable.

Fears have been expressed that many small firms will be unaware of the new requirements. As some recognition of this, the Government granted carriers of construction waste an extra two months, (until June 1992), to apply for registration. The scrap metal industry were also concerned about the imposition of the duty of care and were given extra time to accommodate new arrangements. There are also some exemptions such as British Rail and charities.

Subject to that, holders of waste must ensure that the carrier is registered and is suitable for carrying the particular type of waste.

The Government envisaged that the rules would be enforced mutually by all the holders of waste. As one holder was required to check the credentials of the next holder in the chain in order to satisfy the duty of care, this was perceived as creating a mutual enforcement society.

4. Check the transferor

The transferee of waste must check that waste is not received from a source which is apparently in breach of the duty of care. The transfer note must be properly completed and the registration of the carrier delivering the waste should be checked. This means that a carrier without proper registration should be turned away; hence the concern in the industry that the new rules have not percolated through to the numerous small firms and one man operations engaged in carrying waste.

5. Checking the destination of the waste

There is no specific duty on a waste producer to audit the final destination of his waste. However, there is some encouragement for such a practice in the Code which states that such an audit and periodic site visits would provide evidence that an attempt had been made to prevent subsequent illegal treatment of the waste.

The waste manager should have a look to see that it appears to match the description. The practice of undertaking full checks on the composition of samples of the waste is encouraged.

6. Expert help and advice

Finally, the Code refers to the availability of advice from waste consultants and emphasises the primary responsibility of waste holders to discharge their duty of care.

Who must exercise the duty of care?

All persons who import, produce, carry, keep, treat or dispose of controlled waste, and persons having control of such waste as brokers, owe a duty to take care that an offence is not committed. There is no precise definition of "broker." However, the Code states that a waste consultant who is directing the eventual destination of the waste may be caught by the duty.

The law requires that all reasonable precautions and all due diligence have been exercised. The offence is not absolute. If all reasonable steps have been taken to prevent an escape causing damage then no prosecution will succeed. A trade practice or custom may be evidence of what is reasonable. On the other hand, a court may decide that a custom of the trade is a bad practice. So, a review of working practices may be advisable.

The new regulations, although they do not extend liability from cradle to grave as popular opinion had it, are clearly far more rigorous than the old. They are based on the principle that the polluter pays.

The European regime relating to the control of waste

This is founded on the 1975 framework Directive on waste[28] as amended in 1991.[29] This Directive states that its objectives include the protection of human health and the environment and that the recovery of waste should be encouraged. It provides for a system of permits for the treatment, storage and tipping of waste and provides for the application of the "polluter pays" principle in respect of costs not covered by the proceeds from treating the waste. It also advocates the development of measures at national level to prevent or reduce waste by such means as the development of clean technologies and the development of products which make the smallest possible contribution to increasing waste or other pollution hazards.

As a framework Directive, this has been followed by a number of daughter Directives dealing with narrower areas. For example, the 1976 Directive on the disposal of polychlorinated biphenyls and polychlorinated terphenyls[30] recognises the special hazards of these materials which are used as insulating material in transformers. They are very toxic and the Directive prescribes particular measure to control their disposal.

Of more general application is the 1991 Directive on hazardous waste.[31] This Directive prescribes more stringent rules for dealing with dangerous waste. It provides for the recording and identification of such waste when it is tipped and sets out rules for the mixing of such waste.

---

[28] Directive 75/442: [1975] O.J. L194/39.
[29] Directive 91/156: [1991] O.J. L78/32 and Directive 91/692: O.J. L377/48.
[30] Directive 76/403: [1976] O.J. L108/41.
[31] Directive 91/689: [1991] O.J. L377/20. This Directive replaces the 1978 Directive on toxic and dangerous waste, Directive 78/319: [1978] O.J. L84/43 as from December 31, 1993.

Means of Disposal

Waste can be disposed of by a variety of methods. It can be buried, burned or dumped in the sea or rivers. A major issue relating to the disposal of waste is the question of recycling.

At first sight, the concept of *recycling waste* and using it again is environmentally attractive. To eliminate waste must be a sound manoeuvre and to make something useful out of what would otherwise have been thrown away, appeals to a sense of ethics. Anyone who is accustomed to throwing waste food onto a compost heap and finding it has turned into crumbly brown soil six months later, will understand the charm of the idea of recycling. It appeals to the "waste not, want not" ethic.

But, in order to turn mouldy old food into fertiliser, nitrogen is required. The production of a useful material out of the waste uses up another useful material. Any process involving recycling will have this effect. When old newspapers are recycled, they require a lot of energy. When glass bottles are recovered, a heating process is required which uses energy. The system is even more complicated than that. A lorry must collect the recyclable material and must consume energy to do so.

There are various stages involved. The waste must first of all be reclaimed. It may be possible to reuse it without subjecting it to any further processing. Milk bottles are the classic example of this. We drink the milk, wash the bottle and place it outside the door to be collected by the milkman and refilled for another day. Recycling involves an additional process. Broken glass bottles can be processed and used in the making of new bottles, food waste can be composted and made into soil.

An essential feature of recycling is that the total waste collected, the waste stream, needs to be sorted into its constituent parts. Glass, clothing, tin, paper and other items need to be separated before recycling and reuse can take place. Some attempts have been made to achieve this by local authorities which provide separate bins for different commodities. These bins can be provided in focal places, such as superstore car parks. An alternative is to provide a system of a kerbside collection. The householder is provided with different coloured bags for different types of waste and leaves them for collection outside the property on the public footpath. This system has proved highly successful in Germany where householders have responded enthusiastically. However, this method is more expensive to run as collection costs are higher.[32] A sorting operation is expensive, and much can be saved if householders take responsibility themselves for sorting their own waste and taking it to centralised collection points. It is considered, however, that only a kerbside collection scheme will achieve the government target for recycling household waste which represents an increase of 4-5 times present recycling rates.[33]

The concept of recycling has acquired a moral tone and governments across Europe have succumbed to the political pressure by introducing policies on recycling which require progressively more material to be dealt with in this way. The tool of life cycle analysis is of use in this context, enabling an analysis of each stage of the product's life to be assessed for its environmental impact. This would ensure that the energy savings achieved are not outweighed by the energy costs expended on the process of recycling.

In the United Kingdom the concept of recycling was put firmly on the agenda in the Government's White Paper on the Environment "This Common Inheritance." This White Paper set a target of 25 per cent. of household waste to be recycled by the year 2000. Britain does, in fact, already have a reclamation industry which has a turnover of £2 billion per year. But less than 10 per cent. of the household waste that can be recycled is currently reclaimed. The Government estimates that 50 per cent. of all household waste is recyclable.

European Community policy also advocates recycling as a means of dealing with waste. The draft Packaging Directive is aimed at this end.

The E.P.A. 1990, s.49, imposes a duty on waste collection authorities to investigate what arrangement would be appropriate for dealing with household and commercial waste in their area. They must then prepare a plan setting out their proposals. The object of the Government's proposals is to minimise the amount of waste which has to be disposed of by reclaiming and recovering as much of the waste as possible. A Waste Management Paper No. 28[34] "Recycling" provides further information on this.

In keeping with the philosophy of introducing market forces into environmental regulation, a system of financial credits has been

---

[32] "An Overview of the Impact of Source Separation Schemes on the Domestic Waste Stream in the UK and their Relevance to the Government's Recycling Target." Warren Springs Laboratory, February 1993; "Economic Instruments and Recovery of Resources from Waste" (Department of Trade and Industry and D.O.E.)
[33] Ibid.
[34] HMSO.

introduced by the Environmental Protection Act 1990, s.52. The object of this is to encourage the use of recycling as a method of waste disposal. The system involves the waste disposal authority, (the body responsible for disposing of the waste), making payments to the waste collection authority, (the body responsible for collecting the waste), in respect of waste which they have collected for recycling. The amount to be paid will, eventually, represent the savings made in the long-term by the waste disposal authority in respect of their marginal disposal costs. They will have less waste to take to the landfill site or to the incinerator. If a third party, a charity, for example, collects waste for recycling, then they can receive a payment representing the saving made on collecting the waste and disposing of it. Regulations have been made which provide a method for calculating these costs.[35]

The idea of using financial instruments to encourage recycling is supported by environmentalists. Friends of the Earth, for example, encourage such a method but emphasise that it should only be seen as one way to encourage a reduction in the overall quantity of waste produced.[36]

Landfill is currently the most common method of disposing of waste in this country. At its most basic, this involves digging a hole in the ground and filling it with rubbish. Problems arise from leaching. This is the process whereby liquid seeps through the landfill and takes with it harmful chemicals from the waste. This leachate can leave the land contaminated, and can enter the groundwater supply and get into the rivers and waterways and the drinking water system. Another problem associated with landfill sites is the production of gases. As the waste which is buried rots down it can produce methane gas and carbon dioxide. Methane gas is potentially explosive.

The most usual method used to deal with the problem of leaching is the barrier method. This involves lining the site with a barrier to prevent seepage. A barrier may be a natural barrier formed from the rock or other material underlying the site. For example, a layer of clay soil may be an effective barrier for certain types of waste. Alternatively an engineering solution might have to be sought; that is the construction of a curtain wall out of appropriate materials.

---

[35] Environmental Protection (Waste Recycling Payments) Regulations 1992, (S.I. 1992 No. 462), amended by the Environmental Protection (Waste Recycling Payments) (Amendment) Regulations 1993, (S.I. 1993 No. 445).
[36] Friends of the Earth, "Using Financial Instruments and Other Measures to Reduce Waste and Encourage Re-Use and Recycling" (March 1993).

Such a solution is clearly the most expensive, in particular, if it is undertaken as a remedial solution for a site already in operation.

The problem of leaching is of most concern on sites which have taken hazardous waste. By its very nature such waste is dangerous or difficult to deal with. In the United Kingdom, it is the practice to undertake co-disposal; that is, to dispose of different types of waste in the same landfill site. An argument in support of this method of disposal is that where industrial waste is disposed of with household waste, the latter serves to reduce the concentrations of components leached from the former. In effect, the industrial leachate is diluted. In particular, domestic refuse can serve to neutralise acid wastes which arise in considerable amounts in the United Kingdom. They include heavy metals, for example, titanium in waste acids from the titanium dioxide industry and zinc, copper and nickel from metal finishing processes.[37]

It has, therefore, caused considerable consternation in the United Kingdom waste industry that the proposed Landfill Directive advocates mono-disposal – landfill sites should only accommodate one type of waste.[38] This consternation has also been expressed by the Royal Commission on Environmental Pollution.

Under section 35 of the Environmental Protection Act 1990 it is possible for waste regulation authorities to grant licences subject to conditions relating to the care of the site after it has been filled. In addition, under section 61 the waste regulation authority has power to enter and inspect closed landfills. Where they consider that these are in such a state as to cause harm to human health or pollution of the environment they can undertake such work as is reasonable and recover the cost from the current owner of the land.

Under the C.O.P.A. 1974, there were no such powers as those available under the E.P.A. 1990. The only method of control was through the planning system with the imposition of conditions by the local planning authority when granting planning permission.

The position in relation to the grant of the waste disposal licence has also changed on the coming into force of section 39 of the E.P.A. 1990. Under the C.O.P.A. 1974, once a waste disposal licence was surrendered, then the waste regulation authority had no further control over the site. Under section 39, however, the authority has a choice as to whether to accept a surrender of the licence. They are to inspect the land and seek further evidence from the licence

---

[37] See J.R. Gronow, A.N. Schofield, R.K. Jain eds., "Land Disposal of Hazardous Waste" (1988) in particular Chap. 3.5, p. 125.
[38] "UK Landfill Practice: Co-Disposal" (D.O.E., September 8, 1993) H.M.S.O.

holder if necessary. The NRA are to be consulted about the surrender. If the surrender is accepted then the waste regulation authority are to issue a certificate of completion which states that the authority are satisfied that the condition of the land is unlikely to cause harm to human health or pollution to the environment.

It can be seen that the provisions under the Environmental Protection Act 1990 considerably enhance the powers of waste regulation authorities to control closed landfill sites. Such sites may cause problems years after they have been closed. The holder of the licence will remain responsible for the site if the authority consider there is any risk to humans or the environment, such as the development of methane gas or toxic leachates, emanating from the site. The Act proposes no upper limit to the continuation of such liability.

Landfill accounts for the bulk of waste disposal in the United Kingdom, (90 per cent.). The other method of waste disposal is *incineration*. On the continent the reverse is true – incineration is the major form of waste disposal. When waste is burned in an incinerator there are two consequences: gases will be emitted into the air and residues in the form of ash and sludge will be left behind. Waste incinerators are therefore subject to air pollution control which falls under Part I of the Environmental Pollution Act 1990, (see Chapter 6, section 1 "Integrated Pollution Control.") They are not also subject to the controls on waste disposal under Part II. However, when the residue is discarded this is waste and is covered by Part II of the E.P.A. 1990.

The Royal Commission on Environmental Pollution has published a report on the "Incineration of Waste"[39] which concludes that under the new system of controls, waste incineration should play an increasing part in a national strategy on the management of waste. As a disincentive to landfill as a method of waste disposal, the Royal Commission recommended that a levy should be applied on all waste disposed of in this way. They also encouraged the use of reclamation of waste.

Packaging waste is a major contributor to the waste stream and to the problem of litter. The European Commission has issued a proposal for a Directive on packaging and packaging waste. Over a 10-year-period, it is intended that 90 per cent. of all package waste will be re-used and, therefore, will not enter the waste stream. In addition, the amount of packaging used should be reduced by the manufacturers. Packaging will bear an E.C. mark indicating

---

[39] Cm. 2181 (1993).

whether it is reusable. Member States will have to institute systems for collecting and sorting such waste.

These policies will clearly have a major impact on the manufacturing industry, as well as on the waste industry. It is worth reflecting that the collapsed "East" German system of minimal packaging and recycling, already had many of the characteristics proposed by this draft Directive.

Litter is a form of waste which is an integral part of a consumer society. The discarded cigarette packet or Coke tin in the street is aesthetically unattractive. An accumulation of such litter can attract rats and constitute a hazard to human health.

It is a criminal offence to throw down, drop or deposit in any other way, litter in public open places.[40] In a recent decision in the Ilkeston magistrates' court a fine of £50 was exacted on an offender who dropped an empty cigarette packet on a public road.

Local authorities have a duty to keep land and highways free from litter. This applies, in general, to public land, but it may be extended to areas of land owned privately where the Secretary of State so determines.[41]

There is also a Code of Practice on Litter and Refuse[42] which attempts to prescribe the standard of cleanliness to be achieved according to the nature of the area which is under consideration. For example, it recommends that areas which are heavily trafficked should be cleaned up more regularly than less heavily trafficked areas. It defines 11 broad categories of zones according to land usage and volume of traffic, such as beaches, roads, railway embankments and educational institutions.

The transhipment of waste arises because of the fact that waste is an economic good. Waste is bought and sold on international markets and is shipped around the world. The European proximity principle is applicable to waste and states that waste should be dealt with as near to its source as possible. Moving waste around over great distances – particularly hazardous waste – increases the chances of some environmental damage being caused.

Once waste is accepted as an economic good then the basic European principle of freedom of movement of goods comes into

---

[40] E.P.A. 1990, s.87 replacing a similar offence in the Litter Act 1983, s.1
[41] E.P.A. 1990, s.90.
[42] E.P.A. 1990: Code of Practice on Litter and Refuse issued by the D.O.E. Department of Transport, Department of Education and Science, Scottish Office, Welsh Office, January 1991.

play. The potential conflict between this principle and the principles relating to the protection of the environment become apparent. In the case of the *Wallonia*,[43] decided on July 9, 1992, these issues arose. The Walloon Regional Executive prohibited the disposal of waste from a foreign country in any depots other than installations for the destruction, neutralisation and disposal of toxic waste. In effect, this meant that waste from all sources outside Wallonia was banned. The Commission commenced action under Article 169 on the ground that this was in breach of the framework Directives on waste,[44] and Articles 30 and 36.

There was an initial question to be decided as to whether waste which is unusable and non-recyclable and therefore devoid of commercial value was covered by the rules on the free movement of goods. The court decided that since the waste was being transported across a border as part of a commercial transaction it was therefore subject to Article 30 regardless of the nature of those transactions. The Belgian Government argued that the decree was enacted to satisfy the mandatory requirement of environmental protection and protection of human health. It is unarguable that wastes can cause a hazard to the environment and to human health. The desire of the Belgian Government to limit the amount of waste coming into the country is understandable and probably an aim shared by many of the citizens of Europe, particularly those living alongside rubbish tips, whether that tip is a landfill site or a nuclear waste reprocessing plant. It would seem that Wallonia was in danger of becoming the rubbish tip of Belgium, if not Europe as a whole.

The Court then went on to consider the principle that environmental damage should be rectified at source – Article 130 r(2). From this it was inferred that wastes should be disposed of as near to the point that they were produced as possible – the proximity principle. The court viewed the transportation of waste as bad. They held that, taking into account the special character of waste, the measure was, therefore, not discriminatory. A distinction was made between special and other wastes, in that special wastes were adequately covered by Directive 84/631. For example, a Member State which decided that a particular consignment of special waste posed a potential problem in respect of environmental protection and public health, could ban its import. There was no necessity, therefore, for a general ban.

---

[43] Case C-2/90, *Commission v. Belgium*: [1992] O.J. C195/9. [1992] 1 E.C.R. 4431, [1993] 1 C.M.L.R. 365.
[44] Directive 75/442: [1975] O.J. L194/39; Directive 84/631: [1984] O.J. L326/31.

The reason for the transhipment of waste is likely to be economic. It may be cheaper to dispose of waste by shipping it to a foreign country, even taking into account transport costs, rather than disposing of it at home. This may be particularly apparent when contrasting the cost of disposing of waste in an industrialised country as against a Third World country.[45] Disposal costs in such countries may be cheaper because of the lack of regulatory controls, the lack of enforcement of controls or because of a lower standard of technology. Environmental consciousness in the Third World has been heightened, not least because of some disastrous incidents of waste dumping. One infamous example involved the dumping of toxic and radioactive waste in Nigeria by a private Italian company. When it was discovered by the Nigerian Government they insisted that it should be removed by the Italian Government. Eventually, the waste was shipped onto the ship, the Karin B, which was subsequently refused entry into a number of different countries until the Italian Government was forced to find a final resting place for the waste. The Organisation for African Unity has since signed a Convention banning outright the import of all forms of toxic waste into Africa and controlling transboundary movements of such waste generated in Africa.[46]

In Europe the existing provision is the Council Directive on the supervision and control within the European Community of the transfrontier shipment of hazardous waste.[47] This is to be replaced as from May 1, 1994 by the Council Regulation on the supervision and control of shipments of waste within, into and out of the European Community.[48] This Regulation results from the participation of the EEC in the 1989 Basle Convention on the Control of Transboundary Movements of Hazardous Wastes and their Disposal.

This Regulation provides for a prior notification procedure which will inform the appropriate authorities of the type and method of dealing with the waste. These authorities may then take whatever steps are necessary to protect the environment which may include objecting to the entry of the waste. The export of waste to other countries is banned unless these countries are EFTA countries and are parties to the Basle Convention. The Regulation deals with

---

[45] See Schmidt A., "Transboundary Movements of Waste under EC Law: the Emerging Regulatory Framework" (1992) 4 J.E.L. 57.
[46] Signed in Bamako, Mali on January 30, 1991, reproduced in (1990) 20 *Environmental Policy and Law* 173.
[47] Directive: [1984] O.J. L326/31.
[48] Directive 93/259: [1993] O.J. L30/1.

shipments of waste between Member States, within Member States, and outside the Community. For shipments within Member States a system of supervision and control is to be set up and notified to the Commission. The import of waste into the Community is also covered and limited to specific states. In certain cases, waste may pass through the territory of the Community on its way to its final resting place in another country. Such transhipment is also subject to a notification procedure and must be notified to the last competent authority of transit within the Community. The Regulation lists three categories of waste – green, amber and red – which are subject to different control procedures. Radioactive waste, to the extent that it is not otherwise controlled, is also included.

The earlier 1984 Directive on transhipment of waste is implemented in the United Kingdom by the Transfrontier Shipment of Hazardous Waste Regulations 1988.[49] These regulate the contract for the disposal of the waste, the export and import of waste, the duty of carriers and relevant documentation.

---

[49] S.I. 1988 No. 1562, and see the Department of Environment Circular 16/89 for advice on the Regulations.

Chapter Nine

Radioactive and other hazardous substances

INTRODUCTION

Many objects have the potential for damaging the environment; a potential which may vary according to the way they are handled or stored or disposed of. But some objects and substances have an intrinsically greater capacity for harm than others. Of these, radioactive substances would probably be accepted by most people as the ultimate in dangerous substances. Whereas, many hazardous substances are seen as having beneficial uses, nuclear power is perceived as an instrument of destruction. Its use in weapons makes its peaceable uses suspect in the eyes of many. The construction of new nuclear power stations is surrounded by controversy and opposition and lengthy inquiries take place. The inquiry into the installation of the Sizewell B power station, for instance, took over a year.

Yet, nuclear energy is of considerable significance in many countries. In France, most electric power is provided by the nuclear power stations and in the United Kingdom a significant amount comes from this source. Some countries, such as Sweden, have toyed with the idea of abandoning the development of nuclear power completely. For such countries, however, alternative sources such as hydro-electric power makes the decision to abandon nuclear power sources less difficult.

Many alternative sources of energy have their own environmental problems. Coal-fired power stations produce harmful emissions and HMIP have recently granted permission for a power station to be operated using an emulsion of tar in water, a particularly noxious substance imported from Venezuela. Alternative energy sources are frequently advocated as the environmental solution. These rely on renewable sources of energy. Wind power, for example, uses the action of the wind to drive the windmills which drive the generators.

Wave power has a similar action and solar panels are familiar to many people. But, even renewable energy sources have their environmental problems. Permission has recently been granted for several wind farms to be constructed. Opposition to these has been mounted by environmentalists on the grounds that they are noisy for local people, they spoil the landscape and the manufacture of steel and other materials for use in their construction has a significant impact on the environment. The construction of barrages in Cardiff Bay and on the River Severn have also met with opposition in terms of their appearance and their effect on the tidal flow of these waters.

Yet, nuclear power stands out as the most controversial of all sources of energy. A few infamous accidents have cemented this image firmly in the minds of most people. The accidents at Chernobyl which resulted in widespread contamination, and at Three Mile Island in the United States of America are amongst the most notorious. The plant at Sellafield, Cumbria, formerly known as Windscale, was the subject of a number of leaks and also a deliberate, although unplanned, discharge into the Irish Sea.

The risks of exposure to radiation have long been known to cause cancer. In addition, ante-natal exposure to radiation is thought to make the resulting offspring more vulnerable to certain malign conditions. Exposure which results in a genetic risk has been the subject of protracted scientific and legal argument.[1] The argument is that the exposure may cause a mutation in the genetic make-up of a father which then results in inherited defects by his future children. Many scientific studies have been conducted of children born to mothers resident near the Sellafield plant.[2] There is, apparently, a higher incidence of leukaemia in that vicinity. In a recent High Court decision, the judge, after a careful and length scrutiny of the scientific evidence, found that the case for genetic damage had not been made out on the balance of probabilities.[3] Since the case, a further report issued in October 1993 by the Nuclear Installations

---

[1] See also the Congenital Disabilities (Civil Liability) Act 1976.

[2] See, for example, Independent Advisory Group, "Investigation of the Possible Increased Incidence of Cancer in West Cumbria" (1984); M.J. Gardner et al, "Follow up study of children born to mothers resident in Seascale West Cumbria (birth cohort)" (1987) 295 British Medical Journal 822–827, October 3; Committee on Medical Aspects of Radiation in the Environment (COMARE), Second Report, "Investigation of the Possible Increased Incidence of Leukaemia in Young People Near the Dounreay Nuclear Establishment, Caithness, Scotland" (1988); Sir Douglas Black, "New Evidence on Childhood Leukaemia and Nuclear Establishments" (1987) 294 British Medical Journal 591.

[3] Elizabeth Reay v. British Nuclear Fuels plc and Vivien Jane Hope v. British Nuclear Fuels plc 1990 R. No 880; 1989 H. No 3689 (unreported).

Inspectorate, indicates that the debate on the scientific veracity of these matters is not yet over.[4]

Other consequences of radiation leaks involve contamination to the wider environment. This includes contamination of food sources used by humans. Controls are now available in this event. For instance, after the Chernobyl accident, controls on the movement of lambs and the sale of their meat were imposed as they were believed to be contaminated by eating the grass affected by the fallout.

In addition to radiation, other hazardous substances are singled out for special regulation and control.

Nuclear energy and the United Kingdom

The consolidating statute, the Radioactive Substances Act 1993, came into force on August 27, 1993 and replaces the provisions contained mostly in the 1960 Act of the same name.

It provides *a system of registration for users of radioactive material*; that is, anyone who keeps or uses, or causes or permits to be kept or used, any radioactive material for the purpose of an undertaking carried on by him. An authorisation must be made by the Chief Inspector of the Nuclear Installations Inspectorate, before such material can be kept or used on a site. The authorisation may be issued subject to conditions which may impose requirements relating to equipment or appliances on the premises and may involve structural alterations. The conditions may require the operator to mark the products so as to indicate that they are radioactive materials. The Chief Inspector is required to have regard to the amount and character of any radioactive waste arising from the use of radioactive material on the premises, when imposing conditions. The local authority must receive a copy of the certificate in cases where radioactive material is to be stored or accumulated on land within their area. There are also provisions for consultation with the local authority and any other public bodies, such as the NRA, where disposal of radioactive waste on or from the premises is to take place.

In addition to the well known nuclear establishments, this applies to many smaller or different operations. The radioactive materials, chiefly uranium and plutonium, are used in a range of industrial processes as well as for X-rays and other medical processes. These

---

[4] H.S.E. Investigations of Leukaemia and other cancers in the children of male workers at Sellafield.

materials are used in the manufacture of scientific instruments and clocks, for example. There are also controls on mobile radioactive apparatus, such as mobile X-ray equipment.

The disposal of radioactive waste has long been a matter of concern in environmental quarters. As has been seen in Chapter 8, there are special provisions for the disposal of special waste, that waste which is so difficult or dangerous to deal with. Radioactive waste comes into a category of its own and is separately controlled even from special waste. The Act requires that no person shall dispose of radioactive waste without an authorisation to do so. The controls apply not only to the disposal of radioactive waste but also to its accumulation. So, sites which accumulate radioactive waste prior to to its disposal require a specific authorisation for that. Some plants in the United Kingdom do exist primarily for the reprocessing of waste and, to that end, import radioactive waste from other countries.

The control of radioactive material is a matter for central government, although local authorities have a right to be notified of licensed premises. The National Radiological Protection Board is the national authority responsible for advising on protection standards.

A guide to the 1960 Act states that the objectives of radioactive waste management are to ensure that activities giving rise to radioactive waste are justified in terms of their overall benefit, to ensure that radiation exposure is reduced to levels which are as low as reasonably achievable, taking into account economic and social factors. The guide also lays down a level for determining the effective dose. The guide assumes that compliance with the safe dose for the population will ensure adequate protection for the environment. Disposal is permitted by conventional methods, (for example down the sewers), where this is deemed safe. Otherwise, burial is advocated on land at specified sites, or, suitably packaged, at sea. This practice engendered considerable controversy and was suspended in the 1980s as a result.

Enforcement of these provisions is available to the Chief Inspector through the mechanisms of enforcement and prohibition notices. An *enforcement notice* can be served where an operator is failing to comply with some condition attached to the authorisation. A *prohibition notice* is available where there is an imminent risk of pollution to the environment or of harm to human health. For this purpose, it is not relevant whether the activity posing this risk is in breach of the authorisation. The fact of the risk is sufficient. Breaches of these notices constitute an offence for which the penalty, in line with other environmental offences, is £20,000 or six months imprisonment on summary conviction, or an unlimited fine or five years imprisonment on indictment.

British Nuclear Fuels were successfully prosecuted under these provisions when, in November 1983, personnel at the Sellafield plant deliberately discharged slightly radioactive liquid into the Irish Sea. This incident resulted in considerable publicity as a result of the Greenpeace divers who became contaminated during an attempt to block the end of the pipe.[5]

Information concerning applications, documents, notices and convictions held by the Chief Inspector, is made available to the local authority for the benefit of the public who have access to it.[6] There are the usual limitations in respect of national security and commercial confidentiality.

An accident at the Sellafield nuclear power plant, (then Windscale), in 1957 was the main reason for the passing of the predecessor to the Nuclear Installations Act 1965,[7] although this Act was also passed to fulfil the obligations of the United Kingdom under various international agreements. This is the main Act which controls *the installation of nuclear reactors.* It requires that nuclear reactors may only be installed where a licence has been granted by the Health and Safety Executive. This covers installations for the production or use of atomic energy, preparatory processes, storage, processing or disposal of nuclear fuel or radioactive material.

Particularly hazardous processes such as the extraction of plutonium or uranium are subject to a further specific control. A written permit for this activity is required even though the site is subject to a nuclear site licence.

Conditions may be attached to the grant of the nuclear site licence where the Health and Safety Executive consider that they are necessary or desirable in the interests of safety. This can apply to normal operating conditions or to deal with the possibility of accidents or emergencies. In particular, they may attach conditions relating to maintaining a system of inspections, to the design, siting, construction, installation, operation, modification and maintenance of the plant and its installations.

---

[5] See C. Miller, "Radiological Risks and Civil Liability" (1989) 1 J.E.L. 10.

[6] D.O.E. Circular 21/90, "Local Authority Responsible for Public Access to Information Under the Radioactive Substances Act 1960 as amended by the Environmental Protection Act 1990."

[7] For a report of the inquiry into the accident where radioactive fission products escaped into the atmosphere after the negligent overheating of the reactor causing contamination of cattle and their milk and vegetation, see Cmnd. 302 (1957).

The Act also imposes on the operator of a nuclear site subject to a licence, *a duty to secure that no occurrence involving nuclear matter causes injury to any person or damage to any property of any person.* This includes the emission of ionising radiations from anything on the site which is not nuclear matter or from any waste discharged on or from the site. It might appear at first sight that this provision imposes an absolute liability on the operator to ensure that no such occurrence could possibly occur. In fact, the provision is something less than that. It provides that if there is such an occurrence then there is a duty of strict liability and compensation is payable in respect of the breach of this duty.

This point was considered in *Re Friends of the Earth*,[8] although it does not constitute precedent as the case fell on another point. In answer to the argument of Friends of the Earth that this required a guarantee of absolute safety, Gibson L.J. held that, this would mean that, in practice, no licence would ever be granted since it would be impossible to provide for every eventuality such as an unforeseeable natural event or some act of malice. He considered that Parliament could not have intended such an outcome, therefore, the operator was not required to give such absolute proof.

The extent of the duty was further considered in *Merlin v. British Nuclear Fuels plc.*[9] The plaintiffs owned a house near the Sellafield nuclear site. The house became the subject of a considerable amount of scientific and media interest because of the discovery of radionuclides in the household dust. The plaintiffs were concerned for their own and their children's health and, as a result, decided to move away. When they came to sell their house, they encountered great difficulty in doing so, and eventually sold it at a considerable loss to a Sellafield employee at a public auction. The judge rejected the argument that the presence of radionuclides constituted damage to property. He held that "damage to property" is restricted to physical damage to tangible property. Although he considered that the presence of radionuclides represented an increased risk to the health of the occupants of the house, he held that this was not covered by the Act, which only provided for compensation to be payable in the event of proved personal physical or mental injury.[10] So, although the Merlins had suffered considerable loss, as it was confined to loss of an economic nature, it was held not to be covered by the Act.

---

[8] [1988] J.P.L. 93, C.A.
[9] [1990] 3 W.L.R. 383.
[10] See the case analysis by Macrory, 3 J.E.L. 122 (1991).

The decision is consistent with the development of liability under the common law of negligence where damages for pure economic loss are not available.[11] So, although the decision of the judge is undoubtedly restrictive, it is not unexpected. It does mean that liability for damages within the nuclear industry, which is generally uninsurable, may not be extensive except in the most blatant cases of damage occurring physically to persons or their property.

The provisions relating to compensation where the operator is in breach of the statutory duty place an upper financial limit on the amount of claims payable in respect of any one occurrence. The current ceiling is £20 million for the larger installations and £5 million for the smaller ones. There is also an extended time period prescribed within which claims must be brought. The time period is 30 years from the date of the occurrence which gave rise to the claim. Where the occurrence is a continuing one or was one of a succession of occurrences attributable to one event, then time begins to run from the date of the last event. There is a special time period where the injury has been caused by nuclear matter which has been stolen, or thrown away or abandoned by the operator. In these circumstances the period is 20 years. Time begins to run from the day when the nuclear matter was stolen or abandoned.

Damage can occur when the nuclear matter is being transported from or to the site. The Act extends the statutory duty to the carrier of the material.

There is a *defence* available to the operator, which is that the emission occurred as a result of hostile action in the course of armed conflict. There is no defence, however, where the emission is a result of a natural disaster even if it is of such an exceptionable nature that it could not have been reasonably foreseen. One of the major fears shared by operators of nuclear installations is the effect of an earthquake. A major earthquake could crack the reactor and cause a release of radioactivity. There are, of course, two ways of dealing with such a problem. One is not to build reactors in areas subject to earth movements; the other is to ensure construction design to withstand quakes. However, there have, so far, been no reported cases of accidents resulting from natural disasters. All the accidents have occurred as a result of some human accident or intervention.

---

[11] See *Murphy* v. *Brentwood D.C.* [1991] 1 A.C. 398.

Nuclear energy and Europe.

The Euratom Treaty signed in 1957, was intended to create the conditions for the establishment and growth of the nuclear industries in Europe. Its objectives included the establishment of uniform safety standards for the health of workers and the general public and the development of a common market in specialised materials and equipment.

Directives have laid down basic radiation standards for health protection, and radioactivity levels are to be monitored at Community level. For example, the 1980 Directive lays down such basic standards.[12] There are also measures within the Euratom Treaty which require the Commission to be notified when a discharge of radioactive substances is to occur which may contaminate other states. Further, the Commission is to be consulted when Member States propose to conduct particularly hazardous experiments within their territories. This is subject to the Commission's consent where it may affect other Member States.

However, beyond this, there are few measures at Community level. Nuclear power, and its close links to military and defence purposes, has remained largely a matter for national competence.

Nuclear energy and international law[13]

There has been less reluctance to deal with the issue of nuclear power at international levels, yet, the effectiveness of such international controls as there are, leave much to be desired.

The main agency at international level is the International Atomic Energy Agency, but this is not an environmental protection agency. Its main role is to promote the development of nuclear power for peaceful purposes with safety controls as a by-product of its main activities. Although this agency does lay down safety standards, there is little in the way of monitoring and enforcement at this level.

There are also a number of conventions with varying degrees of support. For example, the Paris Convention of 1960 deals with nuclear accidents in western Europe. The Vienna Convention of 1963 extends this globally, the Brussels Convention of 1962, deals with the liability of operators of nuclear ships, and the 1971 Brussels

---

[12] Directive amending the Directive laying down the basic safety standards for the health protection of the general public and worker against the dangers of ionising radiation, Directive 80/836: [1980] O.J. L246/1.

[13] For a detailed analysis see, Birnie and Boyle, *International Law and the Environment*, (1992) Chap. 9.

Convention relates to civil liability in the field of maritime carriage of nuclear material. These conventions have received limited support from nuclear powers.

For example, in the United Kingdom, the Atomic Energy Act 1989 was passed to provide for the acceptance of the 1986 IAEA Convention on Assistance in the case of a nuclear accident or radiological emergency. But, the United Kingdom is still not a party.

Other Hazardous Substances.

There are other measures which deal with a broader range of hazardous substances.

For example, if an accident occurs resulting in a leak of a hazardous substance, then *contamination of food supplies* may occur. In that event, it may be necessary to take measures to ensure that the food is not eaten or moved. Powers are available under Part I of the Food and Environment Protection Act 1985 to deal with this eventuality. This Act applies to radioactive contamination as well as to contamination by other sources such as chemical leaks. In fact, the Act does not define what substances are covered so there is scope for drawing the widest interpretation of these provisions.

The Act provides that an *emergency order* can be made by the Minister where there are circumstances likely to cause a hazard to human health through human consumption of food. A number of orders under this Act were made in relation to the Chernobyl accident restricting the consumption of sheep. Other orders have related to the presence of dioxin in food at a farm in Derbyshire,[14] and lead in ducks and geese at a farm in Shropshire,[15] for example. The order can prohibit agricultural activities, picking wild plants, slaughtering farm animals, fishing or food processing.

There are also powers in Part VIII of the E.P.A. 1990 for the Secretary of State to prohibit or restrict the *importation, use, supply or storage* of injurious substances or articles. Various regulations have been passed under this provision dealing with such substances as anglers' lead weights, (a cause of lead poisoning in swans), and certain paints. This part of the Act also gives the Secretary of State power to ban the importation or exportation of waste where this is done for the purpose of preventing any risk of pollution of the

---

[14] The Food Protection (Emergency Prohibitions) (Dioxins) (England) (No. 2) Order 1992, (S.I. 1992 No. 1274).
[15] The Food Protection (Emergency Prohibitions) (Lead in Ducks and Geese) (England) Order 1992, (S.I. 1992 No. 2726).

environment or of harm to human health. This is reflective of the decision of the Wallonian Government which banned the import of waste into Wallonia. This was tested by the European Court in the *Commission* v. *Belgium*[16] where the Court decided that this breach of the provisions relating to the freedom of movement of goods was acceptable where protection of the environment was a higher priority.

There are also measures relating to the *transport of hazardous substances*. There are separate measures for radioactive substances and other hazardous substances.

The Radioactive Substances (Carriage by Road) (Great Britain) Regulations 1974[17] prescribes a number of requirements where radioactive materials are being moved by road. A Code of Practice[18] sets out detailed matters relating to packaging and certification.

The Transfrontier Shipment of Radioactive Waste Regulations 1993[19] implement Council Directive 92/3/Euraton on the supervision and control of shipments of radioactive waste between member states and into and out of the Community. Such shipments must be subject to the approval and authorisation of the Chief Inspector.

The Road Traffic (Carriage of Dangerous Substances in Road Tankers and Tank Containers) Regulations 1992[20] deals with the carriage of such substances as are contained in the approved list.

The classification, packaging and labelling of dangerous substances

This is dealt with by Regulations which implement amongst other E.C. directives, the European Chemicals Directive 67/548 as amended.[21] These provide for a system of testing and notification of new chemicals before they are placed on the market. It is a preventive measure which requires dangerous substances to be tested prior to their general use for their effects on people and on the environment.

---

[16] See Chap. 8.
[17] S.I. 1974 No. 1735.
[18] Code of Practice for the Carriage of radiative materials by road issued by the Department of Transport in 1975.
[19] S.I. 1993/3031.
[20] S.I. 1992 No. 743.
[21] Chemical Hazard Information and Packaging Regulations 1993, (S.I. 1993/1746).

Pesticides are specifically provided for under Part III of the E.P.A. 1990. This part of the Act enables regulations to be made for the purpose of keeping under continuous review the development of means to protect the health of humans, animals and plants, to safeguard the environment, and to secure safe methods of controlling pests. Regulations under earlier provisions have been made,[22] and there is in existence an advisory committee on pesticides.[23]

Installation using hazardous substances

This may be as catastrophic in the potential harm which may be done in the event of an accident, as nuclear installations. There are notable examples. The plant at Flixborough which manufactured nylon, suffered an explosion which allowed the release of a substance called cyclohexane. A number of workers in the factory died in the explosion and many people outside the works suffered injuries. Further, the leak of dioxin from the Seveso plant in Italy caused problems for the surrounding population. There are now procedures for notifying the existence of plants handling dangerous substances, and for establishing accident plans. The Health and Safety Executive are in charge of the implementation of these measures.[24] The Control of Industrial Major Accident Hazards Regulations 1984, which implement the European Directive known as the Seveso Directive, list the hazardous substances which are subject to the controls. They do not apply to nuclear installations or installations which are used for defence purposes. The regulations are an example of the preventive principle in operation. They require the manufacturer to identify the major accident hazards and take adequate steps to prevent them and to ensure that the workforce have sufficient information, training and equipment to ensure their safety. In the event of an accident, the manufacturer is obliged to take steps to limit its consequences for the environment and for people. To this end, the manufacturer must prepare on-site emergency plans, and the local authority must prepare off-site emergency

---

[22] See, *e.g.*, the Pesticides (Maximum Residue Levels in Food) Regulations 1988, (S.I. 1988 No. 1378).

[23] See, *e.g.* a report published by M.A.F.F. prepared by the advisory committee on Pesticides "Pesticide Poisoning of Animals 1992; Investigation of suspected incidents in the U.K. A report of the Environmental Panel of the advisory committee on pesticides" (Sept 1993).

[24] The Notification of Installations Handling Hazardous Substances Regulations 1982 and the Control of Industrial Major Accident Hazards Regulations 1984 which implements the requirements of the European Seveso Directive.

plans. There is also a provision for the public living in the locality to be informed of the hazards.

Genetically modified organisms

These organisms have come to be dealt with under the heading of hazardous substances requiring special controls, in part because of their novelty. When James Watson and Francis Crick became involved in research into the structure of D.N.A. in the 1950s at the Cavendish Laboratory in Cambridge, they triggered one of the most radical developments in the history of biochemistry.[25]

D.N.A. is the shorthand name for deoxyribonucleic acid. It is a molecule made up of four separate chemicals which is the basis for all living things. Each D.N.A molecule contains millions of these four chemicals. The four chemicals are identified by the letters A, T, C and G. The basic combination of these millions of chemicals determine whether the living thing is, for example, a tree, a person or cat. But the combinations are more refined than that. When they are broken down, it is possible to know which particular combination in one person causes that person to have, for example, cystic fibrosis or Down's syndrome.[26] Around the world, scientists are examining these combinations and are working out the various sequences which give rise to all the different conditions from which we suffer.[27] This is fundamental research which means we will eventually know the precise chemical structure which determines the predisposition to all the various human conditions, good and bad.

The understanding of the D.N.A. molecule explains the process of evolution. Different combinations of the four chemicals which make up D.N.A. have arisen over the aeons to create different species or different characteristics within species. Man's knowledge of this chemical structure means that we can interfere in the evolutionary process and speed it up or change its direction. For example, we could use our understanding of the consequences of a particular structure of the D.N.A. molecule to abort all embryos containing it, thus eliminating certain types of disease. If the evolutionary process were to take its natural course, the disease might eventually be eliminated because of the factors such as the failure of individuals

---

[25] See James Watson's personal account of the discovery of D.N.A. in "Double Helix" (1968).

[26] For a more scientific description of D.N.A. any of the many scientific textbooks on this subject should be consulted.

[27] This international project is known as the Genome project.

prone to it to breed. Another example of the evolutionary process relates to our discovery and use of antibiotics. Their reaction with bacteria can cause a change in the D.N.A. which might have the effect of making the bacterium resistant to a particular antibiotic. A danger is that this knowledge could be used in hostile circumstances to create germ warfare. If one state manipulated the D.N.A. structure of the flu virus so as to create a new and fatal form, for which they had alone developed a vaccine, this could be spread amongst the enemy troops to deadly effect.

There are various consequences of this development in the understanding of biochemistry. A human embryo can be examined and the structure of its D.N.A. will inform us as to whether it will suffer certain illnesses. But, at this level, the information simply tells us a state of affairs. It may dictate our conduct in that we might use the knowledge to decide whether to abort an embryo. The next and inevitable step, however, is to use this knowledge to manipulate the combination of the millions of chemicals in one D.N.A. molecule to create something different. The Jurassic Park fear is that, knowing the particular combination of chemicals which made up dinosaurs, we could recreate them. Alternatively, the Frankenstein fear is that we could manipulate the combination of chemicals to create something new and fearsome. Having created a new organism, we may not know the effect that organism would have once released into the atmosphere. For example, suppose we create an organism that can consume oil. This would have huge advantages in dealing with environmental pollution caused by marine oil spills.[28] But, having been launched into the environment, could we lose control of it? Could it go on to consume the oil in the holds of our ocean-going tankers or even get into our oilfields? What further unknown consequences could it have? This is the theme of our modern horror stories.

In fact, there is no known evidence so far to support these fears. The uses to which this knowledge is being put have been benign and without unexpected environmental consequences. The knowledge of the combination of the chemicals in the D.N.A. molecule which give rise to cystic fibrosis has been used to develop remedial treatment for the condition. In the plant kingdom, knowledge of D.N.A. structures is being used to create novel foods which may have resistance to certain diseases or which may be able to grow in

---

[28] See Professor Peberdy, "Genetic Engineering" in Garner's Environmental Law Encyclopedia, Vol. 2, VIA/5 and 6, paragraphs 19–22.

inhospitable parts of the world, such as desert regions or areas where the land is saline. In the animal kingdom, combinations of D.N.A. have been introduced into pigs and goats which cause them to produce milk with human characteristics or which contain substances useful to us such as insulin or antibodies.

In the light of these developments, Part VI of the E.P.A. 1990 was passed. Its purpose is to prevent or minimise any damage to the environment as a result of the escape or release of genetically modified organisms. This Act is entirely novel within this field and represents the first attempt to introduce legislation about biotechnological developments. In one sense, mankind has been interfering with the genetic make-up of species for centuries. One glance at our dogs will confirm that. Selective breeding has created different types of dogs with certain characteristics favoured by mankind. The Act is not concerned with selective breeding of this type. The Act is concerned with genetic manipulation which, to give a crude example, can cause a dog to have characteristics derived from a cat.

Environmental damage is broadly defined to include damage to all the media and harm includes harm to the health of humans or other living organisms, or other interference with the ecological systems of which they form part. In the case of man, harm is defined as in other legislation to include harm to any of his senses or to his property.

The organism does not need to be free floating. It has escaped if it is ingested or inhaled by a person for example and is covered by the provisions of the Act.

The Act prescribes general controls which require that a risk assessment should be undertaken where such organisms are to be imported, acquired, kept or released into the environment, or marketed.[29] A record of the assessment may have to be kept. Reasonable steps must be taken to identify what risks there are to the environment and must identify any precautions to be taken to prevent their escape. In addition the BATNEEC principle applies; they must use the best available techniques not entailing excessive cost for preventing any damage to the environment being caused as a result of their release.

Enforcement powers are available to the Secretary of State by virtue of the *prohibition notice*. This can be served where there is believed to be a risk of causing damage to the environment. This can prohibit the import, acquisition, release or marketing of any such

---

[29] Exemptions are contained in the Genetically Modified Organisms (Contained Use) Regulations 1993.

organism.[30] There are also specific consent provisions in relation to organisms which are considered to pose a greater threat to the environment. In these cases it is necessary to have the consent of the Secretary of State before these organisms can be released.[31] Under the European Directive on Deliberate Release, referred to above, there are requirements, in respect of certain organisms, for consent to be given by the Commission of the European Communities, before a release can take place.

Where the Secretary of State gives his consent, he can attach conditions in addition to the BATNEEC condition. Breach of the conditions or any requirement of the Act, is an offence.

The Secretary of State is required to keep a public register of information containing prohibition notices, description of organisms, consents, etc.

---

[30] See the Genetically Modified Organisms (Deliberate Release) Regulations 1992, (S.I. 1992/3280), which give effect to the European Directive on deliberate releases, Directive 90/220: [1990] O.J. L117/15.

[31] See the Deliberate Release Regulations 1992 referred to in note 30, above.

Chapter Ten

Emerging Trends

INTRODUCTION

Politics and science, (or, perhaps it should be more correctly termed technology), remain the two major influences on the future development of environmental law. The growth of the green movement and its sudden decline in the face of an unfavourable economic climate have already been charted. But environmental issues have acquired a momentum of their own. The emphasis on the development of clean technologies and techniques which minimise the use of natural resources means that the industrial world will undertake research and development in these areas. Those countries at the forefront of these developments will become world leaders in the field thus having an economic impact of their own. Technology transfer to the developing world will form another aspect of this development. The environmental technology industries will be good for the economies of their countries thus creating a political will in their favour. Such developments, while good economically for the countries promoting them, present another way in which the economies of the Third World could be further dominated by those of the industrialised states. Thus an objective which appears to be environmentally sincere could simply amount to a strategy to be adopted in a trade war.

GREEN POLITICS

The United States of America

In the United States of America, the change in administration in 1992 was heralded as a bonus for environmentalists. The previous administrations under Presidents Reagan and Bush were perceived as being fundamentally hostile to the interests of environmentalists despite the fact that, historically, the U.S.A has been seen from across the Atlantic as a role model on environmental issues. President Bush's stance at the Rio Conference was clearly against the development of global green policies. President Clinton's campaign manifesto always included the slogan, "Should we not put people first?," but the incoming Vice-President, Al Gore, author of the book "Earth in the Balance" already had a reputation as a keen environmentalist. His policies included technology transfer for the developing countries combined with financial aid, a population programme for the world and the enhancement of environmental awareness on a worldwide scale through internationally agreed treaties. The precise role which environmental issues will play in the administration of President Clinton still, however, awaits clarification. The establishment of the North American Free Trade Agreement raises doubts as to the status of environmental issues. One effect of the agreement feared by environmentalists is that industry will move to Mexico where pollution control and environmental regulations are much less stringent than in Canada or the U.S.A. Prior to the election, President Clinton's support for NAFTA was unclear. Since election he moved firmly in favour of it, showing an inclination to support industry and economic progress at the expense of environmental protection.

The European Union

The firm legal basis for environmental issues in the Treaty on European Union demonstrates a clear commitment at European level to the development of environmental law. Yet, the struggles between the Member States over the extent to which the unification between them was acceptable may, ironically, be paid for by the environment. The European Union is moving into the next stage of its historical development and the development of such a federation will inevitably be tortuous. Indeed, the developments of such federations throughout history have frequently been marked by war and civil strife. The status of environmental issues is part of the struggle for supremacy of the European legal order over the Member States and their desire for national sovereignty. It is not a peculiar British practice; the Germans were the last to succumb to the Maastricht Treaty after it had wound its way through the German constitutional court.

The concept of subsidiarity will be the mechanism used by Member States to argue that environmental matters should be dealt with at national level. The Maastricht Treaty opens up the potential for the development of a unified European policy within the fields of town and country planning, water management and energy supplies. But, with over 200 Directives already issued before the environment was official European policy, the problems associated with over-regulation and under-enforcement have become apparent and may well have weakened the power of the Commission to produce further proposals for harmonising environmental controls across the Union. In many instances, there has not simply been a failure to enforce Community law, but there has been a failure even to check whether compliance has taken place. Where enforcement proceedings are brought, (and they have been brought against every country in respect of the Water Directives, for example), they are normally triggered by a member of the public rather than by a formal process of enforcement controlled by the Commission. Enforcement may, as a result, be erratic, and dependent on the level of environmental education amongst local populations. The establishment of the European Environment Agency may change this in the future.

The United Kingdom argues strongly for the concept of subsidiarity to be introduced into environmental decision-making. The argument is that there is no reason why domestic problems of pollution should be a matter of general European concern. If Lake Windermere is polluted, for example, why should that be of the same concern to other Europeans as would the pollution of the North Sea? However, if there is a diversity in environmental standards, this will affect competitiveness between Member States. If one government imposes lower environmental standards, this may cause a differentiation between health and safety standards and profitability. The Procurement Directives now require that public contracts should be advertised and their criteria set in such a way as to make them available for open competition across the Community. Any distortions caused by local variations in environmental regulations will affect the criteria. But, there may be good reasons for different environmental standards. Some European countries may choose to spend more money on improving the living conditions of their citizens, rather than providing reservations for birds. Conversely, environmental pollution might have a more ravaging effect on local populations in poorer countries than in richer countries. Dysentery is more likely to cause death in a population which is less well fed and clothed than another. In a country where water is drawn and drunk direct from its source, the need for the source to be unpolluted is more critical than in a country where the water will go through a purification programme before being consumed. The issue of subsidiarity, therefore, may not simply be a political protest by the United Kingdom reacting against a supra-national European state. It can raise fundamental questions about the priority, in terms of spending, to be accorded to different environmental initiatives. If the members of the club do not start from the same starting point in relation to their economies and the prosperity of their individual citizens, then, the imposition of harmonised environmental controls will emphasise rather than eradicate, such differences.

The Commission states that 85 per cent. of Directives are transposed into national law, although there are problems with Italy, which is said to have transposed only 59 per cent., and Greece – 76 per cent.[1] There are no figures available on the extent to which countries enforce the laws once transposed into national legislation. This has meant that there has been an uneven application of some environmental measures around the Community which has encouraged a disinclination to comply. In addition, where measures are taken which incorporate the precautionary principle, rather than being based on sound scientific evidence, then the costs of compliance will be brought into question. The Drinking Water Directive is an example of this. It incorporates measures which require the reduction of certain chemicals whose harm is not clearly established. It also incorporates requirements as to the colour of water, a measure which is not necessarily related to health and safety but which is cosmetic. While such measures may be highly desirable, there may be an argument put by the poorer countries that the costs of implementation are too high. It has been one of the candidates for subsidiarity supported by the United Kingdom along with the Urban Waste Water Treatment Directive, which, it is said, will cost £10 billion pounds to implement in the United Kingdom. However, the notion of retreating from universally agreed standards of the most basic kind, that is, those relating to the water that we drink, has perhaps been so radical that it may be abandoned. It is also worth bearing in mind, that the Water Directives were agreed under the former procedure for the issuing of Directives, which required a unanimous approval by the Member States. Under the post-Maastricht procedures such decisions may be made by qualified majority. If there has been such difficulty in implementing decisions made by a unanimous decision, then the future for decisions made merely by a majority looks bleak.

However, although the future for European environmental policy is not rosy, there are still new initiatives being launched and, it may be that once the administration recovers from the turbulence caused by the adoption of the Maastricht Treaty, a new approach to the

---

[1] See Bronwen Maddox, "High Cost of a Cleaner Europe" *Financial Times*, November 3, 1993.

environment will evolve. Initiatives such as the development of carbon taxes are being pursued as draft proposals. As a general policy development, the approach which uses the market as a method of control instead of regulation, appears likely to achieve popularity. It is in keeping with the approach desired by the United Kingdom Government. Proposals relating to the establishment of a régime of civil liability for environmental damage and the introduction of a system for the environmental assessment of plans and policies have not been abandoned, although they remain currently in abeyance. It would be extraordinary if, having formally adopted a clear legal basis for the development of European environmental policy, the Community then retreated from this position.

The United Kingdom

In the United Kingdom a number of setbacks in the development of environmental law have been encountered. The ethos of the Conservative Governments of the last 15 years has been to reduce the intervention of government in the lives of the citizens. This was carried forward in the Deregulation and Contracting Out Bill announced in 1993.[2] Such an approach is antipathetic to the European concept of a regulatory system. The present Government has moved towards a programme of removing a number of regulations such as those concerning clean air and food safety, amongst others. The purpose of this manoeuvre is intended to encourage industry at a difficult time; to reduce the burdens on industry by encouraging free trade. Trade implies a lack of government intervention, whereas for environmentalists, such intervention is perceived as a necessity.

The impact of free trade versus the environment was demonstrated in 1992, when an impartial GATT Dispute Settlement Panel ruled that the U.S.A. could not prohibit the import, from Mexico, of tuna fish which were being caught in nets which also trapped and suffocated dolphins. In effect this meant that the U.S.A. could not prescribe environmental protection rules for another state. Thus, it is argued that, if the United Kingdom promotes unregulated free trade, this will be to the detriment of the environment. The converse argument made by the proponents of the free market, is that if the economy is encouraged, then taxes can be levied, and a revenue will be raised which can be spent on environmental initiatives. This

---

[2] See the proposals of the seven Business Deregulation Task Forces: "Proposals for Reform" published by the Department of Trade and Industry on January 19, 1994.

would result in richer countries becoming more environmentally aware than the poorer countries. However, the Third World, which frequently chafes against the "environmental imperialism" of the industrialised countries, protests that this environmental awareness is born of a longer history of environmental damage in need of remedial treatment; that the "northern" countries have the greatest adverse impact on the world's environment. After all, economic growth has, to date, caused more pollution, not less. This may change if the European emphasis on clean technologies succeeds, but, even then, every process has some negative effect.

One of the problems of the United Kingdom approach of rolling back the "regulatory burdens" and encouraging free trade is that the objective of the traders is to maximise profits without regard to the quality of life or the environmental consequences. Trade is perceived by the managers of many of the world economies as a solution to the problems of recession. World trade is a fact of life. One glance at the clothes we wear and the food we eat is sufficient evidence of that fact. What outrage there would be, if our governments were to ban the import of oranges, for example. Although John Maynard Keynes advocated self-sufficiency and the development of home economies, it is simply the case that a complex and interdependent network of global trading now exists. Little short of wartime exigencies or social revolution can dismantle it. The restriction of trade with its consequent environmental problems is not viable. The issue is whether it is better to control it by regulation rather than allow it free rein.

United Kingdom initiatives. The White Paper, "This Common Inheritance", heralded a new approach by the United Kingdom Government to environmental issues which led to the enactment of the E.P.A. 1990. The Act was to be implemented in stages, and a number of parts of it are now effective. However, some key initiatives have failed to materialise according to schedule: the contaminated land registers,[3] the "clean up" liability,[4] and the introduction of the system for the management of waste[5] were notorious examples. The provision which was designed to implement the system of registration for contaminated land was subjected to a consultation process, and the reaction from the construction and property industries was generally negative. However, the attitude of the concerned

---

[3] E.P.A. 1990, s.143.
[4] E.P.A. 1990, s.61.
[5] E.P.A. 1990, Pt. II.

industries at the apparent abandonment of such proposals is not universally supportive. The effect of the delays is to create uncertainty in the industrial communities at a time when environmental consciousness is very high. Companies which are developing environmental policies or undertaking environmental audits do not welcome sudden changes in policy. Frequently an anticipated regulation will be put into practice in advance on a voluntary basis. In addition, once an issue such as that of the liability for contaminated land has been highlighted, it results in greater awareness of the potential problems and can, for example, result in more detailed preliminary enquiries prior to the completion of the purchase. A proposal has a tendency to acquire a momentum of its own if the climate is right.

New initiatives and policy development on environmental matters have not, however, ceased to flow from the D.O.E. New consultation papers continue to be produced on various aspects of town and country planning policy, and new initiatives such as recent research on the role of social scientists in understanding environmental concerns and their impact on individuals,[6] still flow from the department.

Privatisation. The policy of privatisation has implications for the environment. This has been evidenced by the privatisation of the water industry, where the high capital costs of implementing the Water Directives fall on private companies which will pass the costs onto the consumer. This belies the principle that the polluter should pay. Where the costs fall on the consumer, it is the most vulnerable that are at most risk from the ultimate sanction, that of disconnection. The use of water is not a private health matter, it has implications for the health of the public in general.

The furtherance of the privatisation policy to the rail network in the absence of a coherent transport policy is evidence of the impact that political decisions can have for the environment. The use of the car and the lorry has local and global environmental effects. It pollutes the immediate atmosphere and possibly also causes a greenhouse effect; lorries and cars are dangerous on the roads and have a significant detrimental effect on the amenity of the town and the countryside.

---

[6] Keith Mason, "The U.K. Environmental Foresight Programme" (Centre for the Exploitation of Science).

International environmental initiatives

The United Nations continues to promote opportunities for international progress on global environmental issues. In 1992 the United Nations Conference on the Environment and Development was held in Rio de Janeiro. This conference saw the establishment of the Rio Declaration and Agenda 21. The Rio Declaration establishes 27 principles which include large principles, such as, sustainable development and the eradication of poverty. The principles represent an agreed statement by all the participating parties – over 100 states in all. Inevitably many difficult areas were avoided in order to achieve agreement. Agenda 21 is a document which has a similar import to the European Fifth Action Programme. It sets out a programme for future action and can therefore be seen as the manifestation of future developments in international environmental law. Climatic change, bio-diversity and forestry are all issues which will be explored within the context of the framework for achieving sustainable development.[7]

POTENTIAL GROWTH AREAS OF ENVIRONMENTAL LAW

There are a number of areas which have been flagged for potential future development and where specific proposals have been made. Civil liability for environmental damage, town and country planning, marine oil pollution and controls on dangerous substances are just a few examples of these.

Civil Liability for damage to the environment

Much of the regulatory control for damage to the environment is based on the principle of criminal liability. In the United Kingdom, the common law provides a variable degree of protection within the context of civil law. In 1993, the European Commission produced a Green Paper on remedying environmental damage which considered the introduction of civil liability for environmental damage. The proposal contemplates the introduction of a system of liability which is strict, and, also, the establishment of a compensation fund. This proposal has its roots in the Action Programmes, in particular

---

[7] On January 25, 1994 the U.K. Government responded with a series of documents which comprise four strategic plans on climate change, sustainable forestry, bio-diversity and sustainable development.

the fourth and the fifth programmes. The principles that the polluter should pay, and that prevention is better than cure, underlie the proposal. The idea is that the threat of making the polluter pay will be a sufficient inducement to ensure that pollution is prevented. Common law liability in the United Kingdom is frequently limited, either by the reluctance of the judiciary to extend liability, or by the requirement of some property right which requires protection. Where liability depends on interference with a property right, then the identity of the potential plaintiff is clear. However, the European proposal goes further than this and suggests that the basis of the action should be damage to the environment. This is broadly defined to include such things within the human environment as archaeological remains. But, who is to be the plaintiff? There are various proposals. For instance, groups of local residents or pressure groups could be given the procedural means to bring such an action, or, it could become the role of an environmental protection agency. Damage to the environment could be extensive and there is a suggestion that liability should be limited – a clear compromise between the attempt to make the polluter pay and the pragmatic approach which accepts that there are limits in terms of the financial ability to pay. This raises the question of insurance. The difficulties encountered by the insurance industry in relation to the enormity of claims resulting from a sequence of natural disasters, and, also from some man-made problems such as the presence of asbestos in buildings and the problems associated with contaminated land, mean that the availability of insurance is limited. The question of compulsory insurance remains, therefore, a moot issue. State intervention remains a possibility, but the U.S. experience of Superfund has caused Europe to proceed cautiously with its proposals in this sphere.

Town and country planning law

This is now within the competence of Europe. Article 130s of the Treaty on European Union provides that planning, along with certain aspects of land use and water management are subject to a unanimous voting procedure.

As with the development of many other aspects of European environmental law, the competence of Europe to legislate on issues affecting land use planning was not unduly restricted by the lack of a specific legislative basis in the original Treaty of Rome. European planning law, to date, has fallen into two areas: one area is sectoral using the zoning mechanism to protect vulnerable species; the other is pervasive, seeking to ensure that environmental issues are considered at the root of planning decisions.

The sectoral aspect of European planning law is represented by two Directives: the Birds Directive[8] passed as long ago as 1979, and, the more recent, Habitats Directive.[9] The alternative method is represented by the Environmental Assessment Directive which requires that certain projects are to be assessed prior to their commencement for their effects on the environment. In the United Kingdom, sectoral land use planning is a familiar concept which is well entrenched in the planning system. Conservation areas, sites of special scientific interest, areas of outstanding natural beauty are all examples of such zoning for environmental purposes. Implementation of the Birds and Habitats Directives is through these existing mechanisms. Although such zoning is a familiar concept, it is not altogether successful. The designation of special protection areas under the Birds Directive has only accounted for 1 per cent. of the territory of the United Kingdom. As a group of offshore islands, the United Kingdom is an important stopover for migratory species, and, for many species of birds, represents an important breeding ground. One per cent. is, therefore, an unacceptably low designation, particularly in comparison with other Member States.

Future planning policy could, therefore, concentrate on enforcement of the existing areas of law already in force. Article 169 proceedings have been brought against the United Kingdom in respect of the United Kingdom's failure to designate adequate special protection areas under the Birds Directive.[10] Article 169 proceedings have also been brought against the United Kingdom in respect of its failure to implement the Environmental Assessment Directive in respect of the proposed East London River crossing, (now abandoned), and the B.P. installation at Kinneil near Falkirk, Scotland.[11]

Marine oil pollution

The well publicised incidents of marine pollution by stranded oil tankers has led to a Commission proposal "A Common Policy on Safe Seas." In fact, little has changed between the disabling of the Torrey Canyon off Land's End in 1967, and the wreck of the Braer off the Shetlands in 1993. In practical terms, the dangers are more

[8] Directive 79/409; [1979] O.J. L103/1.
[9] Directive 92/43: [1992] O.J. L27/23.
[10] *Commission* v. *United Kingdom* [1992] 6 L.M.E.L.R. 194.
[11] See [1992] J.P.L. 913; *Commission* v. *U.K.* [1992] 6 L.M.E.L.R. 192; also [1993] J.P.L. 823.

acute now than before, as there is a greater traffic in oil tankers and the individual tankers have a larger capacity. Much of the legislation concerning such incidents is international in origin[12] and is promoted by the International Maritime Organisation.

Further to the Braer disaster, and some earlier spills, the European Environment Committee called for certain measures such as the designation of exclusive zones around European coasts, more controls on tanker design and restrictions on the use of the flag of convenience. Some resolutions were passed and the policy document referred to above, eventually emerged. Proposals in the document include reporting requirements and improved and strengthened standards of navigation and inspection. It remains to be seen whether the policy, once implemented, will be effective in preventing further oil spills.

Chemicals

Further controls on existing and new chemicals are proposed by the European Community. These include new criteria for evaluating environmental risks and the provision of more extensive information before a new chemical is marketed.[13]

THE LEGAL PROFESSION

Practitioners

It was originally anticipated that there would be an explosion in environmental work for the legal profession from the industrial sector as a result of the increasing environmental regime and the growth in public awareness of environmental issues.[14] This does not appear to have materialised as swiftly as thought because of the effects of the recession. However, new developments in respect of civil liability for waste, a proposal currently being debated in Europe, may affect the trend. Major incidents such as oil spills generate an intensive period of activity in the legal arena but such activity does not provide the daily work required to sustain a legal department in the average solicitor's office. Many firms, which had

---

[12] See Chap. 2.
[13] See the seventh amendment to directive 67/548/EEC.
[14] See Chris Clarke, "Green Issues on Hold," and Owen Lomas, "Maze of legislation", *The Lawyer*, October 19, 1993.

set up environmental units, have discovered that there is insufficient work and have either reduced them in size or scrapped them.

Nevertheless, a number of claims are being made which have environmental aspects. Such claims are not confined to those practitioners based in the City of London who service the insurance industries and large commercial concerns, but are affecting provincial firms dealing with small and medium sized operations. After the case in which a firm the size of the Eastern Leatherworks company, based in a Cambridgeshire village, found itself in the role of defendant in a tortious action for damages in excess of a million pounds, the potential, after the Court of Appeal judgement, appeared to be enormous. The House of Lords' decision was greeted initially as a setback for common law liability in cases concerning historic pollution.[15] *Rylands* v. *Fletcher* has, indeed, been confirmed as an ineffectual tool. The potential, however, in cases where reasonable foreseeability can be established remains. With increasing understanding of the causes of pollution and the development of the environmental technology industries, reasonable foreseeability may not be such a difficult hurdle to surmount in future cases.

In provincial firms, the tendency has been, not to set up specialist environmental units, but to pass the work through the existing litigation or commercial sections. This is understandable, given the general downturn in legal work, but it does have potential weaknesses. The body of environmental law is now extensive and multi-faceted. The correct advice may require the consultation of a number of different sources. The need to be prescient in advising a client involves the need to be abreast of an area of law which is fast moving and subject to policy changes and developments at all levels. For the corporate lawyer, or even the general litigation lawyer, to acquire the expertise to advise on the instant case requires a considerable ability in assimilating large quantities of information from sources which may not be readily accessible in the High Street solicitor's office. One large London firm is reported to employ a full-time research officer with a Ph.D. in environmental law to service the data on international legal developments, another employs an information scientist on this area,[16] a resource beyond the capacity of many firms. There are various options available to deal with the problem. One is to pass on the work to a specialist firm, another is to accept the need for some degree of specialism within the existing

---

[15] *Cambridge Water Company* v. *Eastern Counties Leather plc.* [1994] 1 All E.R. 53.
[16] See note 14.

staff in the firm. When the recession lifts, as in a cyclical fashion it should do, the dilemma will become less acute.

The nature of the work that will emerge in the environmental field could be as much in the familiar field of the English common law as in the context of the European Directive and its manner of implementation. Civil and criminal liability could be relevant and forms of criminal liability could increasingly include the liability of company directors under statutes establishing environmental criminal liability which impose fines or imprisonment. Pressure groups are showing an increasing propensity to bring private criminal prosecutions against companies and against the directors of such companies. With access to environmental data on the public registers, the possibility for such groups to bring these actions armed with their motivation and skills, has been considerably enhanced.

The enforcement agencies themselves, have shown a change in the ethos from the conciliation and co-operation approach to confrontation. While this approach has, to some extent been criticised in Parliament, with the increasing public awareness of environmental controls, the trend is unlikely to diminish. The agencies are often in need of informed and expert legal advice.

Insofar as the agencies fail to pursue prosecutions, the general public are showing a greater willingness to become involved. A trend in the number of private prosecutions for noise nuisance, exemplifies this point. The paucity of legal aid in this field, however, limits the opportunities for private clients to utilise the services of their local legal services.

There are further limitations on the scope for environmental actions. For instance, the power to challenge the actions of government, whether at local or central level, is restricted by such questions as *locus standi*, which affects the capacity of individuals to challenge decisions except where they have a direct interest.[17] In addition, the capacity of the courts to intervene may be limited to their role in undertaking a judicial review of the actions of government.

The proposal to establish an environmental court which would provide an appropriate forum for the determination of environmental issues, has been mooted.[18] However, the proposal has not, as yet, been pursued formally. Its implementation would have important consequences for practitioners.

---

[17] Geddes "Locus Standi and EEC Environmental Measures" (1992) 4 J.E.L. 29 and see *R* v. *HMIP and MAFF, ex p. Greenpeace* [1994] Env. L.R. 76.

[18] Sir Harry Woolf, "Are the judiciary environmentally myopic?" (1992) 4 J.E.L. 1.

Academic

While the concern for practitioners is one of immediate import relating to the development of specific laws concerning the environment and their enforceability in practice, there remains many questions of an academic nature underlying the development of this branch of the law. Very often, environmental law is regarded as an offshoot of administrative law in that it simply determines administrative questions affecting procedural issues. But, there are important philosophical questions to be determined which will influence the future development of environmental law.

There are two aspects in particular to this line of enquiry. Firstly, there is the issue as to whether the right to a decent environment is a basic human right. Secondly, there is the question as to whether the environment has rights.[19]

The right to life is a fundamental human right. But the right to life depends on a number of factors such as the provision of sufficient food, adequate housing and a clean supply of water. It could go further and include the right to work. Many international instruments contain a reference to the link between such rights as these and a decent environment. Some national constitutions also contain specific reference to a right to an environment. Some of these emphasise the duties of the state to protect the environment. For example, the Chinese Constitution of 1982 declares that "the State is to protect and improve the living environment and the ecological environment, and prevent and combat pollution and other hazards to the public." Others stress the right of individuals to a decent environment: "all persons are entitled to an ecologically balanced environment," Article 225 of the Brazilian Constitution of 1982. The 1972 Stockholm Declaration proclaims that "man has the fundamental right to freedom, equality and adequate conditions of life, in an environment of a quality that permits a life of dignity and well-being, and he bears a solemn responsibility to protect and improve the environment for present and future generations." This Declaration perceives the right as being mutual; there are rights and responsibilities; man has a right to a quality environment but the environment has a right to protection from man. The 1991 United Nations Report on Human Rights and the Environment[20] concludes that "the right to the environment should fit quite naturally into the normative and institutional structure of protection of the rights,

---

[19] C.D. Stone, "Should Trees have Standing? Towards Legal Rights for Natural Objects" [1972] 59 *Southern California Law Review* 1–154.
[20] U.N. Economic and Social Council. E/CN.4/Sub.2/1991/8, August 2, 1991.

dignity and freedoms of the human person."[21] Clearly, the right to a
decent environment is inherent in all the other aspects of the right to
life of a certain quality.

The question then arises as to the maintenance of this aspect of
human rights. If a child is caned or a prisoner is tortured, then, under
the European Convention on Human Rights, there is the possibility
of seeking the judicial intervention of the European Court of Human
Rights. If, therefore, there is a failure by a state to supply clean
water, is this a matter which is justiciable? The 1991 United Nations
Report states that the right to a decent environment cannot be
reduced to an individual right. Thus, if an individual were in a
situation where their immediate environment was not of a certain
quality, no individual rights to seek redress are available. The right
posed by the United Nations gives no cause of action to the individual. This clearly leaves the enunciation of such rights at the level of
a statement of intent by consenting nations without the power of
sanction and redress.

This theoretical development of the fundamental principles of
environmental law will be explored further, and will reflect the
status which is ultimately accorded to the environment. In turn, this
will determine the extent and impact of new environmental laws and
the enforcement of existing ones.

SCIENCE FACT OR SCIENCE FICTION?

Whether there is a current downturn in active environmental cases,
or whether there appears to be a hiatus in the expansion of green
politics, the fact remains that environmental law is not only here to
stay, but must inevitably continue to develop in the future. It is often
stated that environmental laws are not new and examples of early
legal initiatives are given to demonstrate this.[22] However, while it is
undoubtedly true that the origins of particular aspects of environmental law, such as air pollution, can be traced back in history, the
modern concept of environmental law has expanded since the
Second World War.

The reason for this development has been the interaction of
scientific and technological development with the struggle for economic supremacy. Major scientific achievements can be readily
pinpointed: space exploration, genetic engineering and electronic

[21] Ibid. p. 29.
[22] See Chap. 1, p. 18.

communication are three obvious examples. The technological developments which follow hard upon the heels of these scientific achievements have the potential to transform society, not over a millenium, but over a relatively short period of time. Once a breakthrough is made, then the pace of change can be swift. For instance, the structure of D.N.A. was discovered in the 1950s.[23] The subsequent progress in the fields of agriculture and in the eradication of human disease has been startling. Even so, the potential remains relatively unexplored. If the present developments are taken to their ultimate, then they could result in a leap forward in longevity for the human race. Since these developments will rest upon the eradication of disease and the identification of the causes of ageing, they could result in the Gerontian dream which is not simply of immortality, but of an eternal youth. Consider the example of space exploration. There are no significant technological reasons to prevent a programme of deep space exploration, the development of self-sustaining space stations and the colonisation of the moon. Given the political will, the potential for the human race is, literally, astronomic. In the field of electronic communication, the swift expansion is readily apparent. Electronic mail and the electronic storage of information could remove the need for libraries and postal services.

The effect of such developments may be more difficult to predict. For instance, the expansion of the road building programme has seen an increase in the number and use of cars and further traffic congestion. More roads lead to more cars, not the reverse. But the analogy is more complex than this implies. If the development of public transport had gone ahead at the same pace as the building and widening of roads, then the effect might have been different. If public transport was free and plentiful, the roads would be emptied. Likewise, scientific developments such as those leading to longer life expectancy and space colonisation cannot be viewed in the absence of their political and economic backgrounds. This in turn will affect their potential environmental impact.

It is argued by environmentalists that the exponential growth of technology and productivity cannot be sustained by the environment. But there is no government, at present, that is in a position to prevent such growth. No company, in a market economy, can afford to fall behind in the development of new processes and technologies. To fall behind, means to be taken over or to be liquidated. No government can legislate to prevent or restrict the development of

---

[23] See Chap. 9, p. 229.

technology. In a world where free trade is advocated, then competition is everything.

Even in a market economy which is heavily regulated, no government can afford to restrict its industrial sector so that it cannot compete on a world scale. Where the market is given the power to decide, the concept of sustainable development is a chimera. One solution, seemingly unreal, is to establish a global government. But, even then, what sort of government could enforce a policy which suppressed innovation and exploration? It is arguable that the saving of the environment rests on the future development of technology not the reverse; that alternative sources of energy and cleaner processes which lead to enhanced social conditions for people, will also provide the solution to the protection of the environment.

Future trends in environmental law may be impossible to predict in the long term because of the unpredictable consequences of scientific and technological achievements. Environmental laws are necessary in economies where competition is unrestricted and new developments and innovations ensure success and supremacy in the market place. Such new developments and technological innovations may have completely unexpected consequences and produce social and environmental crises where they have not been expected. Had it been clearly understood that building roads produced more cars and increased the need for traffic management, would they have been built? What impact will space exploration have on society and, therefore, on the environment? Without an understanding of these problems, and without political systems which are competent to deal with the problems as they arise, sustainable development remains an impossible goal.

Index